# QUEEN OF THE MOUNTAINEERS

# QUEEN OF THE MOUNTAINEERS

## THE TRAILBLAZING LIFE OF FANNY BULLOCK WORKMAN

Cathryn J. Prince

CHICAGO
REVIEW
PRESS

Published by Chicago Review Press Incorporated
814 North Franklin Street
Chicago, Illinois 60610
ISBN 978-1-61373-955-6

**Library of Congress Cataloging-in-Publication Data**
Names: Prince, Cathryn J., 1969– author.
Title: Queen of the mountaineers : the trailblazing life of Fanny Bullock
    Workman / Cathryn J. Prince.
Description: Chicago, Illinois : Chicago Review Press, 2019. | Includes
    bibliographical references and index.
Identifiers: LCCN 2018033718 (print) | LCCN 2018057152 (ebook) | ISBN
    9781613739563 (adobe pdf) | ISBN 9781613739587 (epub) | ISBN
    9781613739570 (kindle) | ISBN 9781613739556 (hardback)
Subjects: LCSH: Workman, Fanny Bullock, 1859–1925. | Mountaineering—
    Himalaya Mountains—History. | Women mountaineers—United
    States—Biography. | BISAC: SPORTS & RECREATION /
    Mountaineering. | BIOGRAPHY & AUTOBIOGRAPHY /
    Adventurers & Explorers. | BIOGRAPHY & AUTOBIOGRAPHY /
    Women. | SPORTS & RECREATION / History. | TRAVEL / Special
    Interest / Adventure.
Classification: LCC GV199.92.W67 (ebook) | LCC GV199.92.W67 P75
    2019 (print) | DDC 796.522092 [B] —dc23
LC record available at https://lccn.loc.gov/2018033718

Typesetting: Nord Compo
Image credits: Author's collection: pp. 14, 79, 134, 146, 171, 173, 196, 204,
and 242; National Library of Scotland: pp. 10, 22, 30, 39, 45, 46, 88, 216,
and 246.

Printed in the United States of America
5 4 3 2 1

For my grandmothers,
Sara Sachs Goldstein and Helen Sugarman Prince

*When, later, a woman occupies her acknowledged position as an individual worker in all fields, as well as those of exploration, no such emphasis of her work will be needed; but that day has not fully arrived, and at present it behooves women, for the benefit of their sex, to put what they do, at least, on record.*
—Fanny Bullock Workman

*A woman who has done good work in the scholastic world doesn't like to be called a good woman scholar. Call her a good scholar and let it go at that. . . . Don't call me a woman mountain climber.*
—Annie Smith Peck

# CONTENTS

# AUTHOR'S NOTE

WHEN POSSIBLE, PEAK names and elevations sourced from the Workmans' and Peck's journals have been corrected to reflect modern-day measurements and names.

Fanny Bullock Workman, William Hunter Workman, and newspapers of their day used the word *coolie* when speaking of porters. In the interest of remaining faithful to the source material, this offensive slur has been included in direct quotes from the Workmans and periodicals of the day.

This book neither revisits nor includes every single one of the climbs and expeditions undertaken by Fanny and Hunter Workman or Annie Peck. I encourage interested readers to read their books and magazine and journal articles for more information.

# 1

# MOUNTAINEERING
# FOR LADIES

SWEAT CASCADED DOWN Fanny Bullock Workman's back. Underneath her woolen jacket, her once crisp white shirt, buttoned to the neck, was plastered to her skin. Her heavy skirt was sodden around the hem, and her legs, clad in wool stockings, itched from the heat. On the way to the summit she had noticed how the dust glittered on her hobnailed boots, how the green leaves drooped motionless in the humid air, and how the sedges and mosses carpeted the spaces between the trees. Now, as she caught her breath, her eyes crinkled upward. She could hear her husband's footfalls growing louder as he neared, but for just a moment she owned the view from atop Mount Washington.

It was a clear day in the summer of 1881, and from the summit of the 6,288-foot-high peak in New Hampshire's White Mountains, the earth and sky melded into a misty blue line. Certainly, she thought, few had ever stood here before this panoramic view. All thirty-three peaks in the Presidential Range, including Mount Adams, Mount Jefferson, and Mount Madison, jutted upward. To the east lay the Atlantic Ocean, and if she turned ever so slightly she could see across Vermont to New York's Adirondack

Mountains in the west. To the north lay Canada, and to the south was Massachusetts.

The sight perfectly matched the description in *Among the Clouds*, Mount Washington's famous daily newspaper, the only newspaper printed on the summit of any mountain in the world—and it was printed twice daily.

For Fanny and William Hunter Workman (or Hunter, as she called him) climbing brought a certain sense of liberation. The newly married couple, like so many in their social milieu, enjoyed escaping the cities and towns. As Charles Dudley Warner wrote in his book *In the Wilderness*, "The real enjoyment of camping and tramping in the woods lies in a return to primitive conditions of lodging, dress, and food, in as total an escape as may be from the requirements of civilization."

This was not Workman's first time up the mountain. Many climbers found the rocky terrain too daunting and turned back before reaching the midway point. But not Workman. Marching over the permafrost, a pleasant loamy fragrance in the air, all the way to the top of the tallest mountain in the northeast exhilarated the twenty-two-year-old Yankee. More than that, she was drawn to the peak's mercurial moodiness, although today the sun shone like a brass button. She was grateful to be spared dense fog, driving rain, or worse—hurricane-force winds sometimes whipped through unannounced and every so often blew someone straight off the mountainside into one of the ravines below. The peak deserves its reputation as one of the more dangerous mountains to climb in America—it has claimed the lives of nearly 150 climbers in the past century and a half.

Yet now, as Workman stood on the craggy peak, leaning on her rough-hewn walking stick for balance, her legs pleasantly fatigued from the exercise, she considered where she had come from and where she wanted to go.

---

On January 8, 1859, Alexander Hamilton Bullock and Elvira Hazard welcomed a baby girl into their most patrician household. Fanny joined an older brother, Augustus George, born in 1847, and a sister, Isabel, born in 1849. Both the Bullocks and the Hazards traced their lineage back to the Pilgrims. Fanny's great-grandfather had been a sea captain, and her maternal grandfather, Colonel Augustus George Hazard, had founded the Hazard Powder Company in Connecticut. Through that business, combined with his vast landholdings, Hazard had amassed a sizable fortune and thus secured his family's financial future.

Elvira Hazard, born in Enfield, Connecticut, in 1824, was one of eight children. A family genealogy described her as someone who was "generous, sympathetic and kind, her hand never wearied in the well doing, scattering its bounties into the homes of the poor, and uplifting the fallen." She married Alexander Bullock at age twenty. He was born in Royalston, Massachusetts, and after graduating from Amherst College, he pursued a law degree at Harvard University and got his start in politics at an early age. He edited a weekly Whig newspaper and served in both the Massachusetts House of Representatives and the state senate. Along with his take-charge attitude, financial discipline, and views on equality, Alexander's younger daughter also inherited her father's strong jaw and sober-looking mouth. From her mother, Elvira, Fanny inherited an unflappable demeanor, which as she grew older was often mistaken for aloofness.

Life inside the Bullock family home, a handsome brownstone on 48 Elm Street in Worcester, Massachusetts, was always loud and never still. In spite of the age gap between the children, Fanny was never indulged as the baby of the family. Rather, the trio related like beloved cousins. A keen reader as a young girl, Fanny also loved escaping outdoors to tramp over nearby hills, explore the brooks, and wander through unkempt fields.

In 1866, when she was seven, her father, then the Republican mayor of Worcester, was elected governor of Massachusetts. During his three terms in office and under his financial discipline, another quality Fanny inherited and would later put to good use when leading expeditions, the state paid off its wartime financial responsibilities.

Actively opposed to the expansion of slavery before he became governor, during his tenure Bullock became involved in the Massachusetts Emigrant Aid Society, an organization committed to populating Kansas with abolitionists. In a March 8, 1869, letter to William Lloyd Garrison, who was the editor of the abolitionist newspaper the *Liberator*, Bullock opined on equality; he thought all members of society should be treated equally. Thanks in part to her father's views, Fanny grew up believing women deserved to be considered and treated as equal to men. Although women were still expected to marry and have children, there were changes afoot. Before Fanny was born, Worcester had hosted the first National Woman's Rights Convention in 1850. In 1870 the Utah Territory granted woman suffrage, a sign that things could change. (The territory rescinded the vote in 1887.) Also in 1870, the Grimké sisters and forty-two other women tried to vote in Massachusetts. Their ballots were cast but ignored. Still, the events signaled change to come.

Over at Worcester's Free Church, the Reverend Thomas Wentworth Higginson urged women to engage in physical activity, such as hiking and skating. The progressive thinker would later write an essay, "Saints, and Their Bodies," in which he deemed "physical health . . . a necessary condition of all permanent success."

The city had long been a well of resistance. Settled in 1673 by Daniel Gookin, Worcester had been an outpost during the American Revolution. Its courthouse was besieged during the 1786 Shays's Rebellion, and in 1854 a small riot erupted when US Marshal Asa Butman arrived to enforce the Fugitive Slave Act of 1850. Local citizens kicked and threw rocks at him, chasing him back to Boston.

Alexander Bullock's election as governor bumped the family into a new level of society. Previously, governesses had been given responsibility for educating Fanny, a precocious child with a penchant for testing authority. In keeping with others in their social set, her parents sent their youngest daughter, when she was not quite twelve, to the elite Misses Graham's Boarding and Day School for Girls in New York City. Founded in 1816, the school on Riverside Drive was the city's oldest private school for girls. It counted Julia Ward Howe, Mabel Osgood Wright, and Emily Price Post among its alumnae. There the teachers guided young Fanny in the social graces and cultural rites befitting a young woman of the upper crust. She learned to sketch and paint, how to thread a needle for embroidery, and how to sit ramrod straight, feet planted firmly on the ground, during piano lessons. She also learned she was not fond of this life.

Then, in 1876, as was the custom for wealthy young women, Fanny's parents sent her abroad, to Paris and Dresden, where her education and etiquette were polished until they shone like sterling silver, and where they hoped she might acquire a European husband. The seventeen-year-old had her own ideas, and landing a husband was not one of them. Rather than gush over gentleman callers or agonize over whether she'd perfected the French knot or split stitch, she filled the pages of her slim black leather journal with musings, excerpts from books, and quotations from philosophers and authors. She kept a running list of every book she longed to read, including Leo Tolstoy's *War and Peace*, Thomas Carlyle's *The French Revolution: A History*, and James Bryce's *The American Commonwealth*. In what appears to be the first inkling that Fanny had designs on loftier matters, she also added a list of mountain climbing books under the heading "Alpine Books Worth Reading." Among those noted were William Martin Conway's *Climbing and Exploration in the Karakoram-Himalayas* and Edward Whymper's *Chamonix and the Range of Mont Blanc: A Guide.*

In 1879, three years after she penned her last entry in the journal, Fanny returned stateside. The twenty-year-old woman with wiry brunette hair now spoke French and German fluently, was well schooled in the art of conversation, and knew her way around the Dutch Masters and historical landmarks.

She knew walking through the door on Elm Street meant walking back into a life where silver trays sat on foyer tables waiting to be filled with the calling cards of her wealthy acquaintances, while destitute people begged for alms in the city streets; where corsets restricted her every movement; and where she always had to sit perched on the edge of her chair because of the bustle. Walking through the door on Elm Street meant returning to a life where women sipped cooled sherry and expected to bear children and mind a household. She wanted none of it.

As a means of temporary escape, Fanny sometimes hiked in the hills near Worcester. She soon returned to writing as another outlet. One of her earliest efforts was a short story titled "A Vacation Episode," in which the protagonist, a beautiful and aristocratic young English woman, tires of studying and flees across the Channel all the way to Switzerland's Bernese Alps. In the village of Grindelwald, the gateway to the Jungfrau, she finds her destiny. Rather than wed a rich European, as her parents hoped she would, the unnamed heroine falls in love with an American and becomes a superior alpinist. Though fiction, the short story reads as a thinly veiled account of Fanny's own wanderlust and deep desire to live by her own set of rules.

Observing their daughter after she had spent all those years in Europe without landing a marriage proposal, Fanny's parents worried their youngest child had returned home reluctant to step into the life expected for her. They needn't have worried. Soon enough their gray-eyed and brown-haired daughter caught the eye of Dr. William Hunter Workman, a well-respected Harvard Medical School–trained physician who was eleven years her senior. The youngest of nine children born to William Workman and Sarah Paine Hemenway, Hunter, too, had spent time overseas burnishing his education. He had attended the universities of Vienna, Heidelberg, and Munich. His father had also studied at Harvard University and, before he moved to Worcester with his wife and children, had practiced medicine in Shrewsbury.

Both the Bullock and the Workman families belonged to the Union Church. Fanny's father, as Massachusetts governor, had appointed Hunter a trustee of the Worcester Lunatic Asylum. He held the position while also working as a surgeon and pathologist at Memorial Hospital, which had been founded with funds from industrialist Ichabod Washburn and was first known as the Washburn Dispensary. Finding Hunter Workman's character and credentials exemplary, the Bullocks approved the match.

After a brief courtship, the couple pledged their troth, and Elvira Hazard Bullock ordered twelve hundred engraved invitations sent to members of the bench, the bar, the pulpit, and the medical profession. On June 16, 1881, shortly before seven o'clock in the evening, the denizens of Worcester society entered through the heavy wooden door of the Gothic-style brownstone church on Irving and Pleasant Streets. Above them, watchful gargoyles perched on the iron cross–topped spire.

An announcement in the *New York Times* called the occasion "the great society event of the season, which has been anticipated for months. . . . The church was crowded with distinguished and fashionable people." The paper described the weather as "auspicious" and "so cool that while light silks and other summer materials were appropriate, and most generally worn, there were colored velvets, worn by numerous stately matrons, without personal discomfort."

The justice of the peace ushered guests to their seats. Potted palms and ferns lined the aisle, which was tiled in black and white squares. The last of the evening light filtered through the red-and-blue stained-glass windows. Quiet organ music signaled the start of the ceremony. Draped in blue brocade and Satin de Lyon, the bridesmaids preceded Fanny down the aisle. Bonnets adorned with pink roses perched upon their heads. A vision of maternal pride, Elvira wore a gown cut from heliotrope satin and brocade with black point lace trimming and diamond adornments. Fanny's older sister, Isabel, beamed in white Satin de Lyon with pearl ornaments. Lush floral bouquets dressed the altar and "were in harmony with the rich and becoming costumes worn by the ladies present."

The music transitioned to Wagner's "Bridal Chorus" from *Lohengrin*. Heads turned to see the bride, elegant in white satin and silver brocade with point lace, one hand resting lightly on her father's crooked elbow. The diamond ornaments sewn onto her gown shimmered. Fanny Bullock took a deep breath and walked toward Hunter. One satin-slippered step after another, she could see, like the aisle before her, her life mapped out. A predictable life.

The prominent New Englanders sitting in the wooden pews might have seen a young woman ready to assume the roles of wife, hostess, and mother. They might have seen a woman ready to marry a doctor who grew prized dahlias and sweet onions.

The notes of the wedding march reached a crescendo as Fanny reached Hunter's side. "In the presence of a brilliant assemblage of friends," the couple silently pledged to lead a different sort of life. In William Hunter Workman she had indeed found a wealthy husband who could keep her in comfort for all of her days, yet it wasn't comfort she sought. She wanted, nay, she demanded, a partnership of equals.

A coupé drawn by her own horses, each bedecked with white satin rosettes and ribbons, had carried the bride to church. Now she and her new husband climbed back into the carriage to ride the short distance to her parents' spacious home, where a table groaned under the weight of bridal gifts "profuse and costly." The food was plentiful and the toasts many, and yet, as warm and sparkling as the evening was, the new couple welcomed the moment the last guest left.

With this marriage Fanny Bullock Workman cast off the chains of Victorian womanhood.

———————

Nearly three years after they exchanged vows, on March 23, 1884, Fanny gave birth to their daughter, Rachel, in the upstairs bedroom of their house with bowfront windows. Joyous as the occasion was, the baby's birth curbed neither Fanny's nor her husband's wish to travel beyond Worcester, a city that felt increasingly provincial. Athletic and sharp, Workman couldn't abide her mother's friends and peers who, by the spoonful, swallowed the prevailing wisdom of the time: that motherhood sanctified a woman and that it was the only goal she should aspire to. Well, that and homemaking. Of course, if a woman had free time, engaging in a bit of philanthropy or joining a civic club would not be untoward. Climbing and exploring was not on the list.

Fanny Bullock Workman with baby Rachel.

The young mother knew she was a privileged woman. She knew her grandfather had left her mother means, and she knew that as an upper-class woman she had access to everything—schools, health, and leisure. Yet she wanted more than material comfort. She wanted independence and adventure. Refusing to obey the ossified characterizations of womanhood, Workman was becoming a modern woman of her day. She was formidable. She was independent. She believed in women's suffrage and wished to be judged on her merits, not her marriage. Without realizing it, she was becoming what would in another decade or so be called a "New Woman."

Since returning from Europe in 1879 she had tried several times to publish her short stories but met with little success. Nevertheless, she kept writing. Her persistence paid off in 1886, when her short story "A Romance of King Philip's War" landed on the desk of an editor at *New England Magazine*. Set in 1676 during the First Indian War, or King Philip's War, it told of a captive young white woman named Millicent and her attraction to and ultimate rejection of an Indian named Ninigret. "One bright afternoon early in the month of June 1676, a young girl stood leaning against the trunk of a tree, gazing into the waters of the beautiful Lake Quinsigamond. Her head rested heavily on her hand, as if weighed down by the burden of despair"—so opened the two-part story. Millicent ultimately refuses Ninigret's offer of marriage and protection, telling him such wedlock would spell doom: "Marry you I never can; think of it calmly, and you will see that it is impossible; such a marriage would only bring misery to us both."

Like the protagonist in Workman's first story, Millicent discovers romance on her own terms. Yet, unlike the unnamed English heroine of her first story, who defies parental expectations and marries an American, Millicent recognizes the limitations of a marriage beyond the conventions of class and race, so she does not marry.

Although it's unknown how much Workman earned for the piece, she received a positive review in the *Sacramento Record-Union*: "A most charming romance of King Philip's war is given in the April and May numbers of *New England Magazine* from the pen of Fanny Bullock Workman. It is an incident of the capture and rescue of a white girl, and is told in a very pleasant and infatuating style." In her fiction, Workman rescued her heroines from the claustrophobic life peculiar to her real-life social circles: from heavy dresses worn over tightly laced corsets that restricted movement to the expectation that women regard their husbands as the sun around which all else orbited.

Workman joined a growing chorus of women no longer willing to remain quiet about their lack of agency. In 1886 women protested their exclusion from dedication ceremonies for the Statue of Liberty. And that same year, a women's suffrage amendment reached the US Senate floor, though it was defeated two to one.

---

The young couple returned to the White Mountains summer after summer. They were especially taken with Mount Washington, whose Indian name was Agiocochook, or "home of the Great Spirit." They relished its challenging terrain. Of course, they followed a long line of people who had summited the peak, starting with Darby Field, an Irishman living in Boston, who in 1642 became the first white man on record to stand on the summit.

Prior to the nineteenth century, mountaineering had served primarily as reconnaissance for military strategy or to aid expansion of commercial transportation systems. In the latter part of the century, though, the rising British leisure class began embracing climbing for sport. Closer to home, John Muir, the Scottish American naturalist and author, extolled the virtues of the great outdoors, prompting many Americans to seek respite from city life in forests, mountains, or at the seaside. Hiking and climbing for pleasure in the late 1800s was considered a rather fashionable way for well-to-do city dwellers to pass a holiday. It was quite normal to see wealthy outdoor enthusiasts dressed in tall hats and frock coats as they took to the woods or traipsed across glaciers.

Nevertheless, for the more earnest outdoorsmen, outing clubs had started to crop up across the country. One of the first was the Alpine Club of Williamstown, Massachusetts, established in

1863 (and not to be confused with the American Alpine Club). It guided people on hikes and climbs in neighboring New Hampshire. Following the Civil War, the clubs began expanding their mission. Members began to take it upon themselves to clear and mark trails, provide trail maps, and build trailside shelters. Their work lives on in the numerous outdoor clubs and organizations of today.

The Workmans had yet to join any clubs as of the late 1800s— mountain climbing or otherwise. Still, they delighted in spending time in the great outdoors, particularly in New Hampshire, just a half day's trip from home. Unlike many tourists visiting the region, the Workmans refused to board the cogwheel train that took passengers along nearly three miles of steep track to the top of Mount Washington. Ever since the train had started running in 1868, flocks of tourists had descended on the area. Many were keen to purchase stereoscopic pictures as souvenirs. Some took rooms at the stately three-story Glen House, with its choice of lakeside or mountain views, ladies' writing room, and a smoking room for the gentlemen. Others lodged at the Summit House.

By century's end more than five thousand people had stepped aboard the cogwheel train, from ordinary citizens to political luminaries. President Ulysses S. Grant, his wife Julia, and their son Jesse had taken the train on August 27, 1869, and dined at the Tip-Top House. Eight years later, in 1877, President Rutherford B. Hayes and his family had made the same trip to the top, where the mountain's newspaper, *Among the Clouds*, was published.

Taking a cup of tea at the Tip-Top House was almost always in order for those who reached the summit. Built from rock blasted from the mountain, the hotel's interior felt refreshingly cool after a summer climb. Yet it was the sensation of lacing her hobnailed boots tight and striding purposefully to the top that made Fanny Workman feel most at ease.

"The Presidential Range from Mt. Aggasiz, Bethlehem, White Mts., N.H." vintage postcard.

During Workman's climb that morning in 1881 she likely passed several other women on the lower trails, although most were likely not aiming for the summit. Unlike their European counterparts, American mountain clubs allowed women to join almost from the beginning. The Appalachian Mountain Club (AMC), founded in 1876, had invited women to join starting in 1879. Decades later, when leading climbers and mountaineers established the American Alpine Club in 1902, Fanny Bullock Workman would be a founding member. By contrast in England, women's membership in clubs was entangled with the broader national debate about political enfranchisement. Britain's Alpine Club, founded in 1857, barred women. This discrimination would prompt 250 women to launch the Ladies' Alpine Club in 1907. As reported in the *New York Times*, "For years these lady mountain climbers have rebelled against the stern dictum which has kept them outside the precincts sacred to the men of the Alpine Club in Savile Row." It wouldn't merge with Britain's Alpine Club until 1976.

All this climbing put Workman and other female climbers in close contact and cooperation, as well as occasional conflict, with men who felt the trails belonged to them alone.

For the previous couple of summers Workman would likely have spotted women on the mountainside daring to wear bloomers, named for Amelia Bloomer of Seneca Falls, New York. Bloomer had first introduced the ensemble in January 1851. In May of that year in an article in *Lily* magazine, Bloomer described the garment as pants that extend from waist to ankle, "gathered or plaited up about two inches in depth, and left sufficiently wide for the foot to pass through. . . . Instead of the whalebone bodice, the dress should be made with a sack front extending from the shoulder to the knee, and a tight back, with the skirt gathered in as usual." The calf-length skirt worn over loose trousers kept the wearer warm without petticoats.

The fashion had waned somewhat by the time Fanny started climbing in the late 1880s, although the occasional woman still wore bloomers to express her belief in women's rights—and if truth be told, some women wore them simply out of practicality. A billowing dress was an invitation to stumble over hidden rocks and roots. Still, Workman wasn't quite ready to discard her wide woolen skirts, and for now she would also eschew the latest fashion of sewing rings into the seam of her dress and running a cord through them so she could draw it up at a moment's notice.

Yet anyone thinking her sartorial choices meant she was a stickler for rules would be wrong. As Hunter Workman told anyone who would listen, his wife most certainly was not a conformist. She wore skirts out of personal preference, even if it was a choice that seemed to directly contradict her political beliefs.

There was another reason Workman favored skirts. When she stood at the summit among a group of men, she knew the image of her in a skirt sent an unmistakable message that a woman was more than equal to the task at hand.

---

Workman stood on the edge of Mount Washington's granite peak. Below, the tree-studded ravines looked like parts of a model train set. She thought once again how poorly domestic life suited her; she cared little for a stultifying life of embroidery, teas, and charity work. She craved adventure, and the summer excursions to the White Mountains only whetted her appetite for more.

She knew she was becoming an anomaly within her social circle. Many wives and daughters of well-to-do businessmen, bankers, and politicians thrived under the current system and appeared content with the status quo. Workman yearned for something more. She dreamed of commanding a team of explorers and becoming a pioneer in mountain climbing.

Workman often overtook the other women on the trail, and most of the men too, for that matter, and that got her thinking. The mountain didn't care if you were a man or a woman, tall or short, stocky or slight. Surely women could compete with men. Surely women could have an equal voice to men. She realized two things while waiting for Hunter to catch up. First, she was the better climber and the better organizer—traits he recognized and even celebrated. Indeed, he sometimes said it wasn't she who had married him but rather he who had married her. These first summers of married life climbing in the White Mountains contributed to the happy companionship she felt with her husband.

Second, Workman was bored with the White Mountains. As brutal and challenging as the mountain range was, she had exhausted the region and was ready to move on to higher peaks. She wanted to overcome inhospitable barriers and conquer them. To be sure, climbing here in this little corner of the world had allowed her to perfect her skills, but it was time to go higher. She wanted the thrill of doing something no mortal had done before; she wanted to unlock routes through treacherous landscapes. So, with her steel-gray eyes trained on the horizon, she dreamed of smashing expectations and of the day when Fanny Bullock Workman would be known everywhere as the world's greatest female mountain climber.

2

# NO TIME FOR TEA

I T WAS 1889. In Paris, thirty-two million visitors would pass underneath the lacelike steel arches of the newly built Eiffel Tower on their way to visit the Exposition Universelle, and Daniel Stover and William Hance would patent a bicycle with a back-pedal brake. Meanwhile, across the Atlantic Ocean, Fanny and Hunter Workman prepared to close the door to their brick house on Elm Street. When and if they would return, she knew not.

It was seven years after both Fanny's and Hunter's fathers had died. Both Fanny and Hunter had inherited sizable fortunes, money that made it possible for the family to now decamp for Europe. The couple had fallen in love with the continental lifestyle after spending several holidays hiking in Switzerland and Germany. They planned to settle in Dresden, Germany. Hunter, now forty-two, had recently retired because of an unspecified lung ailment (neither he nor Fanny provided further clarification in their journals), which made their decision much easier. They were unfettered. As for Fanny, she believed living on the other side of the Atlantic Ocean would afford her more independence. She hoped a new continent would allow her room to shape a new identity, much like the heroines of her short stories.

Heavily pregnant with their second child, Fanny glanced around the foyer of their home one last time and considered the possibilities of this new chapter. She looked forward to this next step. Drapes covered most of their furnishings to protect against dust. Clothing, dishes, books, and assorted knickknacks filled several steamer trunks. She slung her handbag over her arm and walked through the door.

Together with Rachel, now four years old, the Workmans settled into a train bound for New York City. Once in Manhattan they went to the harbor, a city unto itself. Barrels of unloaded goods were stacked several feet high. Black smoke spewed from some ships. Wending their way through the crowd, they boarded a Hamburg-American Line steamship bound for Europe. The company's fleet operated primarily between New York and Plymouth, Cherbourg, or Hamburg. The lines were cast off and the ship sailed past the Lady Liberty colossus, dedicated just three years earlier. As the shoreline receded, the city grew ever smaller, and soon they were beyond the harbor, headed into the open ocean.

While on board the ship, the family passed time in the first cabin saloon with its banquettes and paneled ceilings. Each morning, if the weather permitted, Fanny and Hunter took a turn along the polished teak deck. When evening came, they dressed for dinner and descended the carpeted grand stairway.

After nearly ten days at sea, the ship sailed down the Elbe River and docked in Hamburg. Together the family disembarked. Fanny held the rail of the ramp for balance, and Hunter held Rachel's tiny hand in his own. The harbor was a hive of activity. Here a couple embraced one last time. There a young man hefted a duffle on his shoulder before boarding an America-bound ship. Endings and beginnings.

The trio boarded a train; their luggage had already been sent on ahead. Three hundred miles later, they arrived in Dresden, the city they would call home for the next several decades. The elegant couple looked forward to indulging their shared tastes in literature, art, and music, to the philharmonic, the galleries, and the cosmopolitan flavor of the shopping arcades and cafés. Meanwhile, Fanny wasted no time organizing and staffing her household. Her fluency in German came in handy. She hired a cook, a housekeeper, and a governess for Rachel. Life quickly fell into place.

On December 11, 1889, contractions gripped Fanny. The local doctor was summoned to their home, and several hours later, in her upstairs bedroom, Fanny delivered a healthy baby boy.

Taken as Fanny was with newborn Siegfried, who was all blond curls and cherub cheeks, his arrival did nothing to awaken a desire in her to nest. Staying home, head bent over needlework, and being directly involved in housework and caring for her children, would never appeal to her. It was too narrow a life. She had an eye toward the world on the other side of the door.

In their social circle, employing a governess to mind one's children was the norm. However, leaving one's children in the governess's charge so one might head off into parts unknown was something else entirely—if one were a woman. A man could, without question, leave his wife and children in favor of adventure and exploration. It was a double standard that made Fanny bristle as she thought about it, lying in bed recovering from Siegfried's birth.

Fortunately for her, her husband had no interest in dominating their marriage. She had married a man who not only understood but also shared her longing for exploration and adventure. So it was that Fanny had no difficulty persuading Hunter to take a cycling tour. Just the two of them. She had read all about the new craze and was eager to try the newly invented "safety bicycle."

According to the manufacturer, safety bicycles promised a smoother ride thanks to pneumatic rubber tires. Unlike previous models, the front and rear wheels were the same height, which let riders plant both feet on the ground when stopping. The Work-mans bought one each, and Fanny couldn't wait to start navigating the streets of Dresden.

Back in the United States, some department stores emptied their upper floors of merchandise, creating space for women to take cycling lessons. There were also cycling arenas for peo-ple to practice, and dance halls were turned into venues for cycling parties. As amusing as that might have been, Workman preferred to practice outdoors. Once she mastered the art of pedaling, she wanted to explore the rest of Germany on two wheels.

The Worcester native insisted on wearing skirts to bicycle, even though women participating in many sports were pushing dress

Fanny Bullock Workman posing with bicycle in riding clothes.

codes. A fashion show of bicycling clothes in 1895 ranged from the "boldest of knickerbockers to the quietest of skirts."

The American public and the press mocked these women who pursued athletics, politics, and equal rights. Cartoons frequently depicted them assuming a male stance, while their husbands managed the laundry, washed the dishes, and tended to the children. Beyond the lampoons, some states enacted sumptuary laws. In 1895, the same year of the aforementioned fashion show, the male-only Chicago city council passed a law against bifurcated garments for women.

As Workman rode, whether down the wide avenues of one city or the narrow side streets of another, she paid attention to how the traffic rules varied from place to place, with seemingly little rhyme or reason. Some towns and cities prohibited riders from cycling two abreast. Others allowed cyclists only on the right side of the road. All locales required cyclists to fix a bell and a lantern to their handlebars to use after nightfall. In some places riders were to call out and ring a bell when crossing streets. A belt and suspender rule if there ever was one, Workman thought. Like a naturalist observing animal behavior, Workman took careful notes of the rules and regulations and pulled her thoughts together in an article, "Bicycle Riding in Germany," for *Outing* magazine (which had started in 1882 as *Wheelman*, a magazine devoted to cycling). One of her earliest travel pieces, the article's prose was stilted and preachy, similar to the tone she assumed in later pieces. Gone were all traces of the breathless young woman caught in a love triangle between an American soldier and a Native American.

In her short article, Workman described how cycling was a favorite pastime for Germany's men and was fast becoming popular among women. On a personal note, she shared how cycling not only helped her recover from Siegfried's birth but also how the sport allowed her no small measure of independence: "Did women realize what an interesting, exciting and health-giving exercise bicycling is, and to what a new world of pleasure it introduces them, they would more rapidly adopt it."

---

In 1891, two years after the family decamped from Worcester for Dresden, Fanny and Hunter left Rachel and Siegfried at home with a governess and took a sleeper train to Chamonix, France, for a much-anticipated summer holiday. If Fanny felt even a soupçon of hesitation or guilt about leaving her two young children at home, she confessed to no one, not even to the pages of her leather-bound journal. Instead, the young mother wrote about her wish to climb Mont Blanc, the highest mountain in western Europe at 15,771 feet.

Nestled in the Haute-Savoie, Chamonix was first settled in 1091 and originally called Le Prieuré. Until the mid-eighteenth century, most people bypassed the small mountain town, save for the king's tax collectors, clergy, and soldiers. Around this time William Windham, an Englishman living in Geneva, stumbled on "Chamouny." Perched three thousand feet above sea level, the town and its nearby glaciers fascinated the traveler. Here they were on the tip of the Mer de Glace, France's largest and longest glacier.

When the Workmans arrived in Chamonix just over a century later, they found it was no longer a sleepy town. They could also see why the village had charmed Windham. French now dominated the patois mix of French and Italian spoken by its year-round residents. Hotels and inns were filled with droves of British tourists, particularly during the spring and summer months. The little town was fast becoming the center of the mountain climbing world.

An enthusiastic Workman and her husband strolled across the quiet cobblestone streets to meet their guide. She didn't allow herself to be distracted by the horse-drawn carriages clattering by or the meringues and other goodies piled high in bakery windows. She focused her mind on Mont Blanc.

Dr. Michel-Gabriel Paccard, along with Jacques Balmat, a chamois hunter and mountain guide, had been the first climbers known to have reached the top, on August 8, 1786. By the time the Workmans arrived, hundreds of men and a handful of women (the first being Lucy Walker) had followed suit. Most parties attempting to summit the mountain were relatively small, except for those who climbed as part of rather large caravans. Some climbers hired help to carry assorted delicacies to the summit, including champagne, cookies, cheese, bread, and pâté. Some even decreed no successful Mont Blanc climb was complete "without fireworks (sometimes) and cannonade (often) echoing across the valley."

Workman certainly had no plans for firing off a cannonade should she and Hunter reach the top. Instead she strapped rudimentary crampons over her leather boots, tied an ice ax to her waist, and pulled a topee over her brown curls. As she and Hunter climbed, Fanny thought about a story she had heard. Locals often climbed the glacier searching for quartz, hematite, and other crystals. Once in a while some unfortunate soul fell into a crevasse and the body lay preserved under the ice for months, sometimes years. In the distance, almost as a coda to her musings, flew the ominous *choucas*. According to local legend, the jet-black mountain jackdaw nourished itself from the remains of expired and expiring climbers.

Up they went, slowly and methodically, by way of the long and somewhat tedious Grands Mulets and Grand Plateau route. They slept in an alpine refuge about ten thousand feet up. The next morning they stopped now and again to chug water or gulp down a few morsels of dried meat and fruit. While altitude sickness affected their guide, Fanny was impervious to the change in elevation. By late afternoon on the second day, under a cornflower-blue sky, Fanny Bullock Workman became one of the first women to summit the snow- and ice-covered face of Mont Blanc.

———————————

One year after Workman ticked Mont Blanc off her alpine to-do list, she and Hunter decided they fancied another climb in the Alps. Once again they left Rachel and Siegfried home with a nurse-maid. This time, rather than take the train, Fanny suggested they make the journey on their safety bicycles. The couple rode through Bayreuth, Nuremberg, and Munich before they reached Switzer-land. Workman thought it a wonder they made it—for the last several miles of the nearly four-hundred-mile trip, mud pulled at the front wheels of their bicycles. It was like moving through taffy. When they could go no farther, they turned back and took side roads to the inn.

The next morning the Americans settled their bill and pointed their safety bicycles toward Zermatt, a German-speaking village located in the southern end of the Matter Valley. They cycled past apricot orchards and vineyards. High on the lush green moun-tainsides, cows grazed, their bells ringing. Almost completely surrounded by the Pennine Alps, they approached the gateway to the Matterhorn, a solitary peak. Topping out at 14,692 feet, the pyramid-shaped peak sits astride Switzerland and Italy.

It was the end of August, a good time to climb. The snow cover had thinned on the ridges leading up to the summit. Still, the peak was known to be challenging even in good conditions. While the Workmans were in good shape cycling hundreds of miles, Fanny worried their climbing muscles were out of shape.

She suggested they do a warm-up climb up the Breithorn before trying their luck on the Matterhorn.

---

On July 14, 1865, Edward Whymper, the London-born mountaineer, had become the first person to conquer the mountain. Accompanying the twenty-five-year-old were the Reverend Charles Hudson, Douglas Hadow, Lord Francis Douglas, and their three guides: Peter Taugwalder Jr., Peter Taugwalder Sr., and Michel Croz. Hudson, Hadow, Douglas, and Croz were roped together in one group. Whymper and the Taugwalders made up the other group. An hour into the descent, Hadow, wearing boots wholly unsuitable for climbing, slipped and plummeted three thousand feet off the north face to his death. He took Douglas, Hudson, and Croz with him into the void. The story taught Workman an important lesson: the descent is often the most dangerous part of the trek.

In spite of the disaster, Whymper had proven that summiting the peak could be done. In 1881, less than two decades later, Albert Frederick Mummery, another vaunted British climber, followed suit. These highly publicized climbs helped usher in the golden age of mountaineering. The Alps soon became a sportsman's playground, beckoning members of the English, and eventually American, leisure class who had the time, inclination, and money.

After the Workmans checked in to their hotel, they strolled the streets of Zermatt, past shopwindows displaying the latest in climbing gear and warm clothing, as well hunks of hopschil, the local cheese, and bottles of apricot schnapps. As Mummery once noted, Zermatt had indeed become a tourist destination, with "cheap trippers and their trumpery fashions." Trumpery aside, Workman was content. She was here with Hunter, away from home, and they were going to climb the Matterhorn. She was anxious to reach the summit, where thunder, lightning, whirling snow, and rain often visited—sometimes all at once. Just like Mount Washington.

Excited though she was, she was not overconfident. She knew they needed to hire a guide. In this she also agreed with Mummery. She dismissed Whymper's notion that Alpine guides were little more than "pointers out of paths and large consumers of meat and drink." She asked around. More than a few people recommended the Swiss-born Matthias Zurbriggen. Knowing Mummery had once engaged Zurbriggen boosted Workman's confidence.

On August 31, the day of the climb, Fanny arose at 3:30 AM and nudged Hunter awake. They dressed carefully, she in her loden green woolen skirt and thick tights, he in his ash-gray woolen pants. Both wore flannel shirts and woolen coats. After a hearty breakfast, they stepped outside into the quiet darkness. The chilly air bit their cheeks. They met Zurbriggen and set out toward the great buttress upon which rests the Matterhorn Glacier. "The morning was clear, except for a slight mist toward the peak," she wrote.

Like a team of horses, Workman and her husband were attached to Zurbriggen with heavy ropes looped through their legs and about their shoulders. A tingling feeling crawled up Workman's neck as she passed the tree line. The peak looked like one of little Rachel's drawings. Its simple lines belied its challenge. It was, Workman knew, unrivaled as far as Alpine summits went, rising abruptly as it did by a series of cliffs. They trekked along a knife-blade ridge, paying careful attention to the faint ripple lines of snow, which hid crevasses and shadowy crags. They stopped for the night at a hut; they would make the final push for the summit in the morning.

Stepping out into the predawn morning, Fanny tugged her wool sweater over her head and planted her topee hat firmly on her curls. "The snow was thick and the icy wind blew constantly. We had views only occasionally near the summit," she wrote.

The party reached the top just as skies cleared and the pink and gold sunrise washed the distant peaks. In a photograph taken shortly after they reached the summit, Fanny and Hunter gaze steadily into the camera with only the faintest smiles pinned on their faces. With her straight posture and smooth skin, she bore the marks of a well-cared-for life. They stood for a few minutes on the summit, enough time to appreciate the view and their accomplishment, but not so much time as to distract them from the descent. "The wind, very curiously, did not blow on the very top," she said.

However, a third of the way down the mountain, an icy wind kicked up and nearly blew Workman's hat off her head. Her nose and cheeks numb, she murmured a word of thanks that her feet were dry and warm. Before reaching the bottom, Hunter took a flask from his pocket and they each took a healthy sip of cognac. An early but well-deserved celebration, thought Fanny.

A soak in a hot tub soothed aching muscles. A hearty dinner sated a ravenous appetite. Back in their room, Workman opened her journal. She wanted to record everything as it had happened.

After leaving Zermatt, as they rode through the canton of Valais they passed a village where three stray dogs set upon Fanny. One dog managed to get under her front wheel, and as soon as she hopped off her bicycle another snarling dog looked ready to pounce on her arm. It was, she said, "altogether a narrow escape."

Thoroughly exhausted, the couple arrived at the guesthouse in Innsbruck coated in dirt and dust. After tossing their saddlebags on the floor of their room they scrubbed the grime from their faces and under their nails. One "good jolly supper" later they pulled up the blankets and went to sleep. The next morning, feeling somewhat refreshed, the pair mounted their bicycles and

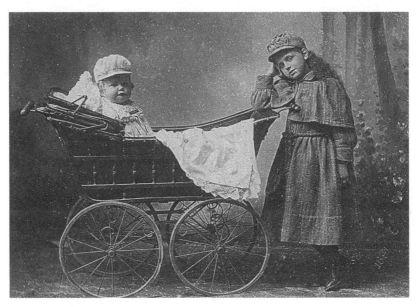

Siegfried, in carriage, with Rachel.

headed toward Lausanne. Lake Geneva reflected the sun and the French Alps looked like decoupage against the cobalt sky. Husband and wife huffed and puffed up the winding hills in the city. They passed the night at Hôtel de l'Ours, a small wood-sided inn. Across the street stood a school and two stately chestnut trees dressed in spring foliage and blossoms. The inn was charming on the outside, but inside "nasty people" ran the lodgings, thought Workman.

---

The couple returned home to Dresden feeling positively invigorated.

Between spending time with Siegfried and Rachel, accepting and declining dinner invitations, and answering correspondence, Workman began to feel a creeping restlessness. She and Hunter had been home only a few months, yet she knew she would be able to ignore the feeling for only so long. Never did she worry that this coming and going might affect her children, now seven and two years old. Never did she worry that they would think of her as the lady with the suitcases. She couldn't think that way if she wanted to be that rarest of late nineteenth-century women: a mother whose interests lay outside the domestic sphere.

---

Meanwhile, back in the United States, unbeknownst to Workman, her rival-to-be Annie Smith Peck had been slowly nurturing her own career.

Peck was born in Providence, Rhode Island, on October 19, 1850, to George Bacheler Peck and Ann Power Smith. She had three older brothers, George Bacheler Peck Jr., John Brownell Peck, and William Thane Peck. An older sister, Emily Smith Peck, had died in infancy. The staunchly Baptist family lived in the house her grandfather had built.

"Our family comes of the best old New England stock, so perhaps we inherited what I could call a strain of endurance. We had great-uncles and aunts galore, who lived into the nineties, our Grandmother Peck to 88. She indeed was a wonder, who at 70 did the work for a family of 12, and once, I am told, lifted a barrel of cider from the ground into a wagon," she would later tell a reporter.

Peck's paternal line descended from Jathniel Peck, whose father and grandfather emigrated from Beccles and Hingham, England, in 1638 aboard the *Diligent*. They sought a new start in the New World after Jathniel's brother, Rev. Robert Peck, had been excommunicated from the Church of England for "contumacious disobedience" sometime around 1636. Centuries later, that "contumacious disobedience" surfaced in young Annie Peck. In that, Peck reflected the nature of her home state, which was colloquially called Rogues Island by some, in part because on May 4, 1776, it had declared independence from England—two months before the other twelve colonies.

A practicing attorney, George Peck Sr. became a coal merchant and then tried his hand in politics. He served two terms in the Rhode Island House of Representatives.

In 1858 Peck's parents enrolled her in Dr. Stockbridge's School for Young Ladies, a school that billed itself for those parents who "felt that daughters ought to be put on footing with their sons in the matter of their mental culture." At thirteen Peck attended Providence High School, which at the time was called Rhode Island Normal School. She hoped to continue her schooling.

Throughout her adolescence Peck recorded everything, a habit she kept her whole life. As her journal revealed, she sometimes worried about her older brother George, who was serving as second lieutenant in the Second Regiment Rhode Island Volunteers, Company G. During the Siege of Petersburg, a musket ball slammed into his left side, near his hip. After a few weeks recovering in the hospital, he tried to rejoin his unit. However, he never fully mended and was honorably discharged on July 5, 1865.

Peck wrote in her journal that she rejoiced on April 9, 1865, when General Robert E. Lee and his army surrendered to the Union, ending the Civil War. Bells pealed throughout the city of Providence, and cannons were fired. In school the students sang hymns of grace.

Five days later, on April 14, all semblance of jubilation was extinguished. John Wilkes Booth shot President Abraham Lincoln as he watched *Our American Cousin* in Ford's Theatre, and Lewis Powell stabbed Secretary of State William H. Seward while he recovered in bed from a carriage accident. On Monday, April 17, Peck, wearing a black-and-white ribbon pinned to her dress, her hair in a neat chignon, entered her high school through front doors trimmed in black and white crepe.

A couple of months later, on June 27, Peck and her parents traveled to New York City. In Central Park they strolled through the Ramble and visited P. T. Barnum's American Museum on Broadway and Ann Street, where, to her wonder, she "saw a giantess, fat lady, and girl with white hair."

Despite his daughter's wishes, George Sr. saw no value in his daughter pursuing an education beyond high school. Her wish to do so confounded him to no end. Peck's rigid mother also gave education for young women short shrift. The elder Ann had been raised to "be a lady." In other words, she felt her daughter should aspire no further than marriage and motherhood. In her view, a woman should strive to provide wholesome, nourishing food for her family. She should aim for frugality and modesty. And indeed, the senior Ann put into practice these firmly held beliefs as she ruled over her household.

In the Peck home, medicine was homeopathic—there were no cathartics or quinine—and mealtimes were noted for their healthfulness. Because the family owned a milking cow, the children drank two large tumblers of fresh unpasteurized milk a day. Breakfast might be a serving of hash or creamed codfish, as well as sweet corn—two to three ears each—sweet potatoes, griddle cakes, corn bread, and rye drop cakes, "but never hot biscuit or warm raised white bread which my mother deemed unwholesome." There was no room in the cupboard for tea, coffee, and most sweets in Mrs. Peck's kitchen. She also frowned on those who used tobacco and alcohol, even the occasional nip. So adamant was she in her beliefs that none of the Peck children ever drank wine or beer or puffed on a cigar or cigarette, even after they were grown adults.

Meanwhile, as she approached her midtwenties, Peck hadn't relented regarding higher education. While her brothers matriculated at Brown University, she wanted to live independently. In

1872 she began teaching language and mathematics at Saginaw High School in Michigan. All the while she pressed her parents on her wish to continue her education.

Still, her parents hadn't budged on the issue. They firmly believed only men belonged in the realm of higher education. Her mother, who subscribed to the view that pursuing a degree was foolish, wrote to her, "I hope you will not study unnecessarily this term. I have felt much anxiety about your health and there is great danger of your brain being overtaxed." Even her older brother John weighed in on the matter:

> I do not esteem it to be at all a desirable thing for you to graduate at a college. If your aim at a high education, for effect first, I would not have you placed upon a par with young graduates of the college. And in the end you could lay claim to a far better education than if you become a graduate of the Mich. University and this claim of advanced study.... I advice [sic] you to take one year of rest and also private instruction.... You have too good talents to take them to a University.

Peck would have none of it. Highly competitive, she had tried to outrun and outdo her brothers at every turn. She could whistle a tune better than her brothers, and she could play tennis and ride horses as well as they could. She excelled in dancing and was a keen whist player. Her growing espousal of women's rights stemmed from this fight to enjoy the same opportunities as her brothers.

Incensed at her brother's letter, she again broached the subject with her father. "Why you should recommend for me a course so different from that which you pursue, or recommend to your boys is what I can see no reason for except the example of our great grandfathers and times are changing rapidly in that respect. I certainly cannot change. I have wanted it for years and simply hesitated on account of age but 27 [the age she would be when her degree was completed] does not seem as old now as it did. I should hope for 20 years of good work afterwards," she wrote.

Finally her father relented, and in 1874 Peck became one of the first women to enroll in the University of Michigan. It had been four years since the university submitted to demands that schools receiving state funds admit women. While attending a university signified class privilege and personal luxury for most women in the nineteenth century, it was part of the growing movement for women to gain equality. Women's rights organizations criticized the argument that women were ill equipped for serious study because they were the "less robust" sex.

For Peck, attending university meant proving to her domineering and chauvinistic father that she could meet the same challenges as her brothers. It meant proving to her exacting mother that she was destined for more than keeping home and hearth. She graduated with honors in 1878, with degrees in Greek and classical languages. She subsequently earned a master's degree in Greek from the university in 1881.

Three years later, in 1884, Peck went to Germany to study the classics. While there she took time to tour, visiting the art museum in Dresden, taking a trip to the Royal Porcelain Factory in Berlin, and spending an afternoon in Potsdam, where she saw the emperor's summer palace. She also traveled to Pisa and Bologna. Tiring of museums and monuments, Peck journeyed to Greece to climb both Mount Hymettus (3,366 feet) and Mount Pentelicus (3,638 feet). She also traveled to Switzerland and climbed several peaks and passes, including the Theodul Pass. Clad in knickerbockers, hip-length tunic, stout boots, woolen hose, and a soft felt hat tied with a veil, Peck's apparel "raised eyebrows and a flutter of gossip."

The following autumn, in 1885, she became the first woman admitted to the American School of Classical Studies at Athens, which had welcomed women students and researchers since its founding in 1881. After her sojourn there ended in the spring of 1886, Peck returned to the States and taught Latin at Smith College.

As Peck worked to carve a new professional niche she courted some but never too seriously. Nothing in her journals indicated she ever seriously entertained the ideas of marriage or motherhood. Even though this widened the gap between Peck and her mother, she chose work as her path forward. She joined the paid lecture circuit as a means to support her newfound passion of travel; her humble teacher's salary didn't cover expenses and, unlike Work-man, she neither had a husband to rely on for financial security nor was independently wealthy. She launched her lecture career in parlors where small gatherings of women enjoyed hearing her speak about the art and architecture of Greece. In no time she moved to more public venues where she could attract a wider audience and earn more money.

Peck also used her lectures to advocate for women's suffrage, an issue she'd been involved in since her days at the University of Michigan. She bristled at the idea that "it is expressibly silly to make a great hullabaloo" about not being able to vote. She wrote to her brother John, the one who'd once argued so force-fully against her attending university, about a lecturer who came and "complimented our sex most highly in regard to intelligence saying we were much brighter and smarter than the men and almost in the same breath declared that if we voted we would cast our ballot for the handsome man with the waxed moustache. We left as soon as possible."

When she wasn't lecturing or teaching, Peck gravitated toward the outdoors, just as she had when she was young. Even now she recalled hiking with her family decades ago in New Hampshire and the Adirondacks. She remembered one hike up Stony Creek Mountain during a summer vacation when she was young and how, many years later, her mother, in a rare display of pride, described the hike to a reporter: "Where a chipmunk couldn't walk, she would go." These memories rekindled Peck's desire to climb.

---

By the time Fanny and Hunter returned from Italy in June 1893 and gathered Rachel and Siegfried in their arms, they'd been gone two months and five days.

No sooner had they settled back into the familiar rhythms of home life than Siegfried came down with the influenza virus. A dark hush fell over the house. At first Fanny thought the baby had one of many childhood colds. But over the next several days his fever rose and fell and rose and fell. Rachel, dressed in her nightgown, padded quietly about the house in felt bedroom slippers; before bed she'd perch on a chair and recite a prayer.

On June 22, Hunter, ever the physician, noted in a little journal that the toddler, pale faced, "cried out great deal and had cramps in arms . . . slept but little, drank much water . . . eyes dull." Two days later, their son was delirious. On June 25, Fanny dipped a small cloth in brandy and milk for Siegfried to suck on, hoping it would soothe him. His breathing labored.

And then the last day.

The virus had severely weakened Siegfried—simple acts of being washed and dressed seemed to exhaust him. Hunter noticed his tiny half-moon nails were cyanosed. "Perhaps within 12 hours we shall lose him, I fear," Hunter wrote.

Fanny couldn't tell whether her little boy was merely sleeping or slipping into a coma. She watched helplessly as Hunter opened the baby's lips to give him medicine. The child's lips and hands grew dusky, and around 4:30 PM Hunter cradled the child in his arms and carried him to his own room. Fanny tucked him into his crib. She tried to will her baby well. Siegfried's chest rattled, but he hadn't the strength to cough. He gasped, ground his teeth, his breath grew shorter. It seemed Siegfried would not live ten minutes more. Death shaded his eyes and a fearful Fanny clenched her heart.

"His eyes closed half turned upwards and outwards, a peaceful look came over his face. His breath suddenly stopped as gently as possible; not a moment indicated that he suffered. Not a muscle stirred. Our Siegfried was no more," Hunter later wrote in his journal. It was 6:15 PM.

Two days later Hunter wrote to his brother Lou:

> I write a line to tell you that Siegfried our pride and joy was taken away from us two days ago by pneumonia complicating influenza, that dread disease which is so often attended with pneumonia and renders the latter so deadly. He was ill 8 days. We are heart broken and inconsolable. Of a rare beauty of form and face, and of disposition amiable and playful to a degree I have never seen engaged in a child, he was beloved by all who knew him and attracted universal attention. He showed qualities, which gave promise of character and future usefulness. Our return is postponed but I think we shall still as soon as we can arrange our affairs, which have been disturbed by his illness and death. I cannot write more. The funeral will be tomorrow.

Siegfried Workman died June 26, 1893, aged three years, six months, fifteen days. He was buried near his grandparents in

Worcester Rural Cemetery. Fanny never spoke publicly about her grief, save for a poem titled "Only a Year":

One year ago, a ringing voice.
A clear blue eye.
And christening curls of golden hair,
Too fair to die.
The silent picture on the wall,
The burial stone
Of all that beauty, life, and joy,
Remain alone!

Siegfried holding watch chain.

3

# THE WHEELS GO ROUND

FOR THEIR FEBRUARY 1894 overnight trip from Frankfurt, Germany, to Basel, Switzerland, the Workmans booked the sleeper car at six marks apiece. Having arrived in Frankfurt from Dresden earlier that day, Fanny and Hunter settled into the compartment. Fanny stashed her holdall in the narrow closet and kept her handbag nearby, her woolen wrap loosely draped over her shoulders. The train rumbled into the night.

She was pleased they were taking a long cycling trip through Algeria. Maybe *pleased* wasn't the right word. Relieved. In the nearly seven months since Siegfried's death she had grown more restive. She hoped this voyage, which would take them hundreds of miles from home, would be a balm for her grief—a grief of which she could not, would not speak. A grief that also propelled her to assume a peripatetic life.

Her baby's death hadn't changed the way she mothered. She wasn't overprotective before, and she certainly wasn't going to become overprotective now. How young Rachel understood the tragedy is unknown; Fanny never mentioned it in her journals. She and Hunter did send ten-year-old Rachel to the Cheltenham Ladies' College after her brother's death. The English boarding school was a feeder school for Royal Holloway College and had been modeled after the boys' school Cheltenham College. Workman admired the ladies' school, particularly because Dorothea Beale, a prominent suffragette educator who founded St. Hilda's College in Oxford, had served as its principal since 1858. In time, Rachel would grow to find the strict regimen of boarding school life stifling, having been raised to believe in freedom and equality for women and in women's education. For now though, she dutifully followed her teachers' instruction and looked forward to letters from her parents.

Workman drifted off to sleep. She didn't open her eyes again until the train pulled into Marseille at 6:30 the next morning; all told they had spent "a very long and tiresome" forty-eight hours traveling by train from Frankfurt to Basel to Geneva to Lyon and finally Marseille. Boats bobbed merrily in the harbor as the couple walked toward the first-class Hôtel des Colonies.

Two mornings later, the steamship whisked them across the cerulean waters of the Mediterranean Sea. The couple relaxed, enjoying the calm passage and the chance to get acquainted with their fellow passengers. That evening they joined the captain for a multicourse meal. Also seated at their table were the first officer, the ship's doctor, and four other passengers, including the wife of the English consul at Grenada and a lieutenant of the English army on his way from India to Gibraltar.

The conversation ebbed and flowed as it does when a group of strangers breaks bread together for the first time. The expatriates' plan to bicycle across Algeria piqued the captain's interest. Yet, he thought he would be remiss if he wasn't completely candid. He suggested the upper-class couple might be more comfortable traveling across the French colony by rail as "the Arab dogs are dangerous, and attack on strangers in troupes." Workman took no offense at the captain's suggestion, though privately she thought him rather small-minded. "This was not encouraging; particularly to a woman whose skirts had previously sustained manifold injuries at the mouths of Swiss and Italian dogs. Even the thought of our revolvers and dog-whips did not quite dispel the gloomy impression produced by this statement of the phlegmatic skipper," Workman recalled.

Ultimately, though, the captain's remarks did not sway Workman in the slightest. She thanked him for his advice and explained that touring on bicycles would add to their adventure. It also meant they could pass through the country at "leisure, stopping where and when we pleased," she wrote.

The steamship docked in Algiers at one o'clock the following afternoon. Instead of lingering at the waterfront, the couple went straight to the Hotel Continental. After checking in, they made sure the bicycles were properly locked in storage before asking the bellboy to bring their luggage to their rooms.

A proper walkabout was in order after spending the night on the boat. The pair was eager to see the city's architecture up close. Workman looked forward to using her camera; "the opportunity offered the kodakist is a rare one," she noted in her journal.

After a light supper they repacked their saddlebags with only the essentials. Eight hours later the couple awoke, settled their bill, strapped their touring bags to the bicycles, and pedaled cheerily away. As always, dangling from Fanny's handlebars was her one extravagance—her teakettle.

---

First stop: the ancient Jewish city of Tlemcen. During the Spanish Inquisition the gates of Tlemcen had opened to welcome Jews and Muslims. Berber and al-Andalusian cultures blended here over the centuries. She saw signs of this blended culture everywhere, from the arched windows and doorways and lustrous mosaics to the array of spices flavoring the couscous and tagine she ate during her trip.

Attired in her ubiquitous woolen skirt, white shirt buttoned to her neck, and hat pinned to her frizzy brown hair, Workman was the picture of modesty. Meandering on foot through the city alone, while Hunter took a leisurely morning for himself, Fanny admired the flat-roofed houses. Most were stained the palest shade of blue with a turquoise *hamsa* adorning the facade. To make this symbol, said to protect against the evil eye, occupants dipped their hands in red or blue dye and pressed them against the wall.

In her journal on February 12 she noted that each house had "spiral stone stairways, hardly wide enough for a single person" and that they were built during the reign of the sultans "who cruelly persecuted the Jews." Yet Workman was not without her own parlor anti-Semitism. In her journals, she remarked how "some of the older Jews, engaged in earnest conversation, gesticulating with uplifted arms and flashing eyes, would make Shylocks such as modern stages cannot produce. Others, sitting in silence, in various attitudes closely muffled in their warm, soft cloaks, the folds of which fall carelessly around them, present figures no less interesting." Unfortunately, Workman's attitude was by no means atypical of the times in which she lived.

Workman ambled about the "particularly characteristic and interesting" area, and before long a Jewish woman invited her inside her home. The alcove-like rooms were cut into the stone and furnished sparsely save for simple pallets and richly embroidered pillows scattered on the floor. Workman inhaled the scent of wood and smoke while women prepared a meal over little pots of fire. Others swept the floors. Workman watched the women and children prepare for Shabbat, or what she referred to in her journal as "the Jewish Sunday." Outside again, she tried in vain to

"Kodak" the children. Every time she pointed the lens their way, they skipped away, laughter tinkling in their wake.

She visited the neighborhood's ancient mikvah, a ritual bath. Inside, many women, young and old, were either bathing or preparing to bathe in one of the old stone tubs. A wrinkled old woman attended the bathers.

As in the Jewish quarter, the Arab women of Tlemcen were equally hospitable and welcomed her into their homes. The inner courtyards, inlaid with colorful mosaics, opened onto a series of small rooms where women and children sat about cross-legged on deep red and blue kilim rugs, eating and relaxing. Peeking inside one room Workman saw a grandmother cooing at a baby. Pots for couscous stood on the packed dirt floor and aside from the door. As she left the house a cluster of children begged her "for a sou."

Fanny Bullock Workman, her back to camera, on her trip through Algeria.

Workman, second from left, in a photo captioned "Children of the Desert. Biskra."

After her morning of solo exploration, she found an overheated Hunter in the town square leaning on the bicycles and wiping sweat off his brow. The couple joined a circle of people standing around an old man, his skin a burnt caramel from the sun. Under a flourish of white hair his eyes swept the crowd. Carefully he extracted two large snakes from his leather bag and held them up before the gathering, making sure to keep the reptiles from getting entwined in his shaggy beard. He whispered to the snakes. Then he laid one on the dirt and tucked the other inside his shirt, near his heart. He raised his arm. As the sleeve rolled back, the serpent slithered out and coiled around his forearm. The serpent struck, and whatever trick the man had planned ended in a flash. Beads of crimson blood ran down his arm. With this picture firmly implanted in her mind's eye, Workman, with her husband following, pedaled furiously away, her Touring Club of France badge pinned to her topee hat, her hands gripping the handlebars.

The captain of the steamship had been right. The Workmans could have afforded to see the country as first-class tourists. Instead they chose to travel on bicycles, and if something happened between cities—if they were stranded, fell ill, or were injured—there was little chance for help. In 1894 that risk taking certainly set them apart from their peers in Europe and America. Here in Algeria, it set them apart for other reasons. The sight of two Americans riding through the countryside on bicycles was a spectacle indeed, especially the sight of Fanny Workman since the sight of anyone, let alone a woman, riding a bicycle was unusual. Occasionally the local population's curiosity evolved into something more exasperating.

One evening the Workmans stored their bikes in the stable of their tiny inn. They thought nothing of it and went inside, ready to wash the day's grime from their hands and faces and change out of their dirt-caked clothes. They sat down to a meal and a glass of water with a splash of grenadine. Fanny found it a "delicious and refreshing drink." Sated, they folded their napkins, pushed back from the table, and climbed up the stairs.

In the dead of night, a terrible racket wrenched them from a deep slumber. They rushed downstairs and pushed open the heavy front door. In the courtyard, screaming villagers fought over who would be the first to hop on the bicycles and take them for a spin. The Workmans shouted. The startled villagers scurried away. In their haste one of them knocked Fanny's bike to the ground, twisting the handlebar and denting the frame. Too tired to do anything about it then, the couple trudged back inside, climbed back up the wooden stairs, and burrowed under the covers once more.

Early the next morning, Hunter opened his metal tool kit and went to work. He hammered out the dent, tightened some screws, and straightened the handlebar as best he could. Repairs completed, the two pushed off, determined to cycle "over the Atlas to the Sahara."

---

The Algerian landscape and wildlife enchanted Fanny as much as the people. As they cycled it became something of a game to spot a dromedary. "Our frequent meetings with this quiet animal, together with the bad condition of the road made us realize that we had reached a land where the Arab and his camel could probably travel with greater ease than the American with his wheel," she wrote.

She quickly learned that dromedaries, which she referred to as camels in her journal, could exacerbate the already poor cycling conditions on the limestone roads, particularly after a rainstorm. "After rains the large feet of the camels, sinking into the soil a foot or more, leave the surface in an impassable condition." Now the cyclists not only had to contend with muddy roads but also had to try to avoid the deep footprints the animals left behind.

When not navigating pitted roads or dromedaries, Workman, a keen "Kodakist," relished snapping pictures of locals with her camera, which at four by five inches was portable and affordable (for the Workmans' purse, anyway) at $25. It was as easy to use as an ordinary field glass. Even Lieutenant Robert Peary had used a Kodak when he'd traveled across Greenland in 1893. The Workmans were mindful readers but were more likely to buy a travel book that included photographs. Likewise, as cameras came into wider use, the public at large developed a hunger to see and not simply read about foreign places.

In the wake of Siegfried's death, the world seemed leached of color. Now, taking to two wheels, Fanny felt her grief subside.

The colors inspired her interest in photography, which helped her deal with her son's death. Against the neutral tones of the desert, colors popped in a way they didn't back home. Pomegranate red, sapphire blue, and parakeet green.

During one stop, Workman reflected on the change of scenery and its effect on her. Sitting on a lawn sprinkled with primroses and anemones, "listening to the babbling brook at our feet, and watching the passing Arabs, some on foot, some on horseback, with their veiled women sitting behind, it is like a scene from the Arabian Nights, and an effort is required to recall the fact that, one week before, we were living under the leaden skies of Germany," she wrote. Here, under the twisted arms of these ancient olive trees, their gray-green leaves fluttering like hundreds of tiny fans, Workman thought nothing could be better than traveling by bicycle.

Their wheels turned. They passed fields abloom with violets and daisies. Green trees dotted with bright cherries fluttered in the breeze. They rode in and out of villages not mentioned on any map and watched the clouds gambol across the sky.

The couple headed toward the Chiffa Gorge toward the end of February. Located in the Tell Atlas mountain range, which runs across North Africa, from eastern Morocco through Algeria to Tunisia, the gorge itself is about six miles in length. Here the "great sight was the monkeys climbing all over the rocks in the mission des singes. . . . We climbed up there and found them swinging wild in all directions. Very curious sight," she wrote of the Barbary macaques. Twenty miles later they arrived in Blida. Orchards and lush gardens surrounded the city. Damage from the 1867 earthquake, which had killed about one hundred people in the vicinity, still marked its buildings.

Along the way Workman stopped to investigate a curious site. To her surprise, she saw people living in caves, similar to the prehistoric troglodytes in the Dordogne, France. She waved. Initially they seemed rather afraid. Once they understood the American couple meant no harm, they welcomed them into their dwellings to see the circumstances in which they lived. Some sold at market the wood and coal they brought down from the mountain. They used the pittance they earned to buy "their *farine* and make *gallettes* or bread of Arab kind." The Workmans met a family whose home was nothing more than a space under a rocky outcrop. Here the profusion of generosity from those who had far less material goods than she genuinely shocked Workman, and she planned to write and speak of it when she returned to Europe.

Nevertheless, Workman's concern for women's rights could be situational; there were occasions where she took a decidedly impe-rialistic attitude toward local populations. Once, on an excursion to Tangier, she wrote about the "bright, pretty slaves . . . in white and pink muslins" who served their coffee, with seemingly little thought given to the enslaved women's quality of life.

After leaving the caves but not the plight of women behind, Fanny and Hunter arrived in a tiny desert village. While sipping cool drinks under the evening sky, they had another memorable encounter. A woman dressed in a man's suit of tight-fitting white jean trousers, high gaiters, and a short sack coat approached their table. In a husky voice she asked them what, if anything, she could do to make their stay more comfortable. Nothing, they replied. Between cigarettes she spoke to them about orange and lemon orchards and regaled them with tales of hunting. Later that evening, when they had moved inside to dine, the couple overheard a group of guests speaking about her. Apparently she was an excellent shot. Who she was and what her story was, they never figured out. Still, the conversation left an impression on Fanny. All night she dreamed of orange gardens where "cordial Amazons in trousers" reigned.

In this way Algeria seduced the woman from Worcester, though she wasn't blind to inequalities and imperfections. Each night she jotted her observations in her leather journal.

———————

Poor roads were not the only hazard. Sometimes people posed the threat, and in those situations Workman was glad of her revolver, like the time the Workmans were headed back to their inn after a long day of cycling. They had hired a guide to ferry them across a small waterway earlier in the day. Upon seeing him on their return journey, they offered him the same fare to recross. He demanded double. Two menacing men popped out of nowhere to back him up. The Workmans refused to double the fare.

"At this he stepped forward, with an ugly expression, and laid hold of one of the wheels," she wrote.

Seeing that he gripped the long steel blade at his waist, Fanny knew talking was useless. "The muzzle of a revolver, within six feet of his face, accompanied by some forcible expressions, convinced him we were not so helpless as we had appeared," she wrote.

The thug and his lackeys turned without another word.

The unnerving experience behind them, they arrived in Kabylie, one hundred miles east of Algiers, thirsty, hungry, and a little shaken. She would leave the place disheartened by what she perceived as unfair treatment of women and girls. According to the guidebooks she had read, the Kabyle women held high positions in society. After spending time in their homes, she strongly disagreed. True, the Kabyle man usually had only one wife, but that was not proof of her emancipated position. Rather it likely spoke to economic necessity, Workman noted.

More than the issue of monogamy, or the occasional lack of it, she was disturbed by the way the Kabyle treated the birth of a daughter. "The newly-born girl opens her eyes on a world opposed to her advent. Her birth is celebrated in a very quiet manner, and only by the family circle—as the Arab would say, without noise," Workman noted. No one showered the parents or baby with gifts, and as the girl grew out of infancy, her education amounted to little. Sometimes a girl attended the village school, but that was the exception. When she turned twelve "the Kabyle girl, without even rudimentary knowledge, with all the innocence and ignorance of childhood, is sold to her husband by her father." The father would rejoice if he got five hundred francs, since the average price was two hundred and fifty francs, she wrote. The most upsetting part of this, in Workman's opinion, was that the girl only learned of her impending nuptials after the deal was sealed and after celebratory gunfire erupted in the village.

The abuse and exploitation of women she encountered and witnessed sharpened Workman's feminist inclinations. The poverty, lack of education, and number of child brides left an impression. "It is to be hoped that a light may fall upon the souls of men, that they may realize the great injustice practiced on the weaker sex, that a day of awakening may come," she reflected. All around her were signs of women's subservience to men. Indeed, Workman wrote, the "advance of a nation in modern ideas may be judged by the position occupied by its women, Germany being a notable exception, so we may form some conception of the degree of civilization existing in the Kabylie at the present time, by a brief consideration of some of the customs pertaining to the women." Professorial tone aside, she made her point: a country's advancement can be judged on the status afforded its women.

———

One year later, feeling inspired by their trip to Algeria, the couple chose Spain as their next destination for a cycling tour. Having read Richard Ford's 1892 *Handbook for Travellers in Spain* before they left Germany, they knew to bring as little luggage as possible. They chose leather saddlebags that when packed weighed about twenty pounds. Over peppermint tea, Fanny and Hunter paged through the red leather-bound Baedeker guide to Spain. Eyelids drooping from fatigue, they turned in for the night.

Months later, while working on a book about their experience cycling through Spain, Hunter would praise his wife for organizing their adventure. He credited her for making sure their luggage got through customs and noted that she carefully plotted the location of railway stations, which often served as post offices, from which they could collect and send correspondence to Rachel, friends, newspapers in Europe and the United States, and, later, to their book publisher. As Hunter was quoted in the *Milwaukee Weekly*, "Without [Fanny's] skill in planning the long route, energy in following it out, and attention to details our journey through Spain would not have been possible."

Before they had left for this trip, Fanny had also consulted Ford's guidebook to find out about the roads. Information was virtually nonexistent. "We neither knew nor could learn of anyone who had made an extensive tour in that country in the manner we proposed," the Workmans later wrote in *Sketches Awheel in Modern Iberia*, their bestselling book about the trip.

The Workmans tried to remember Ford's advice to travelers to learn "thoroughly by heart, and keep constantly at his tongue's end, the three short phrases *Digame usted* (please tell me), *déme usted* (please give me), and *hágame usted el favor* (be so kind). They are soon committed to memory, and they will carry him all over Spain." Sometimes, however, their manners slipped.

At one Spanish inn, the Workmans showed both a low regard for their host as well as their awkwardness in making conversation: "An obese, oily-looking south Spanish woman met us on the landing, and as dinner would not be ready for half an hour, invited us into her private sitting room, where we found her husband and a friend. After a time, becoming weary of our conversation, we took out our notebooks and began writing our notes," Workman wrote.

On occasion their position was reversed and the Workmans themselves were the objects of scrutiny. One Sunday morning in Spain, several Spanish women dressed in black mantillas peppered the couple with questions about who they were and what they were doing. The Workmans, trying to take in the scenery, tried to ignore the ladies, who then set up portable chairs on a lawn to better sit and stare at the American couple.

In Seville, the Workmans joined nearly twelve hundred other spectators to watch a bullfight. Cheers erupted as the toreador entered the arena; Fanny thought he must surely be the most popular man in Spain. Many in the crowd hoped they might catch a glimpse of Isabella II; the queen was known to sometimes attend. The Workmans had just missed the death of a famous toreador, which plunged the city into mourning. His funeral had been a semipublic affair. The spectacle of the bullfight left Fanny shaken, however. "The lead bull [was] worked up with fire crackers. People demanded it. . . . It was horrible, had seemed to please the public immensely," she wrote.

———————

With a steel-corded leather whip dangling from her belt to drive away wild dogs and a broad-brimmed hat askew on her head, Workman drew her pistol from the leather pocket sewn inside her skirt. She trained it on the brigand, quite prepared to pull the trigger. Already it had been a trying morning. A thorn had punctured the front tire of her bicycle, and deep ruts in the muddy road had ripped Hunter's tires nearly to shreds. And now a man with grime-covered hands wanted to hold them up.

Workman hurled a flurry of invectives at the robber. Unimpressed, he stepped closer, brandishing an adze. "He advanced toward us. . . . Threatening to strike us with it, he continued to advance . . . when I drew my revolver and threatened him. At which he let his adze fall and ducked his head like a whipped hound and retreated. We then walked by him and his animal with no further trouble. The revolver had a most quieting effect," Workman wrote in her journal.

---

Dreary skies threatened rain, but as they neared Barcelona the weather lifted. The Workmans were now in the middle of their twenty-eight-hundred-mile ride through Spain.

She was impressed with the plush carpets and double beds in the hotel rooms, the Smith and Wesson revolvers displayed in sporting shop windows, and the establishments advertising themselves as "American bars" and "Coktales."

She was less impressed with the treatment of women. "Barcelona is not a pleasant place for a woman to visit with a bicycle on account of the great number of rough mechanics and labourers [sic] at all times on the streets. Still, as for that matter, even in regulation street gown she cannot walk a block alone without being rudely spoken to," she noted in her journal.

Several mishaps had befallen the Workmans on their way to the coastal city. Sand had clogged Fanny's chain case, rendering the bike inoperative. She'd removed the chain and cleaned the links. Not three miles later, a thorn had punctured one of her tires. Hunter fixed it, but "then after repairing it the damned thing burst. I cut out the hold and cemented the ends together," Workman wrote. The tire had gotten caught in the rim and burst. Out came the repair kit for the third time. The third time was the charm, and after leaving Barcelona they'd pedaled on to Montserrat with no further ado.

Arriving too late in the evening to visit the monastery, which is nestled in the rocky face of the peak Montserrat, the Americans searched for lodgings. After being turned away from several inns, they found modest accommodations where the rooms were primitively furnished but clean and the beds quite comfortable. "We found it very endurable," she wrote.

The next day they rode through rocky country; the mountains stood out in shades of green and gray, sprinkled with box, ilex, myrtle, ivy, heather, and laurel. Storing their bikes at the monastery, they hiked the three hours to the Montserrat summit. It was a most enchanting view, Workman thought. Surely, "he who planned and carried out the path deserves as much credit as any engineer of the famous mountain passes," she wrote.

A thin iron railing on the edge of the cliff was all that stood between her and a several-hundred-foot drop. Workman respected the view from a healthy distance.

Once again seated on their bikes the couple flew along the road, and Fanny admired the wide aquamarine sea, the sweeping vistas of plains and barren mountainsides, and the occasional broken Roman column or crumbling arch.

They cycled over the Guadarrama Mountains, where juniper groves and Spanish broom thickets provided cover for Spanish ibex and wild boar, weasels, and fox. They had it easy for about ten miles. Then the road steepened so much they were forced to dismount and push their bicycles uphill. Four hours later, with aching shoulders and backs, they reached Puerto de Navacerrada, the top of the pass. They got back on their bicycles and rode through pine trees and low-lying bushes until they crossed the eight-thousand-foot-high Peñalara, Guadarrama's highest peak.

In the evening, the couple sipped weak tea, well fortified with whiskey, and Workman opened her journal. In her tightly formed script she reflected that when she started this trip she had dreamed of writing about Spain's architecture. She realized she preferred the stone spires of nature to man-made cathedrals and houses. It was the first sign Workman's work would soon go in a different direction.

Beyond Spain's large cities, few people, and even fewer animals, had encountered bicyclists before. Part of the "attraction" was Fanny Workman herself. Female travelers were often met with curiosity, disbelief, fear, suspicion, and aggression. Once again Workman was glad she had sewn a pocket into her petticoat to carry a gun.

One evening, while riding toward Castellón de la Plana along a coastal road, they happened upon a two-wheeled cart driven by two men who were returning home after a day's labor. Bolting at the sight of the cyclists, the mule overturned the cart, throwing one of the men from the back. While the other man chased the mule, the one on the ground got up, grabbed a mattock, raised it over his head, and "ran towards us in a towering passion, threatening our lives, and swearing we should go no farther. We told him to stand back, and let us pass, but he paid no attention to the request, continuing to advance in the same threatening manner."

His face flushed scarlet, the mule driver closed the gap. Twenty feet. Ten feet. Five feet. For the second time in as many weeks, Fanny drew her revolver from her concealed pocket. His posture changed instantly.

"Lowering the mattock, and raising his right arm before his face as if to shut out the sight of the weapon that glared upon him, he crouched down and stood for a moment very much in the attitude of a whipped cur. Then seeing we did not fire, he quickly retreated towards his cart, offering no further obstruction as with revolvers still drawn we walked by," she wrote.

———————

After leaving Castellón and its richly picturesque Moorish castle under balmy skies on April 17, Fanny and Hunter found themselves on a road so muddy that the spokes of their wheels clogged. It was virtually impossible to pedal through the muck. The couple gave up. Fortunately they weren't far from a small railway station near the ancient port city of Valencia. They took a local train for the remaining seven and a half miles, it was dusk when they arrived in Valencia. In the garden of the inn, orange trees, heavy with fruit, bent down to the ground and filled the air with their perfume.

At the end of the next day the red sandstone hills blazed in the fading light. A stooped man rode out on his mule to see them. Waving arms as knotted as an ancient tree, he beckoned them to stop and offered them a cup of cool wine. While they drank, "women rushed down the hills to see me ride. Evidently more unusual to [see] women riding here than even in other parts of Spain," she wrote. Workman took it all in, the mother with her five children who lived in a tiny cabin and "were so glad to get our cakes and baskets."

A few days later, on a lonely stretch of road near Alicante, the couple spied a team of about twenty mules coming their way. Here we go again, Workman thought. The driver, "a huge bullheaded ruffianly fellow with a bloated sunburned face, jumped down and made for Hunter," she wrote.

Her hand moved. She felt the reassuring weight of the revolver in her pocket. Then just as quickly as she had put her hand to her pocket she withdrew it. Any show of force in the presence of so many was futile. They were a half dozen to her and Hunter's two.

She wasn't quick enough, though, and the driver let go of the reins and sprang to the back of his wagon. She and Hunter tried to continue, but then the assailant rushed them with what looked to Workman to be an eighteen-inch knife, "his fiendish face livid with rage." He was too close for her to draw her revolver. He moved as if to strike. "There seemed to be no chance of escape. The stab of the gleaming blade could almost be felt, the exact spot where it would enter be judged." And then, in the time it takes to blink, it was over. One of his companions caught his arm and stopped him.

Workman huffed. "This sort of adventure was becoming a trifle too frequent to suit our fancy. We had not come to Spain to measure our prowess with that of intoxicated teamsters; we neither aspired to the glory of shooting them," she wrote.

They rode over high rolling hills and along the edges of precipices. They scrambled over dry riverbeds where winter torrents had raced, and sometimes they dismounted because the path was too narrow. Finally, they reached Madrid.

The couple stopped off at a postal center to send mail and forward letters. They had learned that sending or receiving mail often depended on the mood of local officials. Because their mail often spent two, three, or more days lying around before being sent, Workman was always thankful when she learned a letter had been delivered. More often than not their letters never reached their destinations.

News reporters occasionally followed their travels through Spain, and the Workmans were happy to grant interviews. The Workmans sometimes sent word of their adventures to their former hometown newspapers. Additionally, word of the two Americans on bicycles also spread in the towns and cities they were visiting, and so reporters were able to learn of their whereabouts. In their book *Sketches Awheel*, Fanny recounted how "When the press pursued for interviews 'the Englishman Senor Workman and his *sposa distinguida*' who are making the tour of Spain arrived in Cuenca from Tarancon yesterday afternoon. They rode two '*bicicletas magnificas*,' which they understand perfectly how to manage. It cannot be stated positively, but they will probably appear on the track at the velodrome to-morrow before the races. Owing to their limited command of our language, the reporter was unable to learn anything of their future movements." Despite this report, the Workmans did not make an appearance at said velodrome.

In these interviews Workman proved she was a woman of contradictions. She could be a snob with a profoundly colonial attitude toward local people, as evidenced in her behavior in some of the Algerian villages. She was also deeply interested in and sensitive to the world unfolding before her. Sometimes it seemed as if two people resided in the gray-eyed woman. There was the Fanny Workman who saw others in terms of their social status and skin color, and there was the Fanny Workman who championed women's rights and spoke of a day when women would be judged on their deeds, not their dress.

––––––––––

Workman and her husband of more than a decade were fast becoming addicted to the freedom of traveling. The longer they stayed away, the harder it was to return home. But all adventures must end. The couple arrived in Dresden in late 1895 with a new-found sense of clarity and confidence. So ended their several-thousand-mile trip.

As they settled back into the familiar rhythms of domestic life, they decided to collaborate on a book. The entries in their pocket-sized journals provided the framework for *Sketches Awheel in Modern Iberia*. Fanny did most of the writing and rewriting. Hunter searched for a publisher. He found one in Thomas Fisher Unwin, based in London. Unwin wrote Hunter that he was "quite prepared to print, produce and publish your book"; so long as the maps and prints were received on time, he would publish it early in the spring. Though little correspondence between Unwin and the Workmans remains, he went on to publish several of their books, even though the couple was initially displeased that he put their picture on the cover: "We strongly object to any picture in which we appear."

While the book's prose wasn't exactly a selling point, the collaborative nature of the work was. When readers opened *Sketches Awheel*, the first thing they saw, after the title, was the name Fanny Bullock Workman. Most female authors of the day were identified either solely by their initials or as *Mrs. So-and-So*. Workman's name on the title page sent a message to women that they too could claim their position in whatever they wished to pursue, be it climbing, exploring, or suffrage.

Of course, favorable reviews from the American press also helped sales. The *Milwaukee Weekly* found their book entertainingly narrated; the paper was particularly effusive about the photos, which showed the advantage of having a camera for travel writing: "From this it will be seen that the travelers went out of the 'beaten track' into sections in which they had many interesting but often annoying experiences with hotel and inn-keepers."

About two years after their trip through Spain, Fanny decided it was time for another adventure. Only this time she wanted it to be more—more daunting, more difficult, more distant. They decided on a fourteen-thousand-mile cycling trip through India, Burma (now Myanmar), Ceylon (now Sri Lanka), and Java. They didn't know it when they started in 1897, but they would endure sandstorms, rabid dogs, and a walk across a rope bridge suspended thousands of feet in the air.

To the native New Englanders, the flowers and fauna of Ceylon were especially exotic. Monkeys, jackals, and rabbits. Tree ferns, orchids, and jackfruit trees. They passed over ruins and villages nearly camouflaged by vegetation. After watching local dancers perform, Workman distributed money and pies. Green parrots squawked and chattered in the trees. Once, they stayed in a house that had "very simple, beds like stone, no bread no soda water, but we exist cheerfully on tough chicken and mushy rice."

In one village, she observed the women's "curious custom of greeting their husbands or any chief or elder of tribe when they return home . . . falling on their knees and taking first one foot and then the other of the man and lifting and placing on her forehead." At a missionary school, she was bothered to learn the girls were "kept here until 15 and often married from here," but she was impressed that they learned reading, writing, geometry, and algebra. She recorded all of this, the sounds, sights, and scents.

———————

Upon their return to Germany a little more than a year later, their luggage barely unpacked, the Workmans began preparing for their next trip. First, though, they penned their next book, *Through Town and Jungle: Fourteen Thousand Miles Awheel Among the Temples and People of the Indian Plain*. As before, their journals served as a skeleton for the book. It contained the dominant themes of Fanny's first story, "Vacation Episode." It was romantic in tone in a way their five later books on mountaineering would not be. Even though the writing was aloof, it touched on the prominent features of Fanny's life: her restlessness, her interest in women's liberation, and, of course, mountains.

As they wrote the book, they also wrote a few articles about the trip, published in *Harper's* and *Outing* magazines. The pieces helped them court the kind of media coverage in both the European and American press that in turn helped them sell books. They welcomed the name recognition that followed, and in time they would make sure to send word of their trips to various news outlets in the United States.

In 1898, they again sailed to Bombay, then traveled to Cape Comorin, the southernmost point in India and the confluence of the Indian Ocean, Bay of Bengal, and Arabian Sea. They aimed to cycle the length of the Indian subcontinent, ostensibly to study architecture but more likely to break their own record for distance covered on two wheels. This time they hired an Englishman to help carry their luggage. Workman soon found fault with him, unsympathetic to how difficult it was to ride with suitcases strapped to his handlebars. She fired him after he accidently rode off a precipice in the rain, a mishap that damaged the luggage but left him unscathed. She had read Murray's *Indian Handbook*, and while she thought it had "considerable literary taste," she found it lacking in "practical details" that make a guidebook reliable. "We were a number of times led astray and put to considerable inconvenience by inaccuracies," she wrote.

They forded rivers. They pushed their loaded bicycles through sand. They rode in temperatures as hot as 160 degrees Fahrenheit, and on occasion as far as eighty-six miles in one day. Once they mended forty tire punctures in a day. They cycled through plague-ridden villages devoid of a single soul. All the while Workman's teakettle clanked from her handlebars.

Several weeks later, the couple arrived in Kashmir. Looking for some an escape from the heat, they organized their first mountain excursion. They cycled from Srinagar (located in present-day Pakistan) eastward into Ladakh along a "wretchedly kept carriage road . . . so clogged with traffic that the visitor has to undergo a purgatory of discomfort." They went as far as the Karakoram Pass. They spent the summer exploring the area on foot, and toward September they made their way to Darjeeling, a British hill station with winding streets and market stalls nestled in the Himalayan foothills.

Next on the agenda was navigating the local bureaucracy. They needed permission from the Indian officials acting on behalf of the British government and assistance to visit several peaks bordering on the forbidden lands of Nepal and Tibet, so named because they were once closed to foreigners.

Together with their Swiss guide Rudolf Taugwalder (no relation to the Taugwalders who'd climbed with Whymper), they met with the deputy commissioner and his subordinate. Unsure of exactly which permission forms they needed, he reeked of inexperience. After a few minutes of hemming and hawing, he called his superior for advice. He also tried in vain to find two *sirdarsi*, or local leaders. When they finally returned to the office, they too proved ineffective.

Moreover, not a single official admitted to knowing anything about the area the Workmans intended to explore. Each time the couple asked, the "principal *sirdar* would place one hand over his heart and raise the other aloft, turning up his eyes with a pathetic expression, as if to say, 'What you wish to do is beyond the range of human possibility,'" the couple remembered. Additionally, they were repeatedly warned about tigers and wild elephants.

Then, just at the moment Workman thought she had exhausted her last ounce of patience, one of the officials confessed that, why yes, he did in fact know a little something about the region. He then took it upon himself to give Workman a sermon on the route's difficulty and how the dense rhododendron forests, the rivers, the steep and slippery paths, would "make the proposed route almost impassable to a woman," she wrote.

Workman swallowed her exasperation. She assured the civil servant that she was in fact quite accustomed to such challenges. Clutching the permission papers in hand, the trio turned on their heels, walked out the door, and headed for the market.

Though Workman had organizing down to a science, she didn't anticipate the price gouging that awaited. "It was immediately noised abroad in the bazaar that a large expedition was afoot. Stories of fabulous wealth floated through its dusty mazes, and its merchants excited to fever heat," she said. After much spirited haggling, Workman and the guides bought enough supplemental provisions to last eight weeks, including nine sheep and liberal quantities of rum.

In short order they hired an additional sixty porters to add to the forty-five already on the team. After dividing the food into portions, they pitched tents in a thistle-covered field not far from the outdoor markets where they had shopped that morning. A few hours later, angry voices rose over the camp, drowning out the hum of insects. Wondering what the ruckus was about, the Workmans sent for the *sirdar*. He ran to the Workmans' tent. The porters were threatening mutiny and refused to continue unless their rations included curry. Fanny was thoroughly exasperated. Where to find curry, she had no idea. It wasn't as if she could dash down to the corner store and buy curry, or any other spice the porters fancied. Fortunately for her, she didn't have to figure it out. The porters agreed to continue on come morning.

It was not to be. A fierce snowstorm enveloped the camp shortly before first light. The snow piled up high and fast, reducing visibility to less than ten yards. Avalanches rumbled in the distance. After discussing their options, Fanny, Hunter, and Taugwalder agreed there was no way forward. The routes were likely to be impassable. Everyone trudged back to Darjeeling. A disappointed Fanny vowed to return.

Nevertheless, they ventured far enough into the region to see Mount Everest "floating up from a mellow haze to inappreciable height."

Having laid eyes on Mount Everest, the Workmans decided it was time to return home. And so more than a year later, in 1899, back in Germany the couple, now aged forty and fifty-two, stored their bicycles and vowed to return to India as Himalayan explorers.

4

# STEADFAST IN SKIRTS

DURING THAT SUMMER of 1898, Fanny decided that rather than attend the Wagner festival in Bayreuth, Germany, as they had before, they would go to the Himalayas, a range of sky-piercing peaks whose Sanskrit name means "abode of the snow."

It took fifty-five million or more years of tectonic compression, of shifting and colliding plates, for the Himalayas to rise from the earth. Slowly the granitic and volcanic rock formed into the world's highest peaks. The range is home to the world's fourteen "eight-thousanders," those mountains measuring more than eight thousand meters, or twenty-six thousand feet, as well as at least fifty peaks with elevations over twenty-three thousand feet.

The range isn't simply high. It's also long. Separating the Indian subcontinent from the Tibetan Plateau and covering approximately fifteen hundred miles, it passes through the nations of India, Pakistan, Afghanistan, China, Bhutan, and Nepal. The range actually comprises three parallel ranges often referred to as the Great Himalayas, the Lesser Himalayas, and the Outer Himalayas. The Kohistan region sits to the west of the peak Nanga Parbat. The Ladakh region lies between Nanga Parbat and the Karakoram strike-slip fault. In Southern Tibet one will find Mount Kailash, the Gangdese batholith, and the city of Lhasa. Of all the ranges the Workmans could explore, it was the Karakoram that fascinated Fanny and Hunter—so much so that the couple would devote the next decade to exploring and measuring its peaks and glaciers.

It's impossible to know exactly who were the first westerners to visit the region or when they came. There were military men and traders, explorers and religious men. Alexander the Great is said to have made it as far as the Hunza Valley. Buddhist missionaries traveled the region, and legend has it that in 1160 Rabbi Benjamin of Tudela traveled to Baghdad and recorded conversations with those who had traveled in Tibet.

Centuries passed, and by the 1800s the British Empire began intruding from northern India into the Himalayas and Afghanistan. The British brought a more systematic, almost militaristic approach to exploring the region. They also brought a hunger for the region's natural resources, including spices and seeds, cotton and wool, grains and opium. They set about conquering and colonizing enormous tracts of land from Peshawar in the northwest to Darjeeling in the northeast.

For decades the officers of the Crown mapped the region in secret. That changed in 1823 when the Welsh surveyor George Everest was appointed superintendent of the Great Trigonometrical Survey of India. He oversaw the survey of the region from southern India all the way north to Nepal. After he retired in 1843, Andrew Scott Waugh stepped into the position. Three years later, in 1847, Waugh's office launched a survey of Kashmir's Karakoram Range, which extends to the China and Nepal borders. In 1865, despite Everest's objection, the earth's tallest mountain, known as Chomolungma in Tibet and Sagarmatha in Nepal, was named for him.

When the Workmans arrived that late spring 1898, they were keen on setting off for parts unknown. They endeavored to map and photograph their progress in this southwest corner of the Tibetan Plateau. Unlike most explorers of this time period, they had neither government nor geographical society sponsorship. Their itinerary would take them from Srinagar to Ladakh. They knew the area remained largely unmapped in spite of previous survey work and visits to the region by celebrated mountaineers such as Sir Martin Conway, Henry Haversham Godwin-Austen, and Francis Edward Younghusband. The Workmans planned to circumambulate the 28,169-foot Kangchenjunga with their guide, Rudolf Taugwalder of Zermatt.

---

It had taken the Workmans nearly twenty days to travel from Dresden to the British colony of India and another week to reach Karakoram, located in present-day Pakistan. Traveling by rail in India had improved in the past several years. The Calcutta Tramways Company was incorporated in the 1880s, and by 1890 the East Coast State Railway was up and running; seven years later the line introduced lighting on its passenger coaches. The Jodhpur Railway followed suit in 1901 when it outfitted its cars with electric lights.

After spending several tedious hours in line, they cleared customs at the Kashmir border. Having studied the region a bit before their trip, Workman sensed this was going to be far different from any of their Alpine climbing trips in Switzerland, France, Tyrol, or where they first fell in love with climbing—New Hampshire's Presidential Range. Unlike those locales, these summits had no stores or hotels within striking distance. They needed to fully outfit themselves and their team with proper mountaineering and camping gear before they left.

Every piece of equipment, every morsel of food had been shipped ahead in crates. Lanterns, knives, leather punches. Even buttonhooks might come in handy for first aid or repairs. The entire team needed wool boots dipped in alum to make them waterproof and thick flannel shirts, woolen knickerbockers, and woolen tights. They needed gaiters that fit perfectly over their boots and fur hats or knitted balaclavas. Swiss-made ice axes (reportedly better adapted for step cutting than those made in England). Rope and mackintosh-lined rucksacks. Drinking cups fashioned from leather and canvas and treated with wax on the inside to prevent leakage. Crampons made specially to fit over the hobnailed boots. And, of course, sketchbooks, note-books, pencils, maps, compasses, altimeters, barometers, and hypsometers.

For food, there were self-cooking tins of Irish stew and mul-ligatawny, as well as kola biscuits, advertised to curb hunger and give an extra pop of energy. Tins of Lazenby's peas, beans, and soup nestled in the crates alongside containers of beef-tea loz-enges, which some climbers liked to suck on for energy.

Several boxes contained medical and first aid supplies, includ-ing bandages and Seabury & Johnson's adhesive plaster. There was lanoline to protect against sunburn and vegetable laxatives, opium, quinine, saccharin, a small bottle of cholordyn, and a solution of cocaine. Apparently a drop or two of the cocaine solution instantly relieved inflammation of the eyes resulting from exposure to the snow.

Aside from their eiderdown sleeping bags, they packed Mum-mery tents, which weighed about fourteen pounds each. In addi-tion, they packed oilcloths, which had to be laid underneath each tent to block wet snow and ice, and a rug to spread out inside the tent to prevent the climbers' hobnailed boots from shredding the canvas floor. All this added an extra fifty-five pounds.

---

A centuries-old city, Srinagar sits on the banks of the Jhelum River, crowded with houseboats, some two stories high. In springtime, dark storm clouds roll down the valleys, and showy flowers, all scarlet and violet, carpet the mountainsides. After strolling through the city, admiring its gardens and nine old bridges in spite of the summer heat, Fanny, with Hunter's help, got busy purchasing additional supplies. They shopped for spices, teas, chickens, and mutton.

Oftentimes, Hunter tended to watch the planning from the sidelines. That it was his wife and not he who led the team seemed to bother the local men. They bristled at taking orders and advice from a woman—even if she was their employer. Hunter, though, was used to it, and frankly he was proud of the way she took the lead. To be sure, her abrupt and occasionally condescending manner of speaking sometimes added unnecessary friction. She had a habit of arriving in a village like something of a tempest, demanding service and supplies, rounding up food, tea, and tobacco. So too did any man who had ever headed an expedition.

Workman found hiring porters vexing. It wasn't as if she could simply post an advertisement in a local circular. There was a certain protocol. She and Hunter were prepared to pay a handsome sum for the services of porters. After all, they were persuading men to venture into parts unknown for several weeks to several months. But she needed permission from the local *lumberdar*, or chief; he had the final say over who went to work and who didn't.

Yet just how much authority he actually had "we have never been able to determine, but we judge it to be more nominal than absolute, from the fact that, on more than one occasion, our servants have been obliged to drag out unwilling coolies from hiding-places in which they had concealed themselves to escape the service to which they had been appointed by the *lambardar* [*sic*]," she later wrote, using what is now considered a slur for porters.

Once they hired the porters and purchased additional supplies, the expedition went on its way. On July 27, 1898, the party reached Leh, a few days before a religious festival. There they hired an interpreter, a "well-known character, whom we will call Mr. Paul, a sly and cunning Madrasi who had settled in this remote spot and married a Ladakhi lass," Workman later recalled. Mr. Paul favored European dress, but his wife "was richly clad in native costume, her *peyrac*, or head-dress, falling below the waist behind, and being richly studded with turquoise."

Workman applauded Mr. Paul's penchant for sartorial splendor: "When on march, Mr. Paul was an ornament to the party— mounted on an active Nubra pony, with white Ellwood toppe [*sic*], tweed riding coat, knickerbockers and gaiters, and English boots with pointed toes."

The expedition headed toward the Kardong Pass. Once a principal caravan route between Leh and Kashgar, located in westernmost China, thousands of horses and camels crossed the pass annually. While the porters traveled on foot over the dusty and stony path, the Workmans and their guides mounted yaks. With its curtain of dense fur, the bulky bovine was the animal of choice in the region. Weighing upward of thirteen hundred pounds and able to tolerate extreme weather, the animals were ideal for long trekking expeditions.

It was the first time on a yak for either American. Their sure-footedness surprised Fanny. On steep mountainsides where not even a semblance of a path existed and where even the most experienced mountaineer might hesitate, the yaks passed safely and, dare she say, rather nimbly. "Our yaks would examine footprints and walk round the bad places, choosing in every case a firm foothold," she wrote.

Aside from the yaks, about a dozen ponies carried equipment. Where the yaks appeared solid and behaved with discipline, the ponies looked half-starved and behaved rather wretchedly, in Workman's opinion. The ponies made a game of constantly throwing off their loads and then either jamming them one into another or smashing them against the rocks.

Thus the group, resembling a traveling circus, continued on to the Sasser Pass. In the distance, the mountains appeared to graze the sun, the peaks reaching from twenty-one thousand to twenty-five thousand feet.

Vultures circled above. Up and down the line, frightened porters whispered. It was said the birds plucked flesh from human skeletons littering the trail ahead. As it happened, there were no human remains; instead the way was strewn with fresh carcasses and bleaching bones of scores of ponies that had died along the way. "These afforded plenty of occupation to the vultures, so that anyone desiring to investigate the anatomy of a pony could not do better than camp for a few weeks in this equine graveyard. In some places, these skeletons covered the ground in groups of from twenty to fifty, as might be seen after a severe battle," she wrote. But perhaps there was something to the porters' dread. Later, Workman learned that an Englishman who had recently traveled over the route had stumbled upon two human skeletons poking out from the earth.

No such ghoulish encounter took place for anyone in the Workman expedition. They climbed up the snaking 14,000-foot Purkutse Pass (modern maps indicate this is Parkchik La) without incident. Rounding a bend, they spied the 23,540-foot Nun Kun. Upon descending to the Suru River, a tributary of the Indus River, they paused for a moment for refreshment. A village lumberdar offered them a brass vessel filled with sweet milk and a plate of cooked cabbage. As the milk touched her lips, Fanny realized just how thirsty she was.

———

Meanwhile, halfway across the world, Annie S. Peck sat in the cozy confines of her parlor. Several Greek and Latin books, as well as a neat row of red Baedeker guidebooks lined the bookshelves. In the far corner, a nearly eight-foot-long wooden alpenstock leaned against the wall next to an ice ax. A spinning wheel stood in the corner.

The Rhode Island native reflected on her successes to date. It was 1898, and a *New York Times* journalist was interviewing Peck for a profile. Three years earlier, in 1895, she'd triumphantly summited the Matterhorn. She wrote about the two-day excursion in a piece called "A Woman's Ascent of the Matterhorn" for *McClure's Magazine*. Summiting the iconic Swiss mountain had long been a goal for the Latin teacher ever since she'd climbed California's Mount Shasta in 1888, then Greece's Mount Hymettus and Mount Pentelicus in 1884. True, the Greek peaks were only between three thousand and four thousand feet high, "but the scenery was beautiful," she told the reporter while sitting on a couch, her cat curled on a cushion.

As for the Matterhorn, "people had said so much about it that I did not really know what it was going to be, but I was not at all frightened. I told the guides when I came down that I should like to go again immediately," she said.

Only after Peck had made up her mind to scale the mountain had she told her friends about her plans. Her friend David Starr Jordan had suggested she hire a couple of first-class guides and follow their directions implicitly. Perhaps she might engage Jean-Baptiste Aymonod, a forty-year-old French-speaking guide known for his reliability. Jordan cautioned her to avoid joining a large group, "for the danger on that mountain is greatly increased by an excess over the number three in the party."

Not all of her friends were so supportive. Indeed many thought her foolish for even entertaining the notion. Her dear friend Jennie Cunningham Croly wrote:

It makes me shudder to think of it if I were only there to prevent it or if you are determined to win glory at such a risk I would accompany you, and to share the glory or the most horrible of deaths the mind of man could conceive. I have not enjoyed one moment of peace of mind since I read in the *American* that you were to climb to glory on the Matterhorn. I cut out the piece and sent it to you in my last letter. . . . If you are tired of life and wish to shuffle off this mortal clay, return to America and we can climb some gentle, sloping, grassy mountains and lay quietly down and die like good Christians.

Looking back now, Peck was glad she had paid their concerns no mind. Now she found herself once again remembering the day of the climb in detail. She had taken a room at the Hotel Mont Cervin in Zermatt. Opened in 1855, the hotel's first visitors were mountaineers and naturalists. On the morning of the climb, Peck tugged on her woolen stockings and heavy woolen underwear. She pulled first gloves then mittens over her hands. A thick nubby sweater and a felt helmet over a woolen hood completed the outfit. In her canvas rucksack, she packed her black spectacles and a white veil to protect against snow blindness. She was careful not to lace her boots too tightly to account for the slight swelling common at altitude. A local cobbler had added layers of leather and cork and large-headed nails to the soles of her boots, so traction wouldn't be a problem.

As Peck remembered the story, she could almost feel the way the snow had pricked her face like a thousand glass needles. She also remembered how the physical discomfort of that day had paled in comparison with the emotional discomfort caused by the guide's initial attitude toward her. He wasn't used to female climbers. He seemed to have made up his mind that she wasn't mentally or physically capable. She persisted, showing him through her actions she was made of stern stuff indeed.

She recalled how she'd looked up as she walked toward the base of the Matterhorn that day in 1895. A veil of mist parted, revealing the familiar outlines of the massive rock, "clothed in its scanty garb of snow, from which it seemed to be shaking itself free, as if despising the pure white covering in which its neighbors contentedly repose, and proudly raising its uncovered head to the stars," she later wrote in *McClure's Magazine*. Like Workman's fictional prose, Peck's language also tended toward the flowery.

Her guide, Jean-Baptiste Aymonod, who had already summited the Matterhorn twenty-seven times, led her past the churchyard. Stone after stone marked the grave of someone who had perished on the way up the mountain. Surely a visit could wait.

A few hours later, Peck and Aymonod reached the Hotel Schwarzsee, situated on the broad shoulder of the mountain at 8,474 feet. After a bite to eat, the pair kept going. They slept that night on the ridge and after a light breakfast left the following morning. It was still dark. The only light came from the candles in their lanterns. They made their way along a path over rough rocks. Occasionally she felt snow underfoot; occasionally she felt bare rock. The path narrowed. Now barely six inches wide it crossed a smooth and steep slope. Peck knew they would be climbing in snow soon enough, but for now she put all her energy into what was turning out to be a difficult rock climb. She was glad that the other day she had ascended the Grossglockner, one of the most difficult mountains of the Eastern Alps, to strengthen her muscles.

After spending the night in a hut on the side of the mountain, Peck and her guide left in the predawn darkness, holding candles for light. At half past four in the morning, the sky started to lighten and they blew out the last candle. An hour later they neared an old, disused hut, filled with snow and ice. About two hours later,

Peck stood on top of the narrow ridge that is the Matterhorn's summit. Her thighs and calves burned. For the teacher turned climber, the ascent was its own reward, and the risks, the discomfort, the exhaustion were part of it. She and Aymonod didn't spend much time on the top. And so, before long, she bid the summit farewell and started her long descent. "Such a climb is enjoyable, not simply for the exercise, varied and exciting though it be, and for the elation which victory inspires; but also for the intimate acquaintance thus gained with the mountain," she later wrote.

By early evening she was back in her room, where she stripped off her wet and frozen clothes and took a long soak in a tub. After she rested, Peck wrote her friends and assured them they would not be reading about her demise. Her friend Minnie E. Young rejoiced upon hearing the news. "Now don't let it happen again!" her friend said, "Your account in the Herald we read out loud. I could almost hear you telling us."

Another friend was convinced Peck could earn a lot of money lecturing about her Matterhorn climb if she sensationalized the story just enough. Peck agreed and sold the story to *McClure's Magazine* for $400. The National Geographic Society offered her $30 to deliver a lecture on both her Tyrol and Matterhorn climbs. The magazine couldn't offer more as it was "pushed financially." Later Peck would command upwards of $1,000 from magazines such as *Harper's Monthly.*

In the years following her Matterhorn climb, Peck delivered nine lectures in and around Boston. She also addressed several chapters of the Geographical Society across the Eastern Seaboard and spoke at the Art Institute of Chicago. Slowly she gained a following for her illustrated lectures on the Matterhorn, Mexico, Tyrol, and Switzerland.

The Boston Lyceum Bureau, which later changed its name to the Redpath Lyceum Bureau, publicized Peck as one of its most entertaining lecturers. James Redpath, a journalist and abolition-ist, had founded the lyceum in 1868. The organization rose to prominence as one of the most successful agencies in the nation. Its roster of speakers included, in addition to Peck, the likes of Susan B. Anthony, Frederick Douglass, Julia Ward Howe, and Mark Twain. A promotional pamphlet described Peck as one of the most scholarly, most accomplished ladies in the United States, "whose fame as a mountain climber extends over this country and Europe. . . . With a pleasing personality, an unusually grace-ful manner, a charming voice which easily fills the largest halls, and a story to tell of thrilling interest, she holds the audience in rapt attention, fascinating equally old and young of both sexes." Audiences would not be disappointed.

Three years after she climbed the Matterhorn, the press was still eager to talk about how she was one of the few women to summit the Swiss peak. Yet they became positively animated over the forty-eight-year-old's preference for climbing in trousers.

Peck, who sewed her own knickerbockers, found the whole thing quite maddening. She took umbrage at the idea that fem-ininity only came dressed in silk and damask gowns and that women who wore pants were some kind of abomination. She simply believed one should dress for the occasion. Of course, she wasn't so incensed that she refused to use the fascination with her attire to help her secure funding. People were keen to see the pants-wearing lady in person after reading about her and paid to hear her lecture. Nonetheless, she still occasionally posed in long gowns, a flourish of lace at her collar, perhaps a flowered brooch pinned to her bodice. Although when she did, she often included objects that spoke to her success in the field of exploration: ice axes, ropes, and telescopes.

In 1901 the sporting magazine *Outing* published an article by Peck suggesting pants should be considered merely another piece

Annie S. Peck poses for this studio portrait attired in her alpine garb. The photo was used on promotional items, including Singer sewing machines and cigarettes, and to advertise her lectures.

of equipment. "For a woman in difficult mountaineering to waste her strength and endanger her life with a skirt is foolish in the extreme. . . . That men know better what is womanly and what we are capable of than do we ourselves, has not seemed to me logical or proper," Peck wrote.

In her view, climbing in skirts was uncomfortable at best, dangerous at worst. In her article for *McClure's*, she advised women who were nervous about wearing pants or knickerbockers in public to wait until they were out of sight of other tourists to trade their skirts for knickerbockers. She suggested they stash the former under a rock until after they returned from their excursion.

As the Victorian era closed, it was a bold gesture to be photographed wearing trousers, in leather boots with her climbing rope fastened around her waist. There were still isolated cases of police arresting women for wearing men's clothing. In 1895, the same year Peck scaled the Matterhorn, New York City police arrested a young woman for riding a bicycle in men's garb. The case hinged on whether a court believed bicycle bloomers too closely resembled men's trousers.

The topic of women in pants had long been a favorite subject of many feature stories. In 1852, the *Ladies' Wreath*, a monthly journal to which about twenty-five thousand New Yorkers subscribed for one dollar a year, had run an article "The Bloomer Dress." In it, Professor William M. Nevin insisted that women wearing bloomers would usher in socialism or fanaticism. Moreover, he argued such women would undoubtedly "succeed in destroying all moral government and civilization."

As Peck's reputation grew, so too did her fan base. Letters from young people filled her mailbox. There was Fanny Henderson, who delighted at the reports of Peck's escapades: "Our class at school in physical geography have been reading of people ascending the Matterhorn, but they were all men. And as we have read that you were the third woman who ever climbed it, we thought that perhaps you would not mind writing and telling us your experience."

There was young Charles Slacks. Like many people of his day, young and old, his hobby was philography: "Dear Madam, I am a boy fourteen years old. I collect autographs. I have Grover Cleveland's and [comedic stage actor] Sol Smith Russell's and Wm. McKinley's. It will be a great kindness if you will send me yours. Please, send me yours."

Of course adults, too, clamored to hear about her exploits, and so she peppered her lectures with anecdotes about the sport's hazards and its beauty. A skillful orator, she had a gift for spinning her exploits in such a way that it sounded like anyone could rope up and strike out.

She told one rapt audience that bike riding was more dangerous than summiting the Matterhorn. Foolhardiness accounted for at least three-quarters of the accidents that occur in mountaineering, she said. She conceded that extreme weather or falls were always possibilities; however, if one were skillful and prepared, then all should be fine.

She used a calm and deliberate voice when speaking in contrast to her writing. She described climbing thousands of feet high as if it were as easy as a stroll through a flower-strewn meadow. "Obviously a college athlete or one with wholly untrained muscles, need not begin at the same place," she wrote, adding that one simply needed "good nerves, either natural or acquired. . . . Naturally, it is an advantage not to be very stout; one might almost say, the thinner the better, for it is easier to acquire muscle than to reduce flesh."

Though there were a great many people who lauded Annie Peck and even aspired to be her, her mother was not one of them. Just as the elder Ann Peck had disapproved of her daughter's wish to pursue a university education, she looked down on her newfound passion. It was a tired, circular argument between them that would never be resolved.

Fending off her mother's criticism, she was determined to test herself further. For that, in 1897 she chose Mexico's Pico de Orizaba, the third-highest mountain in North America, after Alaska's Denali and Canada's Mount Logan.

Again Peck needed financing. Her income from her lectures helped offset travel costs, but it wouldn't be enough to cover a trip across the border to Mexico. For help, she solicited the *New York World*. She hoped the paper might finance her quest to climb the

18,491-foot peak. American soldiers had first climbed Orizaba in 1848; knowing she couldn't claim it as a first ascent, she pitched the story idea as the first ascent by a woman. She would set a record for highest climb for a woman if she succeeded.

---

In 1897 Peck went south of the border. She climbed the volcano Popocatépetl before turning to Orizaba, the white-capped mountain rising from the tropical forest floor high over the state of Veracruz. For the first time, Peck decided to treat the climb as a scientific expedition. She took along a mercurial barometer, which measured the mountain's altitude. The US Weather Bureau (today called the National Weather Service) calculated the results at 18,660 feet, very close to the current reading of 18,491 feet. The different results in altitudes from the Workmans' era to today occur in large part because of technological improvements such as the development of the Global Positioning System in the 1980s. Today most scientists will place radios on the peaks of a mountain range; satellites will then record the measurements and determine the elevation.

In spite of her success she wasn't satisfied. She decided to aim even higher next time, "to attain some height where no man has previously stood."

Back home, friends showered her with congratulations. She was also greeted with newspaper stories that placed a Miss Irene Wright, who had joined Peck's group, atop the summit first, thereby undercutting Peck's victory. It was a taste of a far greater controversy to come.

Peck wrote to the editor of the newspaper to set the record straight, scolding them for not waiting to hear both sides of the question before accusing her of "filching" the claim to having reached the top. Wright's side of the story is lost to history, and so there is no way to confirm Peck's account.

In her article to the *New York World* Peck explained that she withheld the names of those in her climbing party because the paper had engaged her to focus on her own story, no one else's. Rather than identify them by name, she chose to refer to them as a lieutenant in the army, a lawyer from Michigan, and a young lady from Colorado. She explained that when she reached the summit, the guide told her that she and the Colorado lady "were the first two ladies to attain it. *The World*, not being interested in any other, left out *all* reference to other members of the party and made the statement, which you read."

Peck fumed. Neither the climbing community nor the press gave her full credit for the climb. Moreover, according to Peck, the young lady in question had rushed the summit and arrived before her, which was another source of contention. This was a gross breach of climbing protocol. After all, Peck had secured financing for the expedition. Peck conceded Wright had reached the summit first, but only by a few moments. Additionally, Wright had offered her guide $1.50 extra if he would get her to the top first, according to Peck. So hard and fast had Wright pushed herself that she had a pain in her heart once she reached the top. Peck said she, too, hadn't felt well that morning and had made no effort to reach the summit first and, contradicting herself, said that it was only because of her kindness that Wright had gotten there first. "That she should take advantage of my kindness . . . to win glory at my expense I consider a very contemptible proceeding," Peck wrote.

Peck's celebrity grew. A photo of her in full mountain regalia had been included with every 1895 Singer Sewing Machine. The picture showed Peck wearing a hat tied carefully under her chin, rope about her waist, and what had become her signature canvas knickerbockers and jacket.

Upon her return to the United States, Peck hoped the public and press might have found something more interesting to discuss than the fact that she wore pants to climb. Not a chance. The press continued to obsess over what Peck wore. Even as she continued to scale new peaks, news accounts of her clothing either accompanied her achievements or overshadowed them all together. In 1898, the *Evening Times* in Pawtucket, Rhode Island, appeared to emphasize her "striking costume" more than her climbing. No one remarked on the garments of male climbers.

———————————

Meanwhile, Workman kept abreast of her rival's achievements. Newspapers and magazines routinely covered Peck's exploits, and Workman received newspapers from America. From reading mainstream press, such as the *New York Times*, as well as more specialized journals, such as the *Journal of the American Geographical Society of New York*, she knew Peck had summited Orizaba and Popocatépetl. She also knew Peck was making a name for herself over the Matterhorn climb. "There is a lady who has spent some time in America lecturing upon her climb of the Matterhorn, and she has drawn great audiences," she told a reporter. Already well respected in the clannish climbing community, Workman was not going to let anyone dislodge her from the top.

Aside from staying on top of news about Peck, Workman was wrapping up a grueling series of lectures, something she began shortly after their first trip to India. Women still had a hard time landing speaking engagements in Europe, as men still actively debated whether women should be accepted as full-fledged members to their various societies. Still the Worcester native was one of a small but steadily increasing number of women working to be considered equal to men as explorers, scientists, or geographers. She cared not one whit about offending the patriarchal sensibilities of some of her peers because of her forthright personality and undeniable success. In her heavy woolen skirts and hobnailed boots, she had already climbed higher than most men—a fact she frequently shared with interviewers. In a June 26, 1900, article, the *London Daily News* reported that Workman had climbed four thousand feet higher than "any other lady."

By the 1890s, many botanical, statistical, Asiatic, Hellenic, and anthropological societies already welcomed female members; as of 1884, women had been allowed to join the Royal Scottish Geographical Society. Nevertheless, while many organizations still refused women entry, it was getting harder for the Royal Geographical Society to justify a practice that allowed women to address a society and write papers and textbooks, yet still denied them full membership. In a letter titled "Alpine Club for Women" printed in an August 1907 issue of the London paper the *Standard*, one writer lamented, "It has been a grievance that admission to the Alpine Club has been refused to women, despite the fact that Mrs. Bullock Workman holds the world's highest record in mountain climbing."

Nonetheless, once women were permitted to join these clubs nothing like anarchy or female domination ensued. The men quickly learned the geographical society did not in fact denigrate into a "social club" but rather remained as venerated as before. But for now, women weren't allowed in as members, and that weighed on Workman. She thought about how she needed to break barriers here at home and records out there in the Himalayas.

# 5

# THE GLASS JAR

I N THE FIRST part of 1899, before the Workmans would again
explore the Karakoram, they spent several months on a bicycle
tour through Indochina (now known as Southeast Asia). They were
particularly drawn to Saigon (now Ho Chi Minh City). In Fanny's
opinion, French colonial rule had turned Indochina's southern city
into "a thoroughly modern land . . . [and a] lively over filled French
town," and everywhere she looked she saw echoes of Paris in the
city's aesthetic. There were leafy parks and private schools where
the upper classes sent their children. Railroads now connected several cities, the streets were paved, and new bridges spanned rivers.
There were cafés worthy of the Left Bank and hotels and government buildings whose facades would not have been out of place
in the City of Light. She never remarked, however, on the manner
of colonial rule, the bloody way the French had wrested control
from the people of Indochina and sought to oppress their cultures,
which were thousands of years old.

Over the border in Cambodia, the couple visited the crumbling
stones of Angkor Wat and walked amid the overgrown environs.
They dipped in and out of Singapore and took a trip aboard a
"fairly clean steamer across to Java." Aboard the boat, the normally
indefatigable forty-year-old Fanny suddenly felt unwell. Whether it

was the sea or something she ate, she "had to call a boy to empty my slops and bring washing water both night and morning and then they did it with ill grace." Cool compresses and sips of water and hot tea helped, and by the time they arrived in Java she felt restored in body, if not mood.

Silvery gibbons bounded through the tropical rainforest. Rocky coastal cliffs gave way to rice paddies. The Workmans felt removed from events taking place halfway around the world. On March 2, 1899, President William McKinley signed a bill establishing Mount Rainier National Park in Washington. Two days later, in Queensland, Australia, forty-foot waves crashed

Fanny Bullock Workman in Saint-Rémy, standing next to her safety bicycle. Uncharacteristically, she is wearing bloomers.

ashore when Cyclone Mahina struck, killing more than three hundred people.

All the while, the Workmans pedaled onward. Every day they rode through swampy heat. Every evening they peeled off sweat-soaked clothes. Several thousand miles later, the couple had their fill of Southeast Asia and decided to return to the Himalaya before beginning their trip home. Therefore she and Hunter decided they would return to the Karakoram. She wanted to cross the high-altitude Hispar Pass in Pakistan and then follow the Biafo Glacier, a forty-two-mile-long icy expanse. Such a trip meant they would be at elevations no less than seventeen thousand feet the entire time. Part of the appeal for Workman was the challenge of trekking across largely unmapped terrain.

Ninety-nine percent of the world's glacial ice sits in the polar regions, and there are glaciers on every continent. These frozen expanses are the largest reservoirs of freshwater on earth, releasing it in meltwater as temperatures warm. Glacial ice varies in age. Present-day scientists estimate some Greenland ice is more than one hundred thousand years old, while the glacier on McMurdo Dry Valleys of Antarctica could be over eight million years old. When Workman walked on the ancient ice of the Biafo Glacier she would test herself in a land of extremes. She would find out what it was like to start a day of exploring under a searing sun only to find oneself knee-deep in snow with icy rain pelting one's neck a few hours later.

———————

The Great Trigonometrical Survey of India had executed the most comprehensive survey of India thus far. Founded in 1802 by the East India Company, it had endeavored to map the entire Indian subcontinent. Initially the project was expected to take five years; the work continued for more than seventy.

Ergo, the Workmans would not be the first Europeans to attempt to map the region during this part of their 1899 excursion, even a fraction of the region. Even so, they planned to map the glacier troughs, crevasses, and ice falls. They wanted to detail the direction of the glacier's ridges and whether the ridges were snow-covered or rocky, narrow or broad, steep or gentle. In short, the two aimed to detail the anatomy of the Biafo Glacier. To prepare, Fanny wrote to Sir Sidney Gerald Burrard. The British army officer was then superintendent of the Trigonometrical Survey. She wanted to get information about its work regarding the Hindu Kush at the westerly extension of the Karakoram range. Her letter was the start of an extensive correspondence, for Workman knew the glaciers there were long and unexplored.

With a mind to serious work, Workman invited Matthias Zurbriggen to join their expedition. The experienced Swiss guide had joined them on their Matterhorn excursion and previously had climbed the Karakoram with the renowned British mountaineer Sir Martin Conway, and with Edward FitzGerald had summited Argentina's Mount Aconcagua and New Zealand's Mount Cook, also known as Mount Aoraki.

Zurbriggen was born in Saas-Fee, Switzerland, on May 15, 1856. He was two years old when his family left their small village for Monte Moro, on the Swiss-Italian border, where a more lucrative job in a gold mine awaited his father. The promising future was short lived; in 1864 Zurbriggen's father died in a mining accident. When he was old enough, Zurbriggen took a job in a nearby factory to help support his family. Before long the young man started climbing to escape the daily drudgery, slowly knocking off one peak after another, including the Matterhorn, Breithorn, and Jungfrau. Realizing there was money to be made as a mountain guide, he quit the factory for good. Zurbriggen took clients, including Edward Whymper and Sir Martin Conway, throughout the Alps, Andes, and Himalayas, and to various peaks in New Zealand. Over time he earned a reputation as one of the nineteenth century's great alpinists.

Upon accepting the offer, he agreed to work for "the couple Bullock-Workman" for the whole expedition save for Sundays and religious holidays. Together, they outlined a bold plan to explore the western glaciers of the great Himalayas that drew her "with irresistible power . . . like a magnet."

---

The Workmans arrived in Srinagar, the last stop in civilization, Fanny mused. As usual, it fell to her to iron out the details of their anticipated three-month-long expedition. Although the couple aimed to take turns leading each expedition, the responsibility for each trip usually fell to Fanny as Hunter often assumed a supporting role. Now savvier about organizing, Fanny knew exactly how to go about hiring local labor and which stalls in the bazaar carried which supplies, including curry and the town's famous dried fruit.

Before leaving Germany, Workman had made sure the British government, through its Indian office, sent letters of introduction to the maharaja of Kashmir. In turn, he ordered all village headmen to furnish the expedition with necessary help. But in Srinagar the Workmans ran up against an officious official who tried to stonewall them with a myriad of excuses. First he told them they couldn't go because of regional strife, then he cited the fact that monsoon season was upon them. When that failed, he trotted out Workman's least favorite excuse: it was too dangerous a trip for a woman. He soon gave in.

Before the final permission letters were delivered in a neat stack tied up with a ribbon, Workman hired fifty-five local porters, cooks, and washers. A cursory review of the porters' equipment showed most lacked even basic gear, including climbing boots and woolen stockings. Then there was the matter of food. The Workmans had shipped peas, beans, cheese, and soups, as well as biscuits and bouillon cubes. But they also needed sheep, goats, and chickens. During a long expedition, occasional fresh meat would be a welcome indulgence. Lastly, they needed yaks to help carry the loads into the hinterlands.

––––––––––

Rising at the first hint of light in the sky, the Workmans heated water for their tea. As always, it was black tea, which they'd brought from home. At this point Fanny's slightly battered kettle had as many miles on it as she did; it had accompanied her everywhere, from their first cycling trip through Germany, across the Atlas Mountains, through the streets of Saigon, aboard a ferry in Java. Now here it was in the Himalayas.

This first camp was a flurry of activity. Porters drove stakes into the hard-packed earth to pitch tents, started fires, and unpacked supplies, all under the watchful eyes of Fanny and Hunter. After the campsite was more or less set up, Workman took a moment to talk with Zurbriggen. He told her some of the porters "kept running away from the route to smoke. . . . They are all a nasty lot," Workman noted.

She surveyed the scene for a few minutes. Aside from a few men who were in fact sneaking smokes, the porters were hard at work. Seizing the moment, she ordered everyone to stop whatever it was they were doing. Speaking through the lumberdar, who acted as an interpreter, she announced that while they would spend the night here, no one should get too comfortable. They would move out after first light. The team spent the rest of the day in camp getting ready for "four days in the wilderness."

On the expedition's first full day in what Fanny dubbed the wilderness, while marching across the plateau toward the Biafo Glacier, the team saw "a grand immense white tower of a peak." It was twenty-three thousand feet high. Hours later, they arrived in a valley where they camped on a ploughed field. Dusk brought on clouds of mosquitoes.

"Now, the mosquito is an insect of noble proportions and gigantic voice. He attacks one with persistent virulence from sunrise to sunset; and unlike his *confère* of the tropics, this valiant denizen of the Deosai leaves his victim to rest at night, and is in full possession of both breathing and buzzing apparatus on an elevated plateau of 13,000 feet to 14,000 feet," Workman later wrote in an article for *Wide World Magazine*.

Workman wore rugged shoes studded with steel nails, a heavy skirt, and several sweaters. A helmet on her head and a canvas tote slung across cross her body with a few kola biscuits tucked inside completed the picture. Her husband, in woolen pants and flannel shirts, strode behind. Later, when newspapers in the United States ran stories about Workman, with accompanying photographs taken from the climb, her garb attracted attention.

"The question of dress, especially for women is an interesting one. Mrs. Workman's outfit is exceedingly well shown in the illustration. For climbing about on rock walls it is conceded by everyone that the skirt is dangerous, since it may catch at some critical moment and bring disaster and injury to it wearer. But for the higher snow fields Mrs. Workman wears a short skirt," according to an article in the *Boston Globe*, which ran a photo of Fanny.

The sun reached its zenith on the second day just as the team crossed the Zoji La, a high mountain pass. At 11,578 feet high, it clings to the mountainside between Jammu and Kashmir. The southern branch of the Silk Road, it had remained one of the most important mountain passes in India. It had been used during the Mongol expansion throughout the Asian continent from around 1207 through 1360. Now, instead of bearing spices and dyes, the Workman expedition carried maps and barometers.

Once over the pass, the team, including the yaks and ponies, walked along "the wild and beautiful road." On either side of the red sand shore the rocky banks melted into the green valley. Nearby forget-me-nots and yellow flowers sprinkled overgrown meadows, while "simply exquisite wild rose bushes grew on the perfectly barren mountain sides," she noted in her journal, the pages wrinkled and the ink blurred from water damage.

As they walked, the sun's rays baked their faces and necks. It was like standing next to a kiln. "The sun burns hot all day and the cleanness of the atmosphere is wonderful, likewise the light and shade. At times, every nook and crevice of high mountains on the opposite side looked so clear that one can about grasp them. It seems as if I had never seen such wonderful shadows cast by the sun," she wrote.

---

On July Fourth, the party left the small city of Leh and its many Buddhist monasteries. Sharing a border with Tibet on the east, the city had once been the capital of the northern India Himalayan kingdom of Ladakh. Though modern travelers will find the city fairly easy to reach, such was not the case in the Workmans' day.

They hiked across the Kardong Pass, away from the city, and reached their camp in darkness. No one was complaining about the heat anymore. The temperature had plunged nearly seventy degrees. The camp thermometer registered thirty degrees Fahrenheit. The brilliant moonlight cast a "fine effect on the mountains."

Come morning, the team paused long enough to admire how the mountaintops sparkled against the indigo sky. One snow-covered peak reminded Workman of the Monte Rosa, another of Mont Blanc.

With full stomachs they continued along the bumpy road toward the tiny town of Askole. Today the distance between Leh and Askole can be covered quickly in jeeps. In the Workmans' time it was slow going—one traveled on foot, yak, and pony. Located in the Shigar Valley, Askole was the last human settlement in Gilgit-Baltistan before the wilderness of the Karakoram. It would also be their last chance to supplement their supplies. The town would be their official starting point and, if all went well, their finish line.

On the way to Askole, they navigated paths so narrow that one false step meant falling into a gulch or hollow. Half a day later, they reached the village, with its dwellings shaped from mud and stone, some with cages on the roof to create sleeping spaces in the summer. It took all of five minutes for Workman to make a derogatory remark about the local population. "The Askole people are good mountaineers, but they are great cowards, and they have an aversion to ice, preferring a different and tiresome route over moraine. They rather resemble Polish Jews in dress and appearance," she wrote. Yet, when the rajah came to visit after dinner and handed her "a sweet-smelling nosegay of welcome," she greeted him as an equal.

By late morning the group was packed and ready for the long, steep descent toward the glacier-fed Braldu River. No one spoke much. Several miles into the hike, they stood at the river's edge. Before them lay their first true obstacle of the day—a narrow rope bridge suspended 270 feet above the raging water. It was one of the oldest types of suspension bridges—Chinese diplomatic missions in the Han dynasty had used them while traveling about the western and southern fringe of the Himalayas, the Hindu Kush range in Afghanistan and here in Gilgit.

Workman considered the rope and took a deep breath. Her stomach tightened. She stepped off the bank and put her boot down on the foot rope. She felt the bridge move. She took her next step and tried not to think about how the only thing separating her from the deadly current was one hand-twisted rope. She kept a cool head and focused on the heels of the person in front of her. She took another step. And another. The "bridge sways and swings as we go. . . . One feels as if four pairs of hands would here not be enough to make one secure," Workman wrote.

A couple of days later, Fanny pushed back her tent flap and stepped into the bracing morning air. She raised her German-manufactured Zeiss telescope to her eye. She fiddled with the wheel until the view came into focus. In the valley she saw pink, mauve, and deep red marguerites strewn together with edelweiss flowers, forget-me-nots, wild roses, and sweet columbine.

For twelve hours, they marched over a rocky ridge adorned with cairns and fraying prayer flags. Their destination was the seventeen-thousand-foot-high mountain pass of Skoro La, in the remote Shigar Valley. They stopped often. The rarified air affected several porters. Only when they were on the other side of the pass did they pause to slake their thirst. The change in terrain riveted Workman. Where just a short while ago they had walked on packed earth, they now stood on a moraine ledge in an exposed position with no cover should any rocks fall. The porters built tent terraces on the jumble of schist rocks. Darkness shrouded the camp.

The next morning, the rising sun washed the rocks in yellows and pinks. With virtually no breeze and even less shade, Workman anticipated a difficult day ahead. Still, she was happy—the team had crossed Skoro La unscathed. Of course, she conceded, they had yet to be truly tested. They still faced the most difficult part of the Biafo-Hispar traverse. Steep hillsides and boulder hopping lay ahead. Four major tributary glaciers from the north had to be crossed.

Several days later, after making it over the previous obstacles, on July 17, Fanny and Hunter mulled over the next leg of their journey. They decided to tackle Koser Gunge, which rose a formidable twenty-one thousand feet high. Knowing they'd be eating tinned food for some time, they ordered the cook to butcher one of the sheep. When the lumberdar had purchased it back in Askole, it had been "a lively-looking sheep, but on the following morning, after walking a few steps, it absolutely refused to stir. No amount of coaxing, beating, dragging, or punching with an alpenstock was of any avail," she wrote.

After a savory mutton stew and a few hours of sleep, the Workmans, Zurbriggen, and two other porters departed, carrying tents, ice picks, rations, and first aid supplies. Progress slowed as they approached the glacier's center. They probed for deep crevasses and, when possible, steered clear of enormous seracs, columns of glacial ice, which were frequently the size of a house. Their beauty belies their danger: like a tree rotted from the inside, they could topple without warning.

Zurbriggen was on point. About an hour after they started out they came to a narrow gallery sandwiched between two rock towers. The group waited while Zurbriggen cut a way through. It was tedious work and had to be done slowly. The Workmans were quickly learning how much of exploring was spent waiting, staring at an ice wall or snow-covered ground or the back of the person in front of you. Sometimes she found herself trying to count snowflakes on the ground. Every so often Zurbriggen paused and rested against the rock wall rising alongside the path. His work finished, the group passed through the white-blue ice gallery one by one, leaving their packs behind.

After everyone cleared the passage, Zurbriggen stood on the narrow ledge and handed the packs forward. The team acted like a fire brigade. First the Swiss guide took a pack. Then he slung it across to the outstretched hands of the porters waiting below. By now the rest of the group had caught up, and so Zurbriggen "hefted the whole bundles of 50 men through that gallery, a treacherous task on any man and he did it with perfect dexterity. It was a most precarious position as he stood on one foot mostly balancing the other leg across an opposite serac," Workman wrote.

Two days later the expedition had a most inauspicious start to the day. One of the men stumbled and fell into a thirty-foot-deep crevasse. Zurbriggen fastened ropes around his waist and shoulders. Two well-muscled porters lowered the Swiss guide down into the gap, letting the rope out inch by inch. An hour and a half later, the team hauled Zurbriggen and the porter up and over the side. With no one hurt, save for a few scrapes and bruises, the group advanced at a snail's pace. The troop continued until another huge crevasse yawned before them.

It was too big to cross and there appeared to be no safe way around the chasm. As it was already late in the day, Fanny, Hunter, and Zurbriggen decided returning to camp was the safest course. There they could consider an alternative route up the Koser Gunge. Such was the way of climbing, Workman thought over a bowl of tepid soup. Forward and backward and forward again.

———————————

Something was amiss. Ever since daybreak, Zurbriggen had exuded surliness. He wouldn't speak and made a great show of lagging behind the team. Workman wondered what irritated the guide. Maybe he was sick. Maybe his muscles ached from yesterday's exertion. Perhaps the high altitude bothered him. She decided to ignore his behavior. At least until lunch. "When we sat down on glacier for tiffin I sent for him and he came up . . . unwillingly," she wrote. After a brief exchange about how the morning's exploration would go, the conversation devolved into what Workman later described as a tirade.

He said the Workmans were the first of any employers to be dissatisfied with him. Workman denied ever saying anything of the sort. Nonetheless, she also reminded him that if he wouldn't meet the terms of service she "should not hesitate to speak of it in print." Zurbriggen let loose. The world would believe him, not her, he sputtered, and furthermore, he wasn't getting enough to eat. "He ended his food tirade by saying 'he would . . . help himself before he would starve' which was of course the grossest insult."

Zurbriggen stomped off muttering about how the Workmans shunted him aside, putting him in a tent by himself and treated him as a "native"—"An absurd accusation as most persons regard a tent to themselves as a luxury. Altogether it was the most absurd . . . display of temper and insult we have ever seen in any man we have employed and treated well," she confided in her journal that night.

Workman was discovering, just as her rival Annie Peck had learned, that the greatest challenge for women explorers lay not in the terrain, nor the climate, nor the quantity of provisions. No, the greatest challenge lay in overcoming the doubt and disapproval of a society that preferred women simply stay home. "But like most . . . the guides were rather impatient of what they considered unnecessary advice or suggestions from a woman, even an employer," Peck would later observe. On that point the two women could agree.

Of course, Workman's present circumstances meant she didn't have the luxury to contemplate inequality; not here, not now. She needed to convince the team to continue regardless. Ultimately, they did, and eventually Zurbriggen calmed.

The fight with Zurbriggen had slowed them down and wasted the better part of a day, but the decision soon after by several porters to refuse to go forward ground them to a halt. Workman deployed what little leverage she had: money. "We then refused to pay them and after much talk they said they would all go." It worked. Most of the team went ahead while a few agreed to go to the previous camp and get more food. Just when everything appeared back on track, Zurbriggen lost his cool again.

The guide kicked one older porter in the stomach and "fired a shot from his revolver in the air to frighten them," she wrote. Zurbriggen was showing signs of instability. Fortunately no one was seriously hurt, and the Workmans were able to calm the guide down. Onward they marched. Every step brought them deeper into the Himalayas.

Formed millions of years ago, the Himalayas act as a barrier to the wintertime cold winds that scrape across the continent from Siberia, and the summertime monsoon rains that sweep across from the Indian Ocean deliver rains so drenching it could feel as if water had seeped under one's skin.

—————

"Weird, ice-covered towers" is how Workman described Ogre Camp, their new site. Sitting on a deeply crevassed glacier on the southern spur of the Biafo Glacier at 17,400 feet, it was the highest camp they had made so far.

The camp lay at the base of its namesake, Baintha Brakk, called the Ogre, a craggy 23,901-foot-high mountain in Gilgit-Baltistan. Although Workman had set her sights on the peak, she actually would never even attempt it. It remained unscaled until 1977 when British climbers Sir Chris Bonington and Doug Scott stood at the top. It would be twenty-four years before Thomas Huber, Urs Stöcker, and Iwan Wolf summited the mountain's south pillar. No one in Workmans' party dared attempt the peak; they knew their limits. Nevertheless, the desolate camp cradled by twenty-five-thousand-foot-high peaks made an exquisite backdrop for Hunter to photograph his wife.

They pitched three tents on the small grass-covered terrace, which covered a rocky outcrop hanging two hundred feet above the glacier. That night, when she slid into her sleeping bag she felt a bit like a tin of sardines on a market shelf. It was a strange place to spend the night.

It's not clear from her journal entries when the Workmans and Zurbriggen reached a rapprochement, but somehow they patched their relationship, although the guide's behavior never stopped grating on Fanny; everything he did annoyed the woman from Worcester, even the way he ate. "Z who keeps filling his stomach every two hours and then complains because of diarrhea. He is a fool about taking care of himself and an ass in most respects and his manner exceedingly rude when we are doing all we can for him," she noted. Hunter stayed removed from the drama, making only passing remarks in his journal. Instead he focused on topography, measurements, and distances covered.

Measurements were everything for the expedition. They could write about the flora and fauna, the striations of the rocks, or their climbs up various peaks. But they needed evidence of the altitude for each ascent. They couldn't ask readers, audience members, magazine editors, or society at large to simply take their word for it.

The Workmans used boiling points with a pressure hypsometer to determine altitude. Water reaches boiling point at a lower temperature at higher elevations because lower air pressure means the liquid can change to gas more easily. To make their measurements, the Workmans first recorded the temperature at which the water boiled. Then they looked at a reference chart, which gave an estimate for altitude based on the boiling point.

In addition to the hypsometers, the Workmans also used barometers, which use liquid, such as mercury, oil, or water, to measure air pressure. The atmosphere presses down on a reservoir of the liquid and forces it up a graduated tube. Atmospheric pressure decreases with altitude—air gets "thinner" so the liquid drops lower in the tube when you move higher up the mountain. Like with the pressure hypsometer, a reference chart helped the Workmans convert barometric pressure to altitude. Hunter recorded each measurement in the back page of his journal in scrunched handwriting.

The expedition spent three nights and two days at Camp Ogre. While there they crossed Snow Lake (Lukpe Lawo), a high-altitude glacial basin at the head of the Biafo and Hispar Glaciers. In 1892, just seven years before the Workmans arrived, Sir Martin Conway had become the first European to lay eyes on the frozen expanse. Marking his presence with a rock cairn, he said, "Beyond all comparison the finest view of mountains it has ever been my lot to behold, nor do I believe the world can hold a finer."

While in the region Workman hoped to see markhor goats. Wearing corkscrew-like horns, the wild goats had lived in the region for thousands of years, attracting artists and hunters alike. Elliott Roosevelt, First Lady Eleanor Roosevelt's father and President Theodore Roosevelt's younger brother, had traveled to India in 1880 to hunt markhor. Fanny merely wanted to photograph one for her next book.

High above the lake, they prepared to rappel. The guides secured a rope at a point above the planned descent. Workman ran the rope between her legs and into a kind of loop around her shoulders. Everyone up and down the line followed suit. "Pull on the rope and push back with the feet," Zurbriggen instructed her. And so she pushed off the side and rappelled down. Her cumbersome ice ax slammed against her leg. She winced. It would leave a livid bruise. The descent seemed to take a long time, probably because they were sixteen thousand feet high and because they were tired "after the bumbling gymnastics of the afternoon."

Right after she planted both feet on the ground, Workman stepped forward and landed on . . . nothing. She vanished like a disappearing act. Suddenly her head popped up. The guides pulled her out of a crevasse; she caught her breath and pulled her pith helmet tight on her brown hair. The image was captured in a drawing rather than a photograph, as Hunter was busy helping in the rescue of his wife.

Once she was topside, the party started the ascent anew. By noon they were twenty thousand feet up the mountainside. Workman hollered to Zurbriggen—she needed to change her gloves. Her hands were numb and she couldn't feel the grip of the ice ax. They halted. Zurbriggen rubbed her hands vigorously. She stamped her numb feet. In place of her fur gloves he tied on lined rubber mittens, which, though icy cold at first, restored the circulation after a time. Two-inch icicles dangled from Zurbriggen's beard like so many Christmas ornaments. After navigating a nearly twelve-hundred-foot sheer wall of ice and a series of seemingly endless ridges, slopes, arêtes, and domes, she reached the top of Koser Gunge: twenty-one thousand feet. The snow danced. She glanced at her watch. The hands showed it was precisely 3:00 in the afternoon.

"We had the satisfaction of being first to conquer Koser Gunge," she wrote.

"I had reached the highest point ever attained by a lady climber, and one cannot help feeling some satisfaction in that," she later told a reporter.

Hunter had missed the excitement of the final ascent. He had nearly collapsed earlier, then returned to Camp Ogre to rest with a splitting headache and pain in his lower legs, symptoms of altitude sickness not uncommon above sixteen thousand feet. He pulled off his woolen mittens with his teeth; his fingers, stiff and white, were numb. For the rest of the day he avoided all unnecessary movement. Still, he gasped for air and could not sleep a wink. He hadn't the privilege of supplemental oxygen tanks, which wouldn't be available until the 1920s.

Throughout their many years of exploring, Hunter was more susceptible to altitude sickness than his wife. Although altitude sickness is better understood now than in the Workmans' day, it remains difficult, if not impossible, to predict who will get sick. Scientists now know there is a genetic component making some climbers more susceptible than others. There seems to be a higher risk for those who ascend too quickly and for those who normally live in lower altitudes. And, importantly, it's now understood that there are varying degrees of altitude sickness. Acute mountain sickness (AMS) can cause minor swelling in the brain, headache, appetite loss, fatigue, vomiting, dizziness, and insomnia. It usually begins between six and twelve hours after arrival at a higher altitude and usually takes between one and three days to get better, so long as one doesn't go higher. Today, some first responders treat AMS with acetazolamide, which is thought to accelerate acclimatization. Others treat it with the steroid dexamethasone. In some cases first responders administer oxygen.

Far more serious is high-altitude cerebral edema (HACE). When the brain swells with fluid, climbers will become clumsy and confused, and their speech will be impaired. They may even hallucinate. At the same time, high-altitude pulmonary edema (HAPE), which causes severe breathing problems and coughing, can occur. If hypothermia sets in, climbers might behave even more erratically. They actually might feel as if they are burning up rather than freezing. They will shed their clothes, which is dangerous if, for example, a climber is exposed to the elements on a snowy summit. The only cure for HACE and HAPE is to immediately improve oxygenation—get to a lower altitude. Even then, a hyperbaric chamber might be necessary.

The reasons for altitude sickness remain as much of a mystery today as back when the Workmans climbed. There was, and still is, no way to predict who will succumb to the condition; everyone reacts differently to high elevations. Some people perform better at altitude than others, and anyone can experience AMS regardless of fitness, though good fitness is thought to help speed the acclimatization process. When sickness strikes, though, the signs are unmistakable.

After spending the night on the snow, Fanny and her team set out across the glacier, traversing a labyrinth of seracs and crevasses. They neared the camp where Hunter rested.

"As the sun flung its last flames of fire on the towering ice pinnacles, and the purple fangs of what might be called the Himalayan aurora shot upwards from the dull horizon to the blue zenith . . . one felt not only the overwhelming beauty, but also the intangibility of a scene that seemed in no way of this world," Workman wrote. Here everything was *more*: more remote and more extreme. On any given morning, they had to transport everything with them while wading for four or five hours through miles-long rivers of snow, "bounded by chains of lofty, nameless snow-mountains."

After eighteen days of exploring the snowfields, it was time to return to Askole. Upon their arrival in early August, seven headmen and their families came to honor the group. "And so ended a hard but very interesting trip safe from falling boulders," she wrote.

———

Next up was the Skoro La range, also located in the Gilgit-Baltistan region. Aside from Zurbriggen, the Workmans felt the group needed fresh blood, and so Fanny hired thirty new porters. Lumberdar Kinchin, who carried a battered umbrella under his arm, joined the party.

A couple of mornings later, Workman stood on a remote glacier. The air was so cold and dry that the snow barely melted on her tongue. How different it was to climb and explore here than in New Hampshire's White Mountains, where she and Hunter had first fallen in love with the sport. No matter how frigid and snowy were the New England winters, no matter how dangerous it was to climb Mount Washington in the snow, "there is nothing in it of glacier work and the crevasses and snow bridges," reported the *Boston Globe* about the Workmans' Himalayan trip. Workman lit the camp stove inside the tent and prepared breakfast. Tea drunk, meal consumed, they left their snug tent.

Traipsing over the loose rolling debris was an art. The stones slid from underneath their feet, ricocheting from ledge to ledge like the ball in the eighteenth-century game *billard japonais*. Each member of the Workman expedition relied on his or her alpenstock with an iron-shod tip, used to probe the snow for hidden crevasses. Just a few hours earlier, Fanny's guide had dropped a pebble into a crevasse with a diameter not much greater than a person's head. The stone echoed for several seconds before it was swallowed into the abyss. The risks of death and injury were constant companions on such an expedition. Ending up a grotesquely twisted heap of bones at the bottom of a crevasse was not on Workman's agenda.

Later, while they searched for a place to pitch tents, a "dark, serpentine object" thundered toward the group. The porters barely had time to grab their loads before a "dark, slate covered mass, 60 feet wide and 20 or 30 feet high, consisting of mud, and stones, rolled over and over toward them. And then it shot by and crashed into the river."

The danger passed and the team forged ahead, rather than stay in the unprotected site. For nearly six hours they picked their way over rock debris until they reached the base of the 18,600-foot-high unnamed peak. The summit glittered in the sun like a crystal.

When they reached the top, Fanny and Hunter unofficially named the mountain Siegfried Horn for their dead son. Today it is unclear what the true name is for this peak. She kept her thoughts about her little boy private, about how the cherub-cheeked boy would never again be alive in this world. The summit, which Workman described as a "ragged, shaly wall," was no more than a ledge twenty or thirty feet wide. From here they "gained the most extraordinarily far-reaching views of the Central Himalayas." Several thousand feet below its perpendicular precipice lay the Skoro Nullah. She and Hunter collected stones and, with the help of some porters, erected a cairn. Underneath, they buried a glass jar containing their cards, their names, the height of the mountain, and a record and measurements of the ascent. They kept duplicates of the notes tucked inside their journals to use for their next book.

Their publisher, Thomas Fisher Unwin, was counting on receiving the manuscript shortly after they returned home. This book, *In the Ice World of Himálaya*, would be their first mountaineering book, and they would give it to Rachel for Christmas. In it, Fanny would write, "For the benefit of women, who may not yet have ascended to altitudes above 16,000 feet but are thinking of attempting to do so, I will give here my experience for what they are worth."

Acting the shepherd, Zurbriggen led them in and out, over and around rocky outcroppings. "An ordinary Swiss guide would have been puzzled by and doubtless have lost some hours finding his way through the labyrinth of seracs and crevasses that confronted us. Not so Zurbriggen," she wrote. A few hours after waking, the team took a break and nibbled a light breakfast on a sloping snow plateau.

Standing where she was, in the heart of the Himalayas, Workman reveled in the knowledge that she had climbed higher than any woman before. She would break her own record in short order.

On August 11, 1899, she climbed toward an unknown and unnamed snaggletooth peak. It was their third ascent of the season. The severe cold gnawed her bones. She focused on the crevassed ice slope ahead. After four hours, the group stood at the top. Fanny christened the "monarch among the snow giants" Mount Bullock Workman. It was 19,450 feet. Then, together with Hunter, she erected a large cairn on the summit. Just as they had done atop Siegfried Horn, they buried a record of their ascent inside a glass jar. They had left previously mapped areas and were now charting new regions and peaks.

Zurbriggen actually seemed happy as he watched Workman erect the stone mound. It marked the first time he had guided a woman so high. It seemed to underscore his idea that a good alpinist can reach the highest altitudes.

While peering over the two-thousand-foot drop on the west slope, Workman felt wobbly. She hadn't expected to find the view so grand. To the north stood the great castellated rock peaks of the Biafo and Hispar. It was another altitude achievement for her; she had just broken her own record.

Workman felt vindicated. She had been right to hire this curmudgeon, Zurbriggen. She fully trusted him now. He had helped them steer clear of avalanches, rotten snowbridges, and the like.

Along the way, she and Hunter had studied his every move, becoming more and more expert—leaving behind any traces of their amateurishness.

As Workman predicted, the descent from Mount Bullock Workman was indeed terrible. At one point, the team was forced to crawl along a blade-thin icy ledge, trying to ignore a great chasm yawning below. Workman couldn't remember ever climbing anything quite so steep in the Alps. Once on the other side, they sank into knee-deep snow.

The wind lacerated their faces. Frozen, windblown, and exhausted, the group staggered into base camp. Now Fanny Bullock Workman was triumphant. She now had three successive mountaineering world records for women in her pocket.

———————

It was late autumn when the couple arrived in Nice after several uneventful weeks at sea. They took a spin around the French city on their bicycles before heading to the United Kingdom to see sixteen-year-old Rachel, who was boarding at the Cheltenham Ladies' College.

When they did finally return home to Dresden, the pair caught up on current events. The Dreyfus affair and the impending christening of the battleship SMS *Kaiser Wilhelm der Grosse* were in the news. The couple enjoyed long, unhurried walks along the Elbe River and spent leisurely afternoons visiting museums. Dresden was a jewel box, and they were determined to enjoy it, if only for a few months.

It took several days to unpack their many crates and sort through the equipment. What needed repair was mended, and what couldn't be fixed was discarded. They started reviewing their notes for a book about their bicycle trip through Southeast

Asia. They sat down for interviews with American journalists and firmed up plans for Rachel, who after Cheltenham would attend Royal Holloway College.

———————

Once the Workmans returned to Germany in late autumn of 1899 the American press could not sate its appetite for news about the woman from Worcester. Fanny filled her appointment book and wrote articles for various magazines, including the *Scottish Geographical Magazine*. Over the course of the next year, journalists wrote profiles of her exploits with headlines that shouted her accomplishments: TWO TRAVELERS, ONE A WOMAN, AMONG THE PEAKS AND PASSES proclaimed an article in the *New York Times* on October 7, 1900.

As the *Boston Globe* later reported, "No other woman had ever put foot on this [Biafo] glacier and the only white man who had visited it was the great English climber, Mr. W. Martin Conway." Indeed Fanny Bullock Workman's ascent of Koser Gunge put her in the ranks of the two or three mountain climbers of the world, according to the article. In fact, no other woman climber would brave the mountains of Tibet until well after World War I.

Workman told reporters all the suffering and hardship involved in climbing disappeared with a single glance of the world from such impressive heights. Nothing could replace the thrill of knowing she had done something no mortal had done before. That's what she told the press.

In truth, she never felt like much of a champion the moment she summited a peak. It wasn't fireworks and music. Feelings of triumph were something she expressed later, often in lectures and interviews, as was the case when talking about her record-setting climb of Koser Gunge. When they'd reached the top, she, Hunter, and Zurbriggen had been covered in icicles, and their focus was on the long and often difficult descent to come. Most accidents happened on the way down, and a climb should not be considered over until the team was safely back at base camp. This wasn't something Fanny spoke about before audiences, though. They didn't want to hear even a hint that the immediate moments after reaching the goal comprised something of an anticlimax. They wanted to hear tales of triumph and exhilaration. They wanted music and fireworks.

After this latest Himalayan venture, she was in demand for speaking engagements across Europe as well as several places in the United States. Occasionally Hunter joined her behind the podium, but more often than not he sat in the audience, filled with pride for his wife, this courageous and determined woman with whom he shared the excitement, hardship, and dangers of their adventurous life. He felt inseparably united with her and looked forward to listening to her promote her achievements, especially before the Appalachian Mountain Club in Boston. She was, after all, the most famous woman mountain climber in the world.

Workman knew how to draw a crowd. In Lyon, France, a thousand people jammed into an auditorium. Seven hundred more were turned away at the door. Not only did she lecture on what it was like to live on a mountain—she did it in three languages. In this realm, too, she continued to muscle her way into what had been an exclusively male domain.

Across the United States, even in largely unsettled places like Escanaba, Michigan, on the Upper Peninsula, the press gushed over the New England woman who had begun her career by climbing every summit of note in the White Mountains. In Europe, her lecture "Amid the Snows of Baltistan," addressed to the well-coiffed and elegantly dressed audience at the Royal Scottish Geographical Society in 1900, was standing room only.

Black-and-white photographs from this time show an expensively dressed woman, with dark, arched eyebrows and hair done in an elaborate bouffant. She looks composed and conveys a striking, confidant physical presence. In one photo, Hunter sits next to her, with gray, thinning hair, looking older.

In Aberdeen, Scotland, Workman accentuated her December 1900 lecture with photographic slides illuminated by limelight. The lantern operator set fire to pellets of lime placed in a specially designed lantern. Once lit, the glow illuminated slides.

Attendees delighted at the way "the slides showed the snow-clad peaks, three of which were explored and named by the party, the moraines, glaciers, crags, while several picturesque cloud effects upon the mountains were applauded. At the close of a most interesting lecture Lord Provost Fleming proposed a hearty vote of thanks to the gifted and courageous lady who had lectured to them so entertainingly that evening."

---

The calendar turned. It was 1901. The Workmans rang in the New Year in England. Kaiser Wilhelm II rushed to the bedside of the dying Queen Victoria, his grandmother, and remained in England through her funeral. The death of Britain's longest-reigning monarch superseded all other news coverage. Nevertheless, Workman continued to attract enthusiastic crowds. She used her lectures to pry open the doors for women. Fanny Bullock Workman, well connected, wealthy, and ten years younger than Annie S. Peck, was proving a formidable rival. Indeed, she was on her way to becoming a New Woman.

# 6

# INTO THE DEATH ZONE

IN ENGLAND, EIGHTEEN-YEAR-OLD Rachel Workman was in her first year at Royal Holloway College, studying geology, in 1902. Throughout her childhood, Rachel had never been quite the center of her parents' attention. They were hardly home before getting ready to leave again, and when they *were* home, they remained wrapped up in each other. Now Rachel was a young woman and, like her mother, was keen to pursue her own interests. With little or no attention from her parents, she was blazing her own path.

Meanwhile, that same year, her parents traveled from Germany to Italy by train—first class, of course. From the port of Genoa they sailed to Bombay on a British India Steam Navigation Company ship. They then took the train to Srinagar, and thence it was cycle or walk until they finally reached the Himalayan foothills.

To explore the Himalayas is to tread atop age-old rocks and ice. It is to follow once-active trade routes and to travel between remote villages that seem to melt into the landscape. When the Workmans returned to the region in that summer of 1902, they were poised to become the first Westerners to explore the Nun Kun mountain massif. Located deep in Kashmir, the massif is actually a pair of peaks. The Nun measures 23,408 feet, and its neighbor, the Kun, 23,218 feet.

The couple planned to spend two successive seasons there, the summer of 1902 and again in 1903. They hoped to unravel the great secrets of the twenty-eight-mile-long Chogo Lungma Glacier, which had first been discovered by the Englishman Godfrey T. Vigne in 1835. Zurbriggen once again joined the Workmans. They also hired Giuseppe Müller as a second guide and Dr. Karl Oestreich to conduct the survey and scientific work, which would fine-tune Lieutenant Colonel Henry Haversham Godwin-Austen's survey of 1861. The British officer had completed in just two days the first plane table survey of the area. The official map of the region was based on his survey.

For this trip the Workmans turned to the "capable and energetic" Major George Bretherton for help. They knew the highly experienced director of the Gilgit Transport Department would ensure their expedition got off to a smooth start. Bretherton saw to it they had additional *parwanahs*, or permissions, from the English authorities. He also made sure the maharaja of Kashmir requested the local authorities in Baltistan provide assistance. With the ink still wet on the permission letters, they bid Bretherton farewell. They would never see him again. A few years hence he and two Gurkhas would drown after their boats capsized in the Brahmaputra River, where the rushing, eddying current swept the three men away instantly.

––––––––––

The Bullock-Workman expedition had a hard time finding enough grain since the crops in the villages across the region had failed for two consecutive seasons. Additionally, the husband-and-wife duo made sure their team was outfitted with proper hats, sweaters, woolen trousers, gloves, socks, puttees (similar to gaiters, these are long cloth strips wound around the lower leg for support), boots, and thick woolen blankets. Snow glasses with special smoked lenses were essential gear—at high altitudes, the sun's strong rays could burn not only exposed skin but also eyes, causing snow blindness. The metal glasses frames were often lined in velvet to prevent the wearer from being burned on hot days and frozen on cold ones.

They finished gathering eight weeks' worth of provisions for the team, which now numbered close to a hundred. Aside from the staple items, such as rice and lentils, the traveling pantry also had tea, salt, butter, chilies, plenty of rum, and, because they brought sheep with them, the promise of mutton—stew or chops—for all when they reached the snow line. In addition, there were three yaks to carry the equipment over the granular, hard frozen ground.

Fanny took charge, sticking to the couple's philosophy that only one leader is best, "if that one can endure the loneliness of the situation and the weight of care and responsibility." The arrangements complete, they hoped to officially launch the expedition on May 10, 1902, a bit later than planned. The delay was due in part to a small mishap. The day before their scheduled departure, the couple had cycled from their inn to their camp near Munshi Bagh, a village in Kashmir, to attend to some last-minute details. When Fanny dismounted her bike, she stepped on a small stone. She gasped. She had severely sprained her ankle and wouldn't be able to bear any weight on it for several days.

They agreed that Zurbriggen and several porters should go on ahead. The rest of the team would meet up with them a few days hence. He left May 12, and four days later, on May 16, Fanny, still unable to walk, was "carried in a *dandi* [palanquin] by four kahars" across the brown treeless plains of Ladakh.

They scouted for a campsite. In the past, they had camped on loose sand, ploughed fields, or on ground wet from irrigation. They had pitched tents on the outskirts of villages close to refuse dumps. They were used to less than luxurious accommodations. This time they found a "dilapidated, dust-covered burial-ground, where the tent pegs found precarious hold in the thin crust of earth covering the graves. . . . In Himalayan travel one becomes accustomed to almost anything," she wrote.

With a stew simmering, Fanny, Hunter, and Zurbriggen, turned their attention to the work ahead. Heads bent over maps, they didn't hear the arrival of the local raja, who came to pay his respects and welcome them to the region. His brother and some officials walked a few deferential paces behind. Several more people followed behind them, bringing a hookah, flowers, a sheep, and glistening white and red cherries piled high on large copper plates. A most fanciful end to the day.

---

About three weeks later the Workmans were in Skardu. Lurid streaks of orange and pink tinted the evening sky. A natural amphitheater, the town marked the entrance point to the Indus River and was a gateway to the Karakoram. The region's bustling capital, it was the residence of the tahsildar, the tax officer, and also boasted a post office, telegraph office, subtreasury, dispensary, and bazaar. All offered important services, but as far as the Workmans were concerned the city mattered for one sole reason: it had a government-maintained meteorological station complete with mercurial barometer and thermometers. The Workmans could use it as their lower station for altitude calculations. At precisely 8:00 AM every day, an official forwarded the measurements to the meteorological office in Calcutta. The official agreed to keep a daily record of barometric and thermometric readings three times a day, at 8:00 AM, noon, and 4:00 PM. Three separate readings would ensure greater accuracy.

The Workman expedition continued to their campsite. Nearly a month had passed since her injury, and so on June 27 Fanny decided to take a mini trek to test her ankle. She chose Shigar Fort. Known as Fong-Kahr, or Palace on the Rock, the fort was approximately three hundred years old. She talked Müller into coming along with her on what she promised would be only a small side adventure.

The path was as crooked as it was steep. Workman and Müller picked their way across the narrow ridge. Loose hairs stuck to her glistening forehead. Sweat trickled down her back. Scaling the steep face without ropes was a tad daunting; her swollen ankle still felt tender to the touch. About an hour into the hike, they stood before two narrow rock passages. Less than two feet wide, there was barely enough room for one person. Müller squeezed through on hands and knees first. Then Workman gingerly lowered herself to the ground, mindful of her still tender ankle. Edging through the narrow space, the rocky dirt dug into her hands and knees. On the other side they stood, brushed the dust from their clothes, and took a sip of water.

They reached the top shortly before noon. The two were so focused on reaching the top they hadn't thought through how they would come down. The steep route would be impossible for Workman to navigate. Her ankle throbbed. She had no choice but to send Müller down alone. Perhaps he could find a better route. He balked at the suggestion. He didn't want to leave her. Yet he couldn't carry her down, either. There really wasn't another option. Before he left, Workman asked him to bring back extra tea and water. For the woman who was always prepared, always so organized, this was not her finest hour.

The noonday sun baked the rocks. There was not a solitary cloud in the sky to provide cover. Her skin prickled. Her mind felt fuzzy. "I remained in slight shade of a rock on summit for four hours suffering terribly for thirst," she wrote. She tried to nap. She limped over to a spot between the boulders. There was simply no respite from the sun and thirst. Every two hours she indulged in two swallows of tea from her flask—just barely wetting her mouth.

By three o'clock Workman had only half a cupful of tea left in her flask. She would have to be even more sparing in her sips. In the distance she saw people working their fields. Unsurprisingly, they could not see her waving her arms to signal distress. She tried calling out, but the distance made her cries inaudible. She tried to stand, but her ankle hurt too much, so she sat back on the rock. Time crawled. Her head buzzed. She worried about sunstroke and dehydration. She hoped her skin wouldn't burn too badly. Right when she feared she might finally faint from heat exhaustion, she heard a shout. Then another. She could scarcely muster a whisper from her parched throat. She heard another shout, and then she saw Müller. Behind him a porter scrambled up and over the edge. It was 4:30 in the afternoon.

She guzzled two flasks of water and three cups of tea. She practically inhaled the biscuit, her first since 5:30 AM. She ran her fingers along the inside of the wrapper, licking them for more crumbs. Müller stared at her as if she were slightly crazy. Then again, he'd not spent the entire day roasting on a rocky plateau.

Sufficiently hydrated, Workman and the two men walked to the other side of the plateau until they found a trail with a gentler descent. Before they started, Workman wanted documentation of her day.

"We took a photo and went down an easier route but had one very bad place where I had to slide through a perpendicular hole of an old clay fort, almost 30 feet. I was held by G. [Giuseppe Müller] above by putties [sic] tied together and the coolies stood below on crumbling ledge and caught me as I came down in a cloud of mist, first my feet and then my body as there was no place for a foot hold anywhere," she wrote later, while nestled under her blankets inside the tent.

They moved deliberately over the scree, the rocky shards of debris glaciers leave behind as they flow over a region for hundreds and thousands of years. The rescue team trudged through sand until they reached a village. Parched, they drank four quarts of water each.

When they made it back to camp at last, a relieved Hunter greeted his wife and checked her ankle. He was pleased to see it no more swollen than it had been in the morning. Fanny tumbled into her tent at 7:15 PM, thirteen hours after she had left. It was, she said with characteristic dryness, "a hard day."

———————

On Sunday, July 6, the expedition awoke to a "soft and lovely morning." They didn't feel so lovely, however. On the contrary, they were exhausted. A violent gale had ripped through the camp during the night, keeping everyone awake for hours. Yet, in spite of the fatigue, Workman decided the team would walk back toward the mountains. They could sleep later. Vultures circled above. Knowing they were eating carrion, it nevertheless served as a reminder that climbing in the Himalayas meant climbing alongside death—from a fall, from dehydration, from fever. There were so many ways to die on a mountain, and she knew she had to keep her wits about her, even as she looked ahead. In the distance, Mount Everest scraped the sky.

Later in the day, while resting at camp, Hunter, talked with her about the next stage of their journey: a rafting trip down the muddy Shigar River. With no bridges in this region, the only way to cross was on an inflatable craft fashioned from what looked to be either pig- or goatskins.

The group approached the riverbank, where teams of porters were blowing into the open ends of the legs, inflating the rafts like party balloons. After tying off the legs, they threaded woolen cords through the skins and attached them to poles. With the legs pointed upward, the boat looked like an animal resting on its back. Eyeing the craft suspiciously, the team stepped delicately inside, careful not to capsize the craft. Hunter steadied himself next to his wife. Once aboard he dared not move his feet, not even an inch. He worried he might accidentally poke a hole through the bottom. The crew of four pushed off and steered the lightweight raft down the turbulent stream using eight-foot-long willow poles.

"Whirling round and round, scraping the pig skins on the bottom frequently, occasionally the water splashing up over our ankles at times. The pig skins groaning and creaking when we stuck the pebbly bottoms after a rather exciting journey we reached Yuno (a little village place) at 7 PM," Hunter wrote.

Then the rains came and the expedition, which had set up camp just beyond the village, quite literally got stuck in the mud. Fortunately, mackintosh linings kept the inside of everyone's tent dry. By July 12, an air of restlessness hovered over the small tent village while everyone waited for the first break in the weather. When it came, they moved quickly. Now on foot, they headed deeper into glacier country, and on July 13 husband and wife paused and considered an enormous ice-covered rock "glistening like a gigantic whale."

Days later, after tramping through terrain interspersed with rocks and soft snow, they arrived in Arando, a tiny village on the Shigar River north of Yuno. The chief women called on the entourage bearing plates laden with walnuts and dried apricots. They were dressed in their finery, beaded necklaces and flattened metal discs worn over the bodice. Bunches of keys were suspended from leather thongs cinched around their waists. The number of keys hinted at one's wealth; they opened chicken coops and sheep pens and so indicated how much property each woman owned. Workman learned that the women wore their keys around the clock, lest someone try to "carry off a sheep worth a rupee."

By August 8 the expedition was above sixteen thousand feet. Well northwest of Srinagar in present-day Pakistan, they were now on the doorstep of the Chogo Lungma Glacier. A chorus of hammer blows echoed in the twilight as the porters drove tent stakes into the ground. The Workmans and guides moved equipment into the shelters by lantern light. After a meager dinner of tinned fish, weak tea, and biscuits, it was time for bed. Freezing rain pattered against the canvas.

———————

The next morning, under a light veil of morning mist, the porters set about carving additional tent terraces on the soft snow. Heavy stones weighed down the edges of each tent. Here in the Himalayas, gales blew through the valley, sending whirling clouds of dust, and sometimes tents, into the air.

Snug inside a green denim Mummery tent lined with gray flannel—the tent type the Workmans favored for high snow work—Workman found her accommodations perfectly comfortable. The tents stood about four feet high, and so occupants had plenty of room. During their first time in the Himalayas, in the summer of 1898, the couple had tried a Willesden canvas Whymper tent but found it too heavy to transport. Workman also hated the ground-sheet: "On an exposed mountain-side, one feels a bit nervous in regard to the impossibility of escape, should the tent be carried away by wind and hurled into the depths below." As for the light-weight silk tents some in the climbing community favored, the

Workmans found them neither warm enough nor tough enough to withstand the harsh Himalayan climate and terrain.

At long last the Workmans stood on the Chogo Lungma, ready to test their stamina and agility. Walking on a glacier can be exceedingly dangerous. Glaciers are formed of highly compressed layers of ice. The top layers are quite brittle and can easily fracture. Wide crevasses can form but are often hidden by fresh snow. Where the Workmans now stood the crevasses were visible but were separated by huge chunks of ice. There were no snow-bridges in sight. Zurbriggen led the party in a serpentine course to the middle part of the glacier. There, "in this white wilderness," Zurbriggen spied a safer path.

Just before a tea break, a boulder knocked loose from the ice and careened down the hill. It crashed fifty feet down, smacking into a porter and knocking him out like a bowling pin. The Workmans and Zurbriggen rushed to his side to find the other porters supporting his head, arms, and legs and "singing a dismal chant as they came. The *khansamah* [a steward] said it was a death-song, for they [the porters] thought he was dead. When they arrived he was unconscious, and his extremities were cold, though no bones were fractured, and, in spite of blankets and such measures as could be taken, he remained in this condition till the next morning," Workman wrote.

In this way their exploration unfolded—one hazard after another—until they reached what they thought was the top of Chogo Lungma. They were 18,944 feet high. Workman christened their new site Foggy Camp. The porters erected tents on the sugary snow. In the silvery blue twilight, Fanny, Hunter, and Zurbriggen drew up plans to attack the wall of ice that rose in the distance. Zurbriggen had already cut steps for three hundred feet up to its base.

That night they fell asleep to the lullaby of pelting sleet. The next morning they awoke under a blanket of fog. When Hunter checked the barometer he grew concerned; it seemed a storm was fast approaching. Fanny briskly ordered everyone to make short work of packing the ice-coated tents and rucksacks; the weather precluded them from going further. The party struck out. It was a six-hour trek back to the previous camp.

The storm raged sixty hours. The wind lashed. The snow swirled through the air. Inside their tents everyone hunkered under mounds of blankets. Fanny wore her quilted felt knee-high boots, and a thick woolen cap. She stuffed her hands inside her fur gloves. Each time she or Hunter opened the tent flap to clear the rapidly accumulating snow from the sides of the tent, it whooshed inside. After a while they surrendered. All they could do was lie inside and hope the wind wouldn't carry them off at any moment, or that they wouldn't be snowed in.

"Those not used to camping on snow can scarcely realize what it means to be imprisoned in a small tent during a storm of such length and severity, when the snow increases foot by foot in depth, in spite of efforts to remove it, and the tent, unless cleared often of the load accumulating upon it, is likely to collapse upon you as you sit within," she wrote.

And then just as quickly as the storm had arrived, it left.

Together Zurbriggen and the Workmans surveyed the camp-site. Seeing no damage, the group started off once again. The temperature fluctuations, scorching sun and then freezing cold, conspired to make their march to reach the upper part of the Chogo Lungma particularly difficult. The high walls of the glacier trapped the heat until it felt like the radiation from a blast furnace. "Our faces are burned purple, peeled and so sore that we can scarcely touch the skin from the reflective sunlight from the snow, which burns like fire," she wrote.

Every so often an avalanche tore down a mountainside. Each time, they were stunned at the size of the boulders, some as "large as small houses, some with holes completely through them."

When they reached their next camp, Fanny's feet felt like blocks of ice. Both Hunter and Zurbriggen were in foul moods. Especially Zurbriggen. He screamed he was going down the glacier to a lower camp and shouted that he would not be treated like a dog. They weren't sure what he meant, but they were sure that "he is a perfect brute, a most disagreeable fellow to have with one," Workman wrote.

Perhaps hot soup and a good night's sleep would calm his nerves, she thought.

The next morning, after putting on two flannel shirts, Workman shrugged into her striped sweater. With its filthy cuffs and pilled yarn, the "valley sweater," as she nicknamed it, was her favorite. Then came the thick woolen stockings and drab woolen skirt. She wound puttees around her legs and lastly stuffed her feet into her boots. Away they went. Zurbriggen once again had rejoined their party. Stray rocks peeked out of the snow like marmots from their burrows. They probed the snow for crevasses. "It was exceedingly dangerous and slow as snow was getting every minute softer and there was ice often beneath," she wrote.

They did make it to the top of the col of Chogo Lungma Glacier, which Zurbriggen told Fanny was more difficult than any in Switzerland, according to her August 21 journal entry.

On the way down, the softness of the snow put everyone on high alert for a dreaded avalanche. Every now and then someone slipped. Zurbriggen spoke, his dire words just loud enough for Fanny and Hunter to hear: "Es ist sehr gefährlich. Wir kommen heute nicht hinunter"—"It is very dangerous. Today we do not come down." But come down they must and come down they did, not stopping until they reached the safety of the col.

About two-thirds of the way down, the team stood on narrow ice steps. There was no room to sit, and their feet started cramping from fatigue. They were careful. One misstep and they would slide nearly two thousand feet down the avalanche-gullied ice slope into an abyss. Several hundred feet later, Fanny called for a break. Everyone was flagging and needed to refuel. Word went up and down the line. Workman drove her ice ax into the snow and from her rucksack pulled out a few kola biscuits, a couple of chocolate squares, and a tin of pâté. Hunter took biscuits and chocolate. They swallowed without chewing, eager to be in the relative safety of the camp.

Workman worried they wouldn't reach camp by nightfall. The threat of avalanche remained high, not to mention they were on a precipice several thousand feet up. This time Müller took the lead. They moved single file, putting each foot in the boot print of the person ahead. So they went. One after the other. Suddenly Müller slipped. Everyone on his rope lurched forward. For less time than it takes to blink they believed they would suffer the same fate as Whymper's team. Zurbriggen, who was bringing up the rear, responded in a flash. He wound his rope over his ice ax and yanked hard. The line held.

They made it back just after dark. The night sky glittered with stars. In the privacy of their tent, Hunter turned to his wife. They agreed that climbing the 19,100-foot col was by far the most difficult thing they'd done so far.

They boiled some water using their still relatively new Primus No. 1, the first portable pressurized-burner paraffin stove. Weighing about two and a half pounds, the brass stove was about eight and a half inches high. Hunter prepared what he called his medicinal tea, a special concoction to soothe frayed nerves. He filled a metal tea ball with a half teaspoon of black tea he'd brought with him from Germany and immersed it in two or three quarts of boiling water for about twenty seconds. Then he stirred in a healthy dose of whiskey he kept in a flask out of sight from the porters and guides. After the last sip, they hoped for sleep in what Fanny described as a most uncomfortable camp. Outside it was twenty degrees below Fahrenheit.

Thus the expedition wound down in the early autumn of 1902, and the Workmans prepared for the long journey home. Instruments needed to be wrapped and boxed. Tents were folded and leftover food either given away or stored. Workman kept her journals close at hand. If they lost their notes they'd have nothing to serve as the basis for their planned book or lectures.

From Srinagar they journeyed to Karachi, where they climbed aboard a boat bound for Genoa. This time Fanny was spared the seasickness she had suffered years earlier on the boat to Java. From Genoa they sailed to Marseille, where they caught a train to Dresden. The French station teemed with people. On the train, she started sketching the outline of the book she wanted to write with Hunter. With each mile, they shed a little bit more of the tent life.

————————

Home again. Again they received a warm reception from the press, both in Europe and abroad. *National Geographic* published an article about the pair's successful exploration of the giant Chogo Lungma Glacier and its affluents from its end to its point of origin.

The couple spent time with Rachel, now a young woman living an independent life in England while she attended university. They worked on their lectures and filled their calendar with various social engagements. All the while, they appreciated how being away for much of the year meant they hadn't the same household and social responsibilities of so many of their peers.

————————

One year later, on August 29, 1903, Fanny again shrugged her "valley sweater" over her stout frame. She wrapped puttees around her legs and laced her boots. It was 4:30 in the morning. Carrying her alpenstock, she led the climbing party out of the campsite. Target: Siachen, or the Rose Glacier. She was happiest here in the open air amid scenery that was nothing short of exquisite.

While the Workmans crossed the river near the center of the glacier, Roald Amundsen was attempting to reach the South Pole. In the United States, Leonidas Hubbard, assistant editor of *Outing* magazine, led an ill-fated expedition to canoe the Naskaupi River–Michikamau Lake system in Labrador. Like these explorers, the Workmans intended to add to the body of scientific knowledge. This time they took along B. H. M. Hewett as topographer. During the expedition Hewett would survey the glacier system and fix the positions and altitudes of previously unobserved peaks. In 1904 Hewett would travel to the United States and serve as a resident engineer while workers bored the Pennsylvania Railroad tunnels under the Hudson River. For their 1903 expedition, the Workmans also had hired guides Cyprien Savoye and Joseph Petigax, as well as Joseph's son Laurent as a lead porter.

Thus the band of men and one woman treaded lightly over a narrow tongue of snow-covered ice. The weak bridge spanned a wide blue crevasse. On either side, colossal walls of ice rose. The dark summits of the great moraine lay hundreds of miles beyond.

Matthias Zurbriggen, once again in the Workmans' employ, beckoned the group. Fanny started across but "the tongue began to crack and shiver, as I am heavier and afraid it would break under me. I refused to go. Had it broken, I should have fallen straight [down] as the crevasse was very wide . . . and the fall on my spine and back would have been terrible even with guide ropes holding me," she noted. Zurbriggen tried to convince her the bridge would hold. She could not move. Her feet would simply not obey. Zurbriggen reacted as he often did when frustrated: he unleashed a torrent of curses. Workman ignored the Swiss guide. By now she was inured to his occasional invective. She turned to the group and suggested they return from whence they came. They would find an alternate route.

Now he played deaf. He insisted she come along.

"This was insulting and rude as he is a paid guide and with us to follow orders. He is disgusting and not fit to employ and here end my dealings with him," she wrote in her journal that evening. Of course, she wasn't going to end her dealings with him—she knew it and he knew it. As usual, her temper was extinguished as quickly as it had flared. Still, a draught of Hunter's "tea" and a biscuit would do wonders right about now, she thought. Taken with food, his concoction was the only way, in their opinion, to "take away the jaded sensation in the feet and limbs" after a day's tramp over the mountains.

The couple crawled into their tent that evening nearly frost-bitten, dehydrated, weak from hunger, and slightly sick from the fumes put off by their stove. Workman thought about what the English mountaineer A. F. Mummery had described as the "educative and purifying power in danger that is to be found in nothing other than snow." She also recalled that he had died eight years earlier in 1895, buried under an avalanche while trying to climb Nanga Parbat, known as the "Man Eater." Thirty-one men died before it was successfully summited in a 1953 ascent.

Hunter woke to his wife's low and earnest voice. She suggested he should go on with Zurbriggen and Giuseppe Müller, who also rejoined them in 1903, and attempt a record of his own up what they called Pyramid Peak. (Modern maps indicate this is Spantik Peak.) Not feeling particularly well, he nevertheless warmed to the idea. They crisscrossed their way up to the summit. Hunter stopped to photograph the view from 22,810 feet.

A few days passed before the mountaineers once more attempted to reach the head of the glacier. Five miles from its mouth, five porters suddenly lost their balance. They somersaulted five hundred feet down the slope. One of the porters lost his grip on a box, which rolled down the hill before bursting open. Its contents scattered. Still, the sixteen goats and five sheep meant for meals fared better than the packages. The porters stood unscathed.

Meanwhile, dissension increased among the porters. Many wanted to quit and return to their homes. Not a new sentiment, but this time the timing was nevertheless atrocious. Fanny and Hunter tried to persuade them to stay on for the remainder of the expedition. The local lumberdar was no help. Rather, he refused to supply any more sheep or chickens or eggs for the hungry party. Hunter was supremely annoyed: "These people are a most rotten crowd. They are always begging for tobacco, tea. . . . F. may deal with such people if she will but I won't risk a cent on them. These people have no idea of decency or honour and it doesn't pay to show them any favours."

Despite being down several porters and rations, the team persisted. Inside their tent the couple sipped the last of their evening tea. Outside, a snowstorm raged. Hunter took to his journal to note his frustration regarding the tension with the head guides. He was incensed the porters had simply quit, in spite of the storm. The snow hadn't let up since it had started nearly forty-eight hours earlier. He couldn't understand why they didn't listen to him and stay until the storm ended. "They were in no danger, had tents and fire and there was no reason why they should go away like cowards and leave us here. The whole set are miserable rascals. In the PM some 15 returned, probably not daring to go on in the storm, which increased in violence," he wrote.

All the while, Hunter felt short of breath, like he'd just sprinted a hundred yards. He couldn't stand, stoop, or make any sudden movements. Even when lying down, he felt as if iron bands encircled his chest. Yet, as exhausted as he was, sleep only teased. Hunter was suffering from altitude sickness. He felt better in the morning, but the snow meant he could rest another day in his tent.

Actually, he was able to rest several more days. The severe snowstorms imprisoned them for nearly two weeks before the weather broke. Finally they could dig out of their tents and head back onto the ice, ultimately reaching an as yet unexplored upper branch of the glacier where they took careful measurements to determine the rate of glacier movement.

After the 1903 expedition ended and they had traded the high altitudes of the Himalayas for the paved streets of Dresden, the Workmans spent the next year writing and lecturing. And even though nearly sixty-seven hundred miles separated the Workmans from Worcester, Massachusetts, the press coverage in the United States remained constant. They'd moved away so many years ago, but they returned to the United States now and again for lectures. For instance on October 5, 1904, Fanny, a corresponding member of the Appalachian Mountain Club, addressed some 350 people about "First Exploration of the Great Chogo Loongma [*sic*] Glacier, and Other High Ascents in the Mustagh Range, Northwest Himalaya." Three nights later, on October 8, she spoke before 250 people.

In reviewing her lectures, the *Boston Globe* described the couple as true sportsmen who left "their comfortable home for the excitement of glacier, crevasse and snow peak." Audience members marveled at the dangers they faced and the extreme conditions in which they lived. After all, they conducted their expeditions without the special equipment now available to modern mountaineers.

They had no rugged synthetic outerwear or tents. They lacked radios, dehydrated food, compact tools, and nylon rope. They wore heavy tweed clothes that when wet felt like lead and smelled like mold. Their treks were arduous experiences most in the audience could only imagine.

The Bullock-Workman expeditions had camped in places where knife-edge peaks made for some of the most impressive mountain landscapes. They had climbed icefalls, dined on kola biscuits and congealed meat. They knew what it was like when "absolute silence reigned on the rope, broken only by the sharp click of the axe on the frozen surface." They had seen a sunrise at twenty-one thousand feet; they'd spent forty-eight hours imprisoned in tents. They had seen sights no mortals had ever seen and most never would.

Thus two consecutive summers of exploration in the north west Himalayas ended. Their mapping and surveying work steadily improved, though it would be some years before it was considered professional. As for this 1903 expedition, experts say it is difficult to work out exactly where they went as the map they produced differed in important respects from current interpretations.

Indeed, in years to come their 1903 map of the region would be proven incorrect. For example, they thought Pyramid Peak, known today as Spantik Peak, was three hundred feet higher than Malubiting, also in the vicinity. In fact, unbeknownst to them they had really tried to climb an entirely different glacier called Yengutz Har. As for Pyramid Peak, it's actually fourteen hundred feet *lower* than Malubiting. The Workmans conceded in their 1908 book *Ice-Bound Heights of the Mustagh* that because only a few peaks had been placed on the map as fixed points, "it is not surprising that numerous mistakes in identification have been made by Himalayan explorers and mountaineers."

After two seasons exploring the Himalayas, Fanny was a fairly seasoned mountaineer who had presented papers before the British Royal Geographical Society and continued to rise in its esteem. Yet, the organization remained stubbornly committed to refusing women full membership. In Workman's view, this went against the grain of scientific progress and social justice. Likewise, she found the overall atmosphere at the British Alpine Club "chilly to the woman explorer." She chalked it up to the fact that she was forthright and undeniably successful as well as the driving force in their expeditions.

Meanwhile Hunter continued to champion his wife as one "whose courage, endurance, and enthusiasm, often under circumstances of hardship and sometimes of danger, have never failed."

Thus Fanny persisted in pushing her way inside this male-dominated kingdom. Finally, in November 1905, she delivered an address about the Hoh Lumba and Soston Glaciers from inside the hallowed Royal Geographical Society of London. She was the second woman to do so, after Isabella Bird, the British explorer and naturalist. The *Times* of London covered the landmark event. Only once before had a woman met the society's rigorous requirements for scientific research, exploration, and zeal for adventure, proclaimed the society's president, Sir Clements Robert Markham. For Workman, this was the ultimate in recognition, the ultimate victory.

———————

As Workman regaled her audiences with tales about what it was like to try to boil water at twenty thousand feet or what a treat beef lozenges were on a climb, Annie S. Peck set out for South America.

Peck now had several expeditions to her name. Nevertheless, she remained an object of intrigue for much of the press and public—so much so that the *Phrenological Journal* tried to analyze her by her physical attributes. Phrenology, the idea that the size and shape of the head could reveal something about a person's intelligence and personality, had first taken off in Edinburgh with the work of Dr. George Combe. It reached the United States in the late 1800s when German physician Dr. Johann Spurzheim lectured on the subject at Harvard. Sitting in the audience was Orson Squire Fowler, who popularized it across the United States. President James Garfield and Clara Barton, founder of the American Red Cross, were clients of Fowler. Decades later, in an article about Peck for the *Phrenological Journal*, Orson's niece Jessie A. Fowler wrote, "A combination of good living power as indicated in the bones of the face beside the nose; a strong beating heart as indicated in the chin, good digestive power as indicated by the fullness in the center of the cheeks half-way between the lower lobe of the ear and the other corner of the lips are all essential to the mountain climber."

Whether Peck saw Fowler's article is unknown. At the time of its publication, she was preparing to climb Mount Huascarán in Peru. She (mistakenly) told the *New York Times* that because it is the highest peak in the hemisphere she would break the world's record for climbing if she were successful. Located in the Peruvian province of Yungay, the mountain was named for Huascar, a sixteenth-century Inca chieftain who was the Sapa Inca, or ruler of the vanished Inca Empire.

"The World's Greatest Explorers: Miss Annie S. Peck"
Hassan Cigarettes trading card.

Two peaks, not one, comprise Mount Huascarán. Its southern summit ranks as the highest point in Peru and the fourth highest mountain in the Western Hemisphere, after Aconcagua, Ojos del Salado, and Monte Pissis.

She packed her trunk, making sure to bring her woolen climbing mask. It had a mustache painted on it as a sly comment on men's domination of the sport. She also packed woolen knickerbockers and a woolen tunic. It was always a chore to find proper outdoor gear—nothing was sized for women. Into the trunk went chocolate squares and tea. Next she packed a mercurial barometer, an aneroid barometer, and a plane table to rapidly survey the area. She also packed a compass with a luminous dial and field glasses.

From her too-damp hotel room in New York, where she slept under a thin, scratchy blanket that smelled of mothballs, she penned several letters. In one, she wrote to a professor who apparently planned to write about Peck's adventure. She told him she withdrew her promise of sending a picture of Mount Huascarán. She decided because of their differing views

> as to what is fitting and proper I should not care to contribute a photograph, and thus apparently give my sanction to what might seem to me an inadequate account of my achievement. If you care enough about having the photo to be willing to send me in advance a copy of what you intend to say about my ascent I shall be happy to send you the desired photo with permission to publish if the account seems to me to be a fair one; otherwise I feel obliged to decline giving my apparent sanction to your statements.
>
> A.S.P.

For all her aloofness, Peck cared deeply about her image, so much so that she wanted to approve the article before publication.

Short of funds, she needed to finance her expedition and so offered editors a chance to buy five out of ten articles she planned to write about her forthcoming adventure up the highest mountain in Peru. She would sell them at twenty dollars apiece. The editor would then have the option of buying the remaining five at the same price. "If I can demonstrate this fact [of climbing the highest mountain] it will be of great scientific value and popular interest. In any case its ascent by a woman without the accustomed Swiss guide will be the greatest feat in mountain climbing ever accomplished and one of the large possibilities in the way of striking headlines and illustrations," she wrote.

Peck was confident the trek would be easy. After all, she had easily climbed El Misti in Peru, which was 19,098 feet high. That should have been proof enough that she could accomplish a great deal more.

To sweeten the pitch, she included several additional story ideas. Perhaps an editor would like her to report on the Panama Canal's progress. The French Panama Canal Company had recently offered to sell its rights to the United States for $40 million. The offer had tipped the balance away from those favoring a canal through Nicaragua. She offered to include a bit about the Chimbote railroad, sugar plantations, and life at the foot of Huascarán, as well as a piece on the ascent of Huascarán with a focus on the native people.

Having gotten funding, from both her brother and an editor, Peck now stood on a ship deck dressed in floor-length skirt and lace blouse, a brooch at her neck and a flowered hat pinned atop her wavy auburn hair, the Rhode Island native was a picture of confidence. Next to her stood her guides, carrying pickaxes, and a scientist with rifle. She could not know it yet, but she would to attempt to summit Huascarán not three, not four, but five times.

Days later she arrived in Lima, Peru. Her supplies arrived in tip-top shape—even Admiral Robert Peary's fur Inuit suit. At Peary's suggestion, Peck had written to Hermon Carey Bumpus, director of the American Museum of Natural History. He'd agreed to lend Peck the suit, in part because he knew her brothers from his teaching days at Brown University.

Once in Lima, Peck went about hiring guides. As Fanny Workman had experienced, the guides dismissed her too easily. Already there had been several climbs in Mexico and other places in South America when her guides had deserted her above the snow line. Similar to Workman, Peck was called relentless and overbearing. And like Workman, she noted these were traits widely admired in men.

Although the two women had never met, they chased each other's accomplishments. And as Peck struggled to reach the Huascarán summit, Workman prepared to grab another record. This time she planned to bivouac higher than anyone had before.

# 7

# CAMP AMERICA

I N THE SPRING of 1906, Finland became the first European country to give women the right to vote. That year, in San Francisco, three thousand people died when an earthquake registering 7.9 on the Richter scale struck. Far away in the Himalayas, Fanny Bullock Workman led an army of hundreds of porters and one of her favorite guides, Cyprien Savoye.

Meanwhile, Rachel, now twenty-one, was studying geology and making a name for herself in the academic world. She and her mother had grown closer in the past few years. It was as if Fanny had been waiting all these years for her daughter to reach adulthood and become a peer, something she'd never enjoy with Siegfried, dead now thirteen years. It helped the mother-daughter relationship that the Workmans had spent much of 1905 at home, lecturing and working on their book *Ice-Bound Heights of the Mustagh: An Account of Two Seasons of Pioneer Exploration and High Climbing in the Baltistan Himalaya.*

Much of the heavy lifting for the book fell to Fanny. She struggled with the prose, vacillating between florid and simply factual. Unlike the two fiction stories of her adolescence, where she'd made a poor secret of her personal longings, these new books with their ponderous titles kept readers at arm's length.

During their time at home, the couple pursued their careers as lecturers with the same intensity as they did their Himalayan adventures. A year before, in November 1904, Hunter had delivered his first paper to the Royal Geographical Society. Not to be outdone, Fanny lectured in English, French, and German. In Lyon, a thousand people crowded into the Musée des Beaux-Arts to hear her. Seven hundred more were turned away at the door; there was simply no more room in the hall.

Soon enough it was time to sail east again. In the spring of 1906 Workman pushed aside all thoughts of her books, lectures, Rachel, Siegfried, and Annie Peck. There was room in her thoughts for only one thing now: Pinnacle Peak. At 22,740 feet, it is the third-highest peak in the Nun Kun massif. She and Hunter had first laid eyes on the area in 1898, during that too-hot summer when they'd fled the incessant heat of the Indian plain for the cool reaches of the Himalayas. At the time, she'd felt like they had discovered the world's end. For the better part of eight years, Fanny, now forty-seven, had nurtured a desire to scale this peak. Should she succeed, it would be her greatest mountaineering achievement to date.

Rocky spurs and buttresses surrounded the massif, as if guarding the upper reaches of the ice-covered rock from intruders. Until now, exploration of the region had been largely confined to the valleys below. The Workmans planned a more thorough exploration of this area, "particularly of the upper unvisited portions," Hunter noted.

It took them three weeks to reach Srinagar from Dresden, a journey that was becoming ever-more familiar. They had sailed from Germany for coastal France. Once in Marseille they boarded a second ship. Fair skies graced the crossing to Port Said. Stepping ashore for a few hours, the couple had just enough time to browse the harbor shops. Wanting to send something home for Rachel, they looked at all sorts of trinkets: bracelets, earrings, figurines. They selected four boxes of Turkish delight and an ostrich fan.

From Srinagar, they began a familiar routine, hiring porters, procuring additional supplies, and sorting equipment. The team grouped items based on what they would need for daylong excursions and what they would need for the duration. Climbing gear, food rations, and medicines went into the former pile. The heavier equipment, grouped into the latter, would be either carried by porters or strapped onto the backs of mules and yaks.

This time Matthias Zurbriggen, their temperamental guide, was not part of their retinue. Instead, Savoye would serve as lead guide. Originally from Courmayeur, a village in northern Italy's Aosta Valley, Savoye had accompanied them on their 1903 Baltistan expedition. He had previously participated in the North Pole expedition headed by the Duke of Abruzzi, a Spanish mountaineer and explorer.

The Workmans made other personnel changes in 1906. Aside from Savoye, they had hired a larger European contingent on this trip, including Cesare Chenoz and Emile Gléry, who also hailed from Courmayeur. After so many years of cultural miscues and misunderstandings—largely because of the Workmans' attitudes—Fanny thought changing the team's composition might mean fewer chances for orders to get lost in translation and fewer chances for aggravation. "We had more than enough, in the past, of sitting on cold snow-slopes awaiting the snail-like approach of unwilling coolies, and at snow-camps of hearing their wailing complaints and refusals to march," she wrote.

Savoye double-checked the equipment. He made sure the team had enough crampons, snowshoes, steel stakes, and sharpened ice axes. He checked the ropes were properly coiled and the tents folded neat as table linens. He checked the stoves once more to make sure they worked. He made sure everyone, from the cook down to the last porter, had woolen gloves, trousers, helmets, and snow goggles. In the past, Workman teams had reached the higher-altitude camps only to have a porter point to his cotton shirt and his bare legs and say he must return home.

Everything was in order, save for the food supply. "The crops having failed, the two preceding seasons in *Sam* and Ladakh, no supplies were obtainable there, so we were obliged to forward from Srinagar not only *all* supplies for our party, but also some 16,000 pounds of grain," Hunter noted. They required 243 porters and 60 ponies to transport all the grain. The region had suffered from a crop failure that summer, which had left the markets nearly bare. Farmers stood on the brink of ruin. Just six years had passed since the last famine. Uneven rainfall contributed to the famines. So too did British economic and administrative policies. A system geared toward export crops displaced millions of acres that should have been used for subsistence farming.

---

The quickest way to the pass that would take them to the Suru valley was blocked, necessitating a last-minute change in plans, which in turn meant a long delay. Workman sent part of the group ahead via another route. They took most of the gear and all of the sheep. Another group took a second route in search of additional food. Two weeks later, she dispatched a third caravan. This one included twenty-five ponies, each one carrying two baskets of grain.

Four Kashmiri servants and two Gurkhas, formerly of the First Gurkha Rifles, accompanied the Workmans, some on foot, some on horseback. Feeling ill, Hunter rode most of the way on his wife's horse through the desolate countryside. "It cannot boast of a single tree, but the swampy land along the river is covered with bush-growth two to six feet high," Hunter noted. The trail clung to a precipitous slope overlooking the turbid river. To the south, the spires of the Nun Kun massif rose nearly twenty-three thousand feet high.

Personnel changes weren't the only difference on this trip. Workman decided the guides and porters should prepare their own meals, not because she wanted to increase their workload but because she wanted their complaints to cease. On every prior expedition, the porters had griped about the Kashmiri khansamah, or cook. He served the most unappetizing fare. He didn't thoroughly cook the meat. He didn't make enough to eat. Others had grumbled the cook squirreled away most of the butchered sheep to eat later, alone. Workman had had it. They could cook for themselves. If they didn't like what was served up, well, they knew whom to blame.

———————

At Kargil, the second-largest town in the region after Leh, the Workmans haggled with a local headman until he agreed to furnish a permanent corps of sixty porters. Five and a half hours later, they reached Baltistan, where they crossed the Zoji La in "nasty and rainy" weather. Fires were lit. Everyone ate a spot of lunch. Then Hunter went to bed with fever and sore throat. His illness and the atrocious weather sidelined them for a full day. Later, before night fell, Fanny, Savoye, and a porter trudged down the slick hillside in the rain to negotiate with villagers for more food and extra supplies.

A skilled bargainer, Workman haggled for forty chickens. After agreeing on a price, one of the porters crowded the chickens into two baskets. Seven died immediately for want of air. Another half dozen died during transit, greatly diminishing their food supply.

Three days later, the group arrived in Suru, where livestock fodder dried on the roofs of stone houses and a whitewashed Buddhist monastery perched on a hill. A certain Mr. Hogg greeted the party. In the manner of a concierge in one of Europe's grand hotels, he showed them to a field where they could camp beneath weeping willow trees. A longtime resident of the village, Hogg helped procure additional sheep and fowl. This time, however, the birds were not stuffed into too-small baskets. Instead, a woolen thread was wound around the legs of each bird and then tied to the top of a porter's pack with the free end of the thread. Now with their chicken supply replenished, the party continued on its way. What a sight to see these chickens bouncing along on their human perches, Workman thought.

Normally the chickens would be allowed to hunt and peck for their own food. It made them tastier, Workman said. However, the vegetation was scarce here, and the birds had a hard time finding food, so the porters carried extra grain for them. After all, a starving chicken did no one any good, she mused. "If the traveler wished to have the benefit of the fowls he takes with him, he must himself see that they are fed till killed for his table," Workman remarked.

By the time the group crossed the Purkutse La into the Rangdum valley, the expedition now also included thirty sheep, fifteen goats, and the dozen fowl.

So far the new porters hired in Kargil didn't impress Workman. "They seemed to take no interest in their work, and did nothing to make themselves useful or to further our interests or those of the coolies they had charge of. . . . They were slow in starting, took up their loads grudgingly, complained of their weight although they were not heavy . . . and stopped to rest every sixty to a hundred steps," she wrote. She didn't think they'd last long.

Scorching heat blasted the sandy and shadeless ground. Each step kicked up a puff of dust. Most of the team tucked kerchiefs under their hats to block their necks. Relief came when they chanced upon a small oasis in the Nagar region. A porter climbed a rocky slope overlooking the village and lit a small fire. The smoke column announced to the local raja that the Bullock-Workmans had arrived. Shortly afterward, they climbed down the hill and "under a shade tree we threw ourselves down for lunch. Food and all covered with thousands of flies as well as our selves so that tiffin was a poor meal," Workman wrote.

On Sunday, July 1, the Americans awoke to a peacock-blue sky. Gone were yesterday's plump clouds. Situated 11,998 feet above sea level, this new camp was tucked in an isolated pocket in northern India's Ladakh region. In the distance, a glacier appeared to tumble into the roaring Suru River. Enormous chunks of ice bobbed along until they plunged over a sheer two-hundred-foot drop. Ice blocks sprinkled the shoreline for at least a mile. Workman found "the whole scene is one of wild and mighty chaos."

The next morning, they were once more walking along the riverbank. Suddenly, out of the corner of Workman's eye she spied a Ghurka and his workers waving to them from the other side of the river. He had tracked them from the opposite shore. They waved back. He waved again. He slipped into the water and swam across holding a leather bag above his head. Water ran down his body in rivulets as he handed Workman the bag filled with letters from Hogg. He refilled the bag with letters from Workman. Mission accomplished, he turned on his heel and returned the way he had come. Such was the rudimentary system of staying in contact with the outside world.

This time of year, the intense daytime heat melted the snow's surface. Glacier-fed streams swelled, and their muddy waters became virtually impassable. Flash floods were common. Swimming was the only way to cross the river, as "impossible a feat for our loaded caravan as flying would have been."

Workman sorts equipment amid a tangle of ropes.

After discussing it with Hunter and Savoye, Fanny agreed the best time to ford the river would be soon after dawn. They followed a sixteen-mile path to a little village where the water was at its lowest point. Acacia, poppies, vetch, thistles, and chickweed grew alongside the trail. Even here, the slate-colored waters remained waist high. One by one, the porters waded through the ice-cold rapids, holding on to each other for security. The stream was over two hundred feet wide.

"Armed with our bergstocks they stepped into the water, and we climbed upon their shoulders. As they advanced to mid-stream they swayed and floundered in the rapid current, stopping every few feet to secure toting on the cobble-paved bed of the river, and to preserve their balance, while we clung to their shoulders and necks with all our strength, our feet and backs lashed by the cold waves, realizing the insecurity of our moving perch and expecting every moment to be precipitated into the seething waters," she later recounted. Likewise, most of the twenty-six sheep and fifteen goats balked. The porters "had to play the part of good shepherds and carry them over on their shoulder." After three hours every person and animal, every piece of equipment and food was safely across. Soon three campfires blazed, clothes dried, and chilled limbs warmed.

The village head took advantage of the lull in activity to settle accounts. "A bakhshish [*sic*] of money, silk, handkerchiefs, and a liberal supply of tobacco, had already been given him, but he did not hesitate to ask for more tobacco, and in addition to payment for the ponies on the last two days, a bakhshish for each pony and *pony-wala*. In fact, the word bakhshish fell from his lips constantly during the half-hour of settling, and, as he rode away, it rang in our ears as long as his voice could be heard," she later wrote. After so many seasons in the Himalayas, the Workmans were well versed in this ancient system, which was more than a gesture of gratitude, more than a negotiating language; it demonstrated respect. It was an integral part of daily life and supported those living at poverty levels. As she explained to readers, the village head had done a valuable service for their group and so she did "not grudge him the pocketful of rupees he got from us before and after the river was forded."

On the other side of the river, they discovered a large marmot colony. "Burrows pierced the ground at short intervals in all directions," Workman wrote, adding, "Were this place of sufficient importance to have a name, it might appropriately be called Marmotville."

Roughly the size of a large house cat, the squat rodents hurried to and fro on short, stocky limbs. They retreated into their deep burrows at the slightest hint of human footfalls. They were swift, she thought. And polite—crying out warnings to each other when they heard noises. Though she wasn't an expert naturalist, Workman often included personal observations on a locale's flora and fauna. And the marmots simply delighted her. It was with reluctance she left them behind to discuss how best to map what she and Hunter named the Fariabad glacier.

———————

Great moraine masses yielded to slopes of barren ice sliced through with crevasses. It was slow going. Looking at how the packed snow filled the spaces between the rock ridges, Fanny felt as if she were walking on a giant whale skeleton. Just seventeen degrees Fahrenheit at midday—it was going to be cold. They'd have to be careful of the subfreezing temperatures; the strong wind increased the risk of frostbite. The night before, the wind had blown "down upon us in strong gusts the whole night, shaking the tents so that we feared we should be carried down in to the *bergschrund* with the altitude, the effect of which all felt decidedly, effectually prevented sleep," she wrote of her fear of being swept into a crevasse. The group was now ensconced in their new home at an elevation of 15,100 feet. The sound of pounding ice axes and hammers echoed through the site like Verdi's "Anvil Chorus."

Like a royal court procession, they left the camp on July 17 and climbed up the glacier to base camp. "For more than a mile we followed the steep, torn, and boulder-covered left or west bank, and then descended to the glacier, where for another mile we picked our tortuous way over, up and down, in and out of, its rock-smothered ravines, hillocks," she wrote. Fanny, Hunter, and the porters unpacked the nine Mummery tents and spread them out so they could check the canvases for any holes in need of a patch. The cook lazily stirred a cauldron of soup. Savoye sharpened his alpenstock. Some porters lazed about, smoking. Others darned socks.

The new spot was a grazing paradise for the goats and sheep. They roamed freely over the slope, nibbling on purple asters, edelweiss, crimson orchids, and grass. For the people, the spot was less than ideal. As the camp sat well above the tree line, there was nary a shrub or a twig to burn for fuel. Each day, twenty porters went down to the nullah, the dry riverbed, and fetched wood for fires and tent pegs.

Come morning, husband and wife heated water for tea and tried not to break their teeth on the biscuits. They wrestled their feet into semifrozen boots and buttoned their flannel shirts with fingers stiff from the cold. Then they waited. A hard rain beat against the tents. That was the thing about monsoon season, which began in early June. It was as if someone sliced open the clouds and released all the water contained in the sky.

When it let up, they moved out. A few hours and twelve miles later, the rains started again.

———————

The "snow work," as Fanny called the higher-altitude explorations, was about to begin.

"Ice-axes were tested and polished, and thick clothing was stowed in our clothes-bags in place of thinner garments heretofore worn. Extra mountain-boots were brought out and oiled, and those already in use re-nailed and repaired where necessary," she said.

A vast white field of nieves penitentes lay before them. Charles Darwin had first described such snow formations in scientific literature in 1839. He had seen them in 1835 during a trip to South America. Closely spaced, the elongated thin blades of hardened snow and ice pointed skyward toward the sun, resembling a procession of pennants. It was an apt name.

The Workman expedition picked their way through what felt like the first challenge on a high mountain obstacle course. "First we went over a short sharp snow wall, but it was easy without cast iron mummery nails hammered into the soles of our boots," Fanny wrote. They stopped to strap on crampons before moving "over long ascending snow côtes, steadily up. We passed very fine icicled crevasses and snow scenery before reaching camp which was on a long sloping plateau." Welcome to the newly christened Nieve Penitente Camp, elevation 17,657 feet.

Icefalls and sharp peaks flanked the camp, and Workman was thankful she didn't suffer from claustrophobia. Singed chops and kola biscuits served as dinner. Several fires kept the camp warm through the waning light of day and into the night.

———————

Hunter shouted to his wife. She was slipping and sliding her way up a sharp incline, and he wanted her to be careful of the icicle-lined bergschrunds. Here the deep crevasses interrupted the landscape with increasing frequency. Save for the team, there wasn't a single living creature in sight. They sensed the head of the glacier must be near. For a time the party moved apace, but soon the steepness slowed them down. They forged ahead until they reached their new site. Workman called it White Needle Camp. They were now just under twenty thousand feet high.

Bellies full, everyone settled in to sleep, but it would not come. Insomnia reigned. Several porters complained of headaches and pain in their backs and limbs. The symptoms grew more pronounced at night. Some coughed and others lost their voice. Sleep remained elusive. As soon as they began to doze, they started gasping for breath. No one was getting enough oxygen. "This did not tend to fortify us any too well for the coming struggle, tired, as we were, by the three days of hard snow-climbing," Hunter wrote.

So it went. Each night they slid under their blankets hoping sleep would claim them. Each night Fanny listened as Hunter tossed and turned and tossed some more. The cold gnawed her bones; reaching an arm from beneath her covers, she grabbed another layer. She tried to will herself to sleep to no avail. Such was the climber's curse—the low oxygen that comes with high altitudes can sometimes cause insomnia.

They hardly had space to move while hiking along the trail A misstep here meant falling into the schrund. "Or if we passed that, down gruesome precipices to the glacial ice-fields thousands of feet below," Workman noted. There was nowhere else she'd rather be.

Climbers endure a great deal of mental strain on prolonged expeditions. "There is plenty of opportunity to observe and realize one's precarious position, the longer time occupied suffices to create considerable nervous tension," she wrote.

Risk is as much a part of climbing and exploration as the cold and fatigue. When climbing, the body and spirit must operate at full capacity; otherwise the consequences can be fatal. Some climbers maintain focus by breaking up the ascent, others by breaking the whole expedition into sections. Additionally, climbers cannot let their minds wander while climbing.

Some climbers liken high-stakes mountaineering to war— "physical suffering, but also long periods of boredom," says Hayden Carpenter, editor of *Rock and Ice* magazine. "The element of the unknown and the threat of death are always present to some level, and can slowly wear away at morale." Like any climber, the more experienced she got, the better Workman would have been at coping with the physical and mental strain as time went on.

———————

At 20,632 feet, Camp Italia occupied the lower flank of the Nun Kun. The expedition would pass two nights here. "And if any snow-leopards were prowling about, they must have viewed with some curiosity the scene which ensued—men engaged in pitching tents, lighting stoves, preparing dinner, setting up cameras, making observations, and doing other things which showed, that this uppermost plateau in the very heart of the Nun Kun had been successfully invaded by human beings," she noted.

In spite of the ever-present avalanche threat, and one very sick porter, Workman urged everyone to press onward. With the arrival of the summer monsoon season, the climb would be too risky to attempt in a few short weeks.

Just before they reached twenty-one thousand feet, Hunter collapsed to his knees. Removing his woolen mittens, Fanny noticed his hands were impossibly white and stiff. A severe headache gripped the fifty-nine-year-old. His back and lower limbs seized in pain. She insisted he go to bed. Upon lying down, he complained of shortness of breath. The symptoms grew worse, especially at night. He gasped for breath and feared he wouldn't last the night.

No woman—or man—could last long working at these altitudes, she thought. And yet, Fanny and Hunter, now with a smaller group that included Savoye, worked hard, and as soon as they thawed they made their way back to Camp Italia. A cup of hot tea, a few spoonfuls of pâté and crumbling biscuits, and breakfast was finished. They descended to White Needle Camp.

Still a keen photographer, Workman snapped the angles and ice. Suddenly, a sharp pain bit deep into her legs and back. It persisted, and she felt worse during the wee hours of the night. Even after taking a tonic, she couldn't sleep. It seemed Fanny Workman, ever immune to altitude sickness, had succumbed.

She felt a little better in the morning, so she and Hunter left their frozen tent to trek up a rising plateau. By midafternoon they were 21,300 feet high.

The Workmans and their guides scaled the steep curving slope. They cut steps into the ice and squeezed through narrow passages between ice walls. They passed along the sixty-pound packs one at a time. Here the seracs loomed higher and sharper. The fissures appeared longer and wider. The snowbridges more treacherous.

The group waded through thigh-deep snow for five more hours until they were brought up short. Perpendicular walls of ice and stone rose from the snow. They stared. Either they went up or they returned. If they returned, they could mark the expedition as over.

---

While the Workmans were considering their next move, a dense mist rolled in back at Camp Italia and cloaked the area. Savoye and the porters had returned to collect the tents. It proved a futile mission. Aside from heavy snow and fog, mountain sickness felled the group like dominos. The first man to fall appeared strong and healthy until they reached twenty-one thousand feet. Then he collapsed in a heap. He murmured something about not feeling his hands. His fingers were white and stiff beneath the woolen mittens. The man was too sick to be moved; the team would have to pass the night in these dangerous conditions. "We did not fancy the prospect of being left in such a place, at such an altitude, cut off entirely from all communication with the outer world, in weather which appeared to be uncertain, and in a temperature which, though now too warm for comfort, was sure to fall to or below zero before morning, but this contingency had to be faced," Fanny wrote.

Unable to continue, the Workmans unpacked the instruments and provisions. They tried to make themselves comfortable inside the tents, but the tent walls felt too close and the ground too hard. To distract themselves, they checked over their equipment. None of the Primus stoves and hypsometer lamps seemed to be working. They went through about a half dozen matches to heat alcohol in the stoves' lighting cups. When smoky, ill-smelling fumes filled the tents, they opened the flaps to let in fresh air. The sun's rays reflected off the snow, and daytime temperatures rose. At one point Fanny and Hunter wound wet towels around their heads for some relief from the oppressive heat. After sunset, the sky shifted. Out of the mist, the great Nun Kun emerged. "So we camped here alone until 8 AM next day. It was the highest camp made by mortals and called 'Camp America,'" Workman wrote.

Despite the illnesses and hardships, the elevation record was quite an achievement. However, a few months after they returned to Germany, Workman would hear a story claiming that a Mr. W. H. Johnson had camped at an altitude of twenty-two thousand feet, one thousand feet higher than Camp America. She didn't believe the story. She examined Johnson's published reports and found no evidence that he himself ever made such a claim. The information, first pushed in a story written by noted British explorer Dr. T. G. Longstaff, was now being perpetuated by an attorney named H. F. Balch. But why? She couldn't say for sure.

She said she didn't want to wade into this controversy, yet she also said she wanted to set the record straight. If mountaineering and glacial exploration were to be considered through a scientific lens, then one had to measure altitudes using accepted standards.

Throughout this 1906 trip, and on future trips, the Workmans observed and noted the physiological effects of high altitude. They recorded the structure, movement, and phenomena of ice and glaciers. Their journals contained records of maximum and minimum sun and shade temperatures, as well as altitude measurements taken with both aneroid barometers and boiling point thermometers.

There was no room for guessing. What "a man 'personally thinks' was not a sufficient measure of altitude," Workman said. There was a certain irony to her complaints, though. Many of the Workmans' early maps would fail the test of time, no matter how extensively she and Hunter explored the region, and no matter how careful they were in taking measurements. Many of the trigonometrical points given for the region would eventually be rendered erroneous.

In any event, on that cold night in July 1906, she planned to summit Pinnacle Peak in the morning. The next day's climb and the sheer remoteness of their camp was all she could think about as the shadows lengthened and night fell. She stepped outside her tent, wrapped in a vicuña coat. She felt "but an atom" standing here in this wide arctic basin, this frozen nothingness. Utter silence. A "mountain-stillness more potent than speech." The cold penetrated, and "leaving the ice-wilderness to the fast-encompassing pall of darkness, we turned shivering into our tents."

---

On the other side of the world and several months earlier, Annie S. Peck prepared for another trip over the equator. It was May 24, 1906, and she was back in New York City's harbor. Tomorrow she would sail for Panama.

Peck had just completed a year of lecturing, to rave reviews. The audience at the Geographical Society in Baltimore loved her lectures on Bolivia and the Matterhorn—even when interrupted by a gaggle of rowdy children. One woman wrote to Peck asking if it might be possible to have police patrol the hall at future events. A man in Springfield, Massachusetts, wrote to her, dismayed that his church never held lectures. There was no one he would rather hear than Peck, he said, she being a distinguished woman who had climbed so high with such courage and ability.

She arrived in Peru some two weeks later, in June 1906, once again arriving by the port of Samanco. She checked into what passed for a hotel. Ignoring the room's grime-covered floor, she threw her journal and maps on the wobbly wooden table and draped her traveling clothes on a chair. The room, which cost ten dollars a day, was cold, and there weren't enough blankets. The clerk denied her request for more.

Peck scrubbed her face and hands in the bedside washstand and went downstairs to dinner. The waiter set the table with a bowl of noodle soup, a serving of rice and potatoes, and a platter of tough, cold meat. In the morning, her guide joined her for breakfast. Peck ate heartily of soup, fish, eggs on toast, pureed bananas, and coffee. She chased it with a cocktail of egg yolk brandy.

Even with the shabby state of her room, Peck felt almost at home here in Peru. During a previous trip, she had visited a private school where she was pleased to see young women preparing for university. She wanted to see more of this in the United States. True, this opportunity was only for children born into wealth; poor students hadn't a chance, and in most places the priests opposed education for girls. Nevertheless, she thought it a good start.

After breakfast the second day, she looked for additional porters to round out her team.

The day of departure, Peck awoke early. She stood outside and waited for the rest of her group. At last they got underway. They rode past ruined mills and dried-up riverbeds. They saw cultivated fields and overgrown meadows. In the distance, snow fell, thunder rumbled, and lightning raged across the sky. The weather turned so violent that she and her guide were forced to seek shelter until the worst had passed.

At the inn where they stayed, dinner was served. Peck relished the soup, meat, peas, and tomatoes. Famished, she helped herself to a second helping of meat and fritters. For dessert there was rice pudding, cake, and pie. Fine wafers came out with the coffee and tea. Sated, Peck went to bed soon after 9:00 PM and slept deeply until around 4:30 AM. It was too early to get up, even by her standards, so she lay in bed until 6:00. A plate of eggs, a cup of coffee, and she was ready for her fifth assault on Mount Huascarán.

# 8

# PINNACLE PEAK

L IKE A GEM CUTTER, Workman guided her ice ax. If she struck too hard, the blade might pop out and hit her in the eye. Or worse, splinter off a slice of ice and send it careening down on the porter below. It was all about precision and patience.

Even with the sun shining, the day held the cold. Workman tied her neckerchief a little tighter. She curled and uncurled her toes inside her boots. The cold burrowed inside her bones and she worried about frostbite. Now at 21,300 feet, the team was engaged in what Workman called high "snow-work."

At the new campsite, empty tents sat in straight lines. Several of the porters were on their way back down to the previous campsite to retrieve the remaining supplies. They planned to rest a bit and then return before nightfall. Then the snow came.

As the line between earth and sky blurred, it dawned on Workman that she and Hunter would pass the night here alone, without guides or porters. "The absolute silence that reigned during the watches of the night, in the absence of sleep, proved almost as nerve-wearing as an excess of noise. The feeling of having completely no touch with the material world and the imagination uncontrolled . . . runs riot," she wrote. Hunter agreed.

Only a thin skin of canvas separated the couple from the blizzard. The tent shook and shuddered. The wind gusted through the camp, threatening to send the tent sliding across the mountain like a skiff. Fanny shivered in her sleeping bag. She was so cold she thought her teeth might shatter. Her throat was aflame and her head pounded. Sleep stayed away.

Wide awake, she prepared letters to send to *Pioneer* magazine about their work thus far. Hunter tried to write in his journal, but he couldn't keep his thoughts in order, all the while hoping the gale wouldn't lay waste to the camp. The snow piled up on the roof, which sagged under the weight. Once or twice they ventured outside to clear it away lest their tent become a snow crypt. It was mercilessly cold, even inside the tent. Their hands cramped and their fingers turned ghostly white. They took turns massaging each other's hands and feet to stave off frostbite. The hours dragged.

Finally the light streamed through the green tent, casting supernatural shadows on their faces and hands. Hunter reached for his water. There was none to be had; the water in the flasks was frozen solid. Try as she might, Fanny couldn't pull on her boots. They, too, were frozen stiff. She looked at her husband and suppressed a smile. Ice flecked his push-broom mustache.

"On putting our heads out of the tent-flaps we were greeted by Savoye and two porters, who, with red eyes, purple faces, and moustaches fringed with icicles, looked as if they had fought a hard battle with the elements," she noted. There wasn't really anything funny about it, but she chuckled to herself all the same. A release from the stress. Some climbers considered themselves tough if they spent the night in a rustic but warm hut before making an ascent, she mused. They should try spending the night in a frigid tent on the snow, waking in below-zero temperatures, boiling coffee over a Primus stove that, because of the rarefied air, takes five times longer to light, "and, last but not easiest, wrestle with frozen boots."

After Workman bid Savoye good morning, she ducked back inside the tent to begin melting snow for tea. Preparing food, or tea or coffee, on high-altitude glaciers was just as tedious a process as when they had first started exploring the Himalayas six years earlier. First they had to gather snow. If it was the first night in a new camp, they had to assemble the stove. Then they had to heat the snow so it melted. If the bottle of water froze, they would immerse it in the warm water to melt that as well. Today there is far less actual mountainside cooking; dehydrated precooked meals and energy bars for nourishment are widely available.

She and Hunter nibbled a few kola biscuits and shared a tin of room-temperature tongue. Workman always found it tasty and easy to digest. The meager meal finished, they layered themselves against the cold and stepped back into the thin air to assess the scene. Black rock and blue ice as far as the eye could see. The snow danced about like will-o'-the-wisps. It was time to climb.

She, Hunter, Savoye, and two other guides roped themselves together and started upward. In truth, neither Fanny nor Hunter felt entirely up to it; three sleepless nights on the mountain hadn't been exactly restorative, though as the sun warmed Fanny's neck she felt her muscles wake up and her energy return. They maneuvered up the incline. Savoye led the way, cutting steps when needed.

A constant, cold breeze blew down from the heights with chilling effect. Their feet suffered most, and Workman was anxious that one of them would get frostbite. They wore fleece-lined rubber mittens to keep their hands warm. All the same, the cold chewed Workman's bones. She windmilled her arms and clenched and unclenched her fingers. She wriggled her nose and stomped her feet. Nothing worked. Her blood was turning to ice. Her cheeks burned from the cold. She glanced at Savoye, hoping to commiserate. Yet, other than the puffs of air when he exhaled, he seemed resistant to the frigid air. Mind over matter, mind over matter, she repeated, lifting one foot after another.

"It would be a boon to mountaineers if someone would invent a certain means of keeping the feet warm at 20,000 feet. Some of us were scarcely conscious of having any feet by the time we reached that height, but by beating them vigorously with our axes until they tingled sufficiently to denote safety, we were spared the extreme exertion required in the rarefied air of taking off boots and rubbing our feet with snow," she would later write. They had tried fur-lined boots and plain leather boots and Norwegian goat-hair boots . . . Nothing worked as well as she would have liked.

Cold wasn't their only adversary. Altitude sickness stalked the expedition. Altitude affects people differently, regardless of their physical condition. Some experience appetite loss. Others feel nauseated. Rapid heart rates and insomnia are common. In rare cases, cerebral edema and death can occur. Even the simplest of actions, "which one recognizes as of great importance and which at ordinary altitudes are not difficult processes become bugbears. . . . One has therefore, often to call the will into play to its utmost power to force oneself to carry out what has been proposed. Those who are destined to raise the mountaineering altitude-record much higher than it now stands will undoubtedly be persons of strong will and self-control," she wrote. Even the act of taking basic measurements became a challenge at such great heights. It would be decades before climbers had the advantage of bottled oxygen.

When they reached 22,720 feet, Hunter stopped to photograph the landscape while his wife went on with the other two porters to complete the ascent, attaining an altitude of 23,300 feet. When Hunter caught up with the trio, he reached into his pack and traded his camera for his notebook and pen. Then he set up the hypsometer. He and Fanny took altitude measurements to prove this was "the highest point up to date, to which tents have been taken and occupied, and the highest measured point at which mountaineers have passed the night." As was their practice in all high camps, peaks, and passes, they took hypsometric observations and compared their readings with the lower station mercurial barometer readings, which a government official in Skardu took thrice daily. The calculations were then measured against three different tables, and the average was the figure the Workmans accepted as the true height. They also brought along two Watkins patent aneroid barometers, graduated to 25,000 feet, and checked those daily using boiling point as a reference.

Several hours later, after finishing the work, the couple stumbled into camp. Fanny sank to her knees, grimacing; her alpenstock fell out of her hand. Her entire body ached, but she did not want to stop the expedition. She still felt unwell several days later. She "suffered much the last few days from headache and backache and pains in limbs. Cough nearly gone. I think the marching exhausts her and she has not her former energy," Hunter wrote in his journal. He was worried. He didn't know what ailed his wife. All he could do was give her analgesics, tell her to rest, and hope it wasn't anything too serious. If she were gravely ill—if anyone on the trip fell gravely ill—there was nothing to be done. They were thousands of miles and weeks away from adequate medical treatment.

Fortunately, Fanny rallied. Outside the tent, no one knew she was unwell. As the lone woman on the trip, she had to be twice as stoic and twice as resilient. If she weren't, the porters and guides would snigger about the too-weak woman who fancied herself an explorer.

———————

On August 2, at precisely 8:45 AM, Fanny stood atop the summit
of Chogo La. She allowed herself a moment of elation. Hunter
snapped five photographs of the party on the rocky peak. Clouds
fluttered above, and the whole Hispar Glacier spread forth below.
They felt suspended in the air. "The view . . . is one of the finest
and most comprehensive topographically I have ever seen. It is
unobscured in fine weather on all sides . . . the peak so near," she
wrote in her journal about what it was like to stand there at such
a tremendous height.

A boom interrupted their meditation. A thick cloud of snow
rumbled. From their perch they were in no actual danger, but
they were sharply aware of the power of an avalanche and the
destruction one might bring. They stood for several moments
more and then got to work. Using an aneroid barometer, they
calculated their altitude at 22,000 feet. Later, a more considered
calculation showed the actual altitude to be 21,250 feet, 750 feet
less. Hunter made the correction in his journal. Gathering altitude data was fiendishly difficult; there was always ample room
for errors. Corrections were neatly listed on the back pages of
Hunter's journals.

On their return to camp Fanny and Hunter learned all sorts
of items were disappearing from camp: glasses, handkerchiefs,
socks, even biscuits and lozenges. They casually asked several
porters about it, but either no one knew who it was or no one
wanted to give up the thief. In truth, there wasn't much Fanny
or Hunter could do to unmask the culprit. So long as nothing
violent occurred and so long as their progress wasn't impeded,
they would let the porters settle the matter themselves.

A day later they hiked down to the valley under an egg-yolk-
yellow sun. The calm weather didn't last; strong winds chased
away the fleecy clouds bringing snow. Their visibility much dimin-
ished, they stepped carefully on the fresh snow. The terrain was

brutal. Here the earth rose to dizzying heights. Savoye raked the terrain with his eyes to discern hidden cracks in the ice; he didn't want anyone stepping in the wrong place. If they did, they could crash through. They decided not to take a shortcut. Instead they retraced the path they'd taken on the ascent. Studded with rocks, the route back to their previous camp threatened to trip even the most alert trekker.

This time it was Hunter who flopped to the ground. He suffered from an angry abscess that had formed around a loose molar. It was so sensitive he couldn't touch the area with his tongue. His jawline burned and red spots flowered on his cheeks.

The retired physician slowly sipped a cocktail of peppermint and cognac. For dinner he ate a softened kola biscuit. The cracker-sized biscuits, prepared with kola nut extract, sugar, and wheat flour, were a staple in the climbing world. By the late 1800s factories turned them out by the thousands. Usually he ate the biscuits to curb hunger pangs during the day, but right now it was all he could manage.

Sometimes they made a meal of little more than two chocolate Plasmon biscuits and a French preparation of kola nut with brown sugar. At the turn of the twentieth century, the dried milk biscuits were considered a health food. During his 1902 Antarctic expedition Ernest Shackleton had eaten the biscuits. Samuel L. Clemens, more familiarly known as Mark Twain, had invested in Plasmon Milk Products Company and reportedly ate them daily. As for the kola, Fanny approved—mostly: "Taken in moderate quantity [it] is excellent for maintaining the vital force, but if taken in too great doses produces dizziness. On rocks climbing at 23,000 feet, persons of ordinary strength must have some stimulant as they cannot eat meat and all cognac and whisky should be left untouched as they reduce the strength in their secondary effect a little cold."

Later that night of August 3, Savoye stopped in their tent. Apparently a few porters had seen snow leopards roaming in the vicinity. No one worried too much about the elusive cats with their snowshoe-like paws. They weren't known to attack people. In any event Workman was more worried about the severe cough nagging Cesare Chenoz. Before long nearly everyone in the camp was coughing incessantly. They had become a high-altitude infirmary.

---

A few weeks later, toward the end of August, the entire party, now fully recovered, reached Nun Kun. A large black crow and its mate cawed a greeting. An eagle nested nearby. "Some days ago he carried off a piece of a sheep that had been buried within snow," wrote Workman. Occasionally she sighted black-throated thrushes, rose finches, and majestic Himalayan monals, also known as impeyan pheasants. The males had a long metallic-green crest, coppery feathers on the back and neck, and a white rump. Females had a white patch on the throat and white strips on the tail. She would never be an ornithologist, but she enjoyed watching the different birds.

Frost feathered the rocks, and Workman wasn't sure her hobnailed boots would keep her from slipping on the ice-glazed snow. She glanced behind her. Hunter was also having trouble, as were the porters who'd come along. Cutting steps was the only way.

In all the years they spent exploring, the Workmans never made much effort to develop better relationships with their local hires, though as leaders it was their responsibility to do so. Their expeditions carried an inherent tension because seasonal conditions required that they stick to a certain time line. Workman sometimes grew frustrated with the porters because they "showed no spirit in marching," although what she meant by that is unclear.

Perhaps they didn't match her steady and determined pace. The woman from Worcester was known to forge ahead.

Seen from the plateau on which the last two camps stood, Pinnacle Peak slants upward to its apex in a broad surface covered with an ice sheet. Perpendicular precipices make up its northeast face. The two faces meet at the skyline in a sharp ridge, which projects above the snow. High winds in the region keep the summit bare.

Savoye led the way. "A misstep here might hurl us into the bergschrund just below, or, if we passed that, down gruesome precipices to the glacial ice-fields thousands of feet below," Workman mused.

They stopped for a bite of Plasmon chocolate.

Once more fortified, the team rose to their feet. They were now climbing at sixty- to sixty-five-degree angles. The crampons strapped to their boots helped. On the surface the snow had hardened to a consistency not unlike spun sugar. If the temperatures stayed constant, the snow would remain like that for the rest of the day. Two and a half hours later, at 22,750 feet, Workman called for another break.

Hunter and a porter stepped aside and rested on a ledge. Fanny, Savoye, Chenoz, and one other porter continued up over the arête. In the distance the sharp line of the mountains looked like stitches across the sky.

Fanny's chest constricted. It was the most arduous ascent she'd made so far. Even Savoye, who always seemed immune to altitude sickness, felt the effects once they hit 23,300 feet. On the final push to the summit, her fingers locked. The cold was through and through. She couldn't grip her ice ax. She hesitated to pull off her mittens and check the color of her hands. Every few feet she bent down to chip ice from the bottom of her boots. Sweat streamed and froze across her brow.

Five steps. Eleven steps. Five steps. With her bearlike, lumbering approach Workman forged ahead. Three steps. Five steps.

One. More. Step. Workman stood on the narrow peak.

Beneath "a wide galaxy of mountains running in snaky lines surmounted by winding crests, equally tortuous glaciers, and ribbon-like valleys" spread before the trio. Peering down she saw the sharp ice slant "we had ascended plunged down to the Nun Kun basin covered with a sheet of driven snow, while on the east, a perpendicular precipice fell from where we stood some thousands of feet to a savage, rock-bound abyss." Farther to the north, the Nanga Parbat, also known as the "Man Eater" towered. Rolling mists shrouded the eastern Karakoram. To the east was the Shafat Glacier.

The lack of oxygen hit Workman. Her camera, which weighed a pound or two at most, now felt four times as heavy. The glacial wind swept across the summit as Fanny added stones to a cairn, to mark the simple fact of having stood here, on this ridge, at this moment. At forty-seven, Fanny had just broken her record ascent for women and joined the small band of mountaineers who reached a height higher than 23,000 feet. Later, triangulation would show Pinnacle Peak to be 22,740 feet high, 260 feet less than Workman had measured. Nevertheless, her record, the altitude record for women, would stand for twenty-eight more years.

But she didn't feel jubilant. Not yet, anyhow. She knew the climb wasn't over until they reached base camp. She knew mistakes most often happened on the descent. They rechecked the ropes and the crampons. And then they turned around. They would not make it back to camp until well past nightfall. On the way down, the party ascended a projecting rock needle, where her always-patient husband was waiting to photograph the trio of guides and his quietly triumphant wife. An imperceptible smile graced her face as she posed on the crag for Hunter, who was so proud.

Going down turned out to be more stressful than any of them had anticipated. The snow was softer, and with each step their feet sank several inches before hitting the ice buried below. They fought against a penetrating fatigue. No one spoke until they saw the fires of Camp America flickering in the distance.

"I made another record placing me now with the few men holding world altitude for the time being," Workman wrote before she extinguished her lamp. "That a single glance of the world from such impressive heights and the thrill that comes from doing what no mortal has done before fully compensates for all the suffering and hardships involved."

––––––––––––

In fact, Pinnacle Peak, which the Workmans asserted to be the highest peak in the Nun Kun group, was not the highest. It was the third-highest, after the 23,409-foot Nun and the 23,218-foot Kun. The Workmans had not provided all necessary points to do a proper triangulation. It took several more expeditions by other mountaineers for the massif's elevation to be determined, most notably the 1911 retriangulation of the peaks by Dr. Arthur Neve, a Christian medical missionary. He showed the elevation to be approximately 22,742 feet. Even so, the prestige of making a first ascent, as a woman in the early 1900s, cannot be overstated: her altitude record would stand until 1934.

When he sat down to write his twelve-volume study, *Southern Tibet*, the celebrated Swedish explorer Sven Hedin would pay a rare compliment to the Workmans for their work in the Nun Kun: "Of great importance for the knowledge of this world of icy mountains are the several journeys undertaken by Dr. Hunter Workman and Mrs. Bullock Workman."

A proud Hunter later described his wife, a slow and deliberate climber, in glowing terms. With unabashed admiration, he wrote:

> [Her] enthusiasm for what she undertook was unbounded. She concentrated her attention on the end in view, often disregarding the difficulties and even the dangers that might lie in the way of accomplishment. She went forward with a determination to succeed and a courage that won success where a less determined effort would have failed. She believed in taking advantage of every opportunity. She was no quitter, and was never the first to suggest turning back in the face of discouraging circumstances. She frequently urged her Alpine guides on to renewed effort where they began to hesitate.

Fanny Workman's addiction to climbing knew no bounds.

———————

Once home in Germany, Workman returned to the lecture circuit, employing her considerable fame to speak out in support of women's rights, particularly the continued hostile and patronizing reception women in climbing encountered in Europe. Below the snow line she met with sexism from her male society peers, just as she had from porters and guides on the mountain who had difficulty respecting a woman's authority.

While the only condition for membership into the American Association of Geographers, established in 1904, was that applicants proved their "mature scholarship," the Royal Geographical Society was still debating whether to admit women. In spite of the

A porter carries Workman, attired in her favorite "valley sweater" and a pith helmet, across a raging river.

fact that Workman had already addressed the forum on several occasions, she was still denied full membership. She decried the unfriendly reception she received in Britain. She felt she suffered from sexism. Nevertheless, she would not be cowed.

She crammed her calendar with speaking engagements; at one point she delivered thirty lectures in thirty-seven days, splitting her time between Munich, Vienna, Dresden, Berlin, and Hamburg. Each time, she made no effort to smile as she approached the podium. She merely adjusted her blouse, shuffled her papers, and started speaking, a knob of graying brown hair piled high atop her head and her cheeks still burnished by the Himalayan sun.

She took her show on the road and presented at geographical and scientific societies in the United States, the United Kingdom, France, Germany, and Italy. Audiences listened to her talk about life in hostile climates where howling winds and below-zero temperatures were the norm. The lectures were well received. In Scotland, a John Clarke of the University of Aberdeen thanked Workman after one particularly energetic lecture. Aside from the subject, which he thoroughly enjoyed, he gushed about her fluency in both French and German. As well as lectures in Boston, the Workmans also spoke to International Geographical Congress in Washington, DC, New York, Philadelphia, St. Louis, and the Appalachian Mountain Club.

Around this time, they were working on the final edits for their book *Peaks and Glaciers of Nun Kun*, which would be published in 1909. The prose still came across as somewhat detached. Fanny and her husband seemed to observe, rather than join in, local culture and customs. The writing style wasn't particular to their published books. While both of the Workmans' journals remained mostly devoid of emotion, Fanny's, even more than Hunter's, were products of control. She literally went to the ends of the earth to escape society's rules and expectations. She liked mountaineering more than people.

———————

On June 9, 1908, Annie S. Peck was once again sailing to Peru, this time aboard the *Prinz August Wilhelm*. The night before she'd left, she had hosted a farewell dinner at the Hotel Alabama, in New York City. The fifty-eight-year-old Rhode Island native planned a rematch with her nemesis: Mount Huascarán. Intuitively she knew this would be the last time.

Before Peck had left New York, her literary agent had told *Collier's Weekly* they should not miss out on an opportunity to buy climber's story. Later, *Harper's Monthly* bought an exclusive five-thousand-word story and photographs for $1,000.

Peck and guides heading to Peru for another attempt to summit Huascarán.

Peck once again hired Swiss guides: Rudolf Taugwalder, who had climbed with the Workmans, and Gabriel Zumtaugwald.

As the boat crossed the Isthmus of Panama, Peck marveled at the transformations taking place in the region. What was once wilderness was now a place of industry and building. She arrived in the Port of Samanco, Peru, on July 23, and went in search of saddle horses and baggage mules. Task completed, she and her party traveled nearly three hundred miles over the sparsely inhabited Cordillera Negra, or Black Range. From there they continued to Yungay, just west of Cordillera Blanca. As in the past, Peck boarded with a local family and hired local porters.

Over the next several days, Peck found herself confronting a familiar obstacle: male guides trying to tell her what to do and how to do it. "One of the chief difficulties in a woman's undertaking an expedition of this nature is that, whatever her experience, every man believes that he knows better what should be done than she. So it is not strange that, in common with my previous helpers, the Swiss guides should conclude that my experience in three abortive efforts counted for nothing in comparison with their own judgment," she wrote.

The way up Huascarán was long, with many nights spent bivouacking. She melted snow for soup or tea and on more than one night hoped her tent, though fastened by iron spikes driven into the snow and weighted down, wouldn't blow away.

On the morning of the final push for the summit, Peck donned every stitch of clothing she had—three suits of lightweight woolen underwear, two pairs of tights, sweaters, and four pairs of woolen stockings. But most of the clothing was permeable and did little to block the wind. How she lamented the Inuit suit Admiral Peary leant her; she had lost it on a previous excursion and it now lay at the bottom of a ravine somewhere along the way to Huascarán's summit. "I had not really needed it before, nor worn it except at night. Now when I wanted it badly, it was gone. I am often asked if my progress is not impeded by the weight of so much clothing, to which I answer, No. All of the articles were light, and garments, which cling closely to the body, are not burdensome. I never noticed the weight at all."

A pair of vicuña mittens covered her hands. She said a silent thank-you to the tailor in La Paz who'd lined them with two layers of fur. As the sun rose higher, her hands started to sweat. She exchanged the vicuña mittens for two pairs of wool mittens. The only thing Peck didn't wear was her poncho. She asked Zumtaugwald to carry it for her, thinking she would want it when they paused for luncheon at altitude.

Repeatedly she warned the men in her team to watch carefully for the telltale signs of frostbite. She relayed a cautionary story from Sir Martin Conway's 1899 attempted ascent of Mount

Aconcagua. It was one of the early tries to reach South America's highest mountain. At daybreak one of Conway's guides felt his feet turn to ice blocks, even with two pairs of stockings. He was forced to turn back. She also shared with them the story of Matthias Zurbriggen. He, too, had suffered from frostbitten feet on Aconcagua in 1897 and Sorata in 1894. (His feet healed, and the frostbite didn't prevent him from participating in later expeditions.) Either her guides paid her no mind or thought they knew better than she did. In her experience, it was likely the latter.

The last rays of the sun gone, Peck poured a bit of alcohol from her canteen to light her kerosene stove. Each night, inside her tent, she enjoyed a small draught of liquor. If only her mother could see her now—installed inside her canvas tent, wrapped in heavy woolen blankets, notes and instruments strewn before her feet. She visualized the ascent over and over, knowing she couldn't depend on chance.

Peck also thought about the way the press tried to cast her sometimes as the symbol of all women and at other times as a pants-wearing oddity. She found it infuriating. One woman could not be representative of all women, any more than one man could represent all men. As for the obsession with her pants, Peck was tired of explaining the idea of choosing clothing appropriate to the activity. She wore pants to climb and skirts to lecture or socialize. She often argued that women who tried to act like men did a disservice to the cause. In Peck's opinion, they were essentially saying "they aren't as good as men, that they know they aren't, and that they are going to try to be just as good by the usurpation of all the masculine trimmings."

Her thoughts turned to the first time she had heard about the formidable Huascarán, back in 1903. A Peruvian engineer had suggested she try her hand at his country's highest peak. He'd told her about its lofty views.

For Peck, though, the challenge of climbing brought more satisfaction than the view: "Many persons suppose that people climb mountains solely to enjoy the view. . . . This view is erroneous. . . . To the mountain climber every moment is a pleasure, from the time when he sets forth for the little mountain hut, until the hour of his return, triumphant and happy even though weary and footsore."

They progressed slowly, spending several nights on the mountainside, sometimes in the midst of ice walls and "yawning chasms." They were almost at the steepest part of the saddle when they hit an ice wall. Zumtaugwald cut steps, but, Peck wrote, "the steps were so far apart that my thigh was often horizontal; the wall so nearly perpendicular that in taking a step I was frequently embarrassed by my knee striking the snow above." Zumtaugwald hefted the adze of his ice ax and cut steps.

Bad weather delayed the ascent; the team waited for Zumtaugwald to recover from a headache. Three days later, after trying to ascend the slope, which was coated in brittle ice, they reached the saddle. They were now about twenty thousand feet high. The twin peaks of Huascarán loomed several thousand feet above.

In the morning they "toiled upward." The wind was strong and the day frigid. Zumtaugwald was roped to Peck and began cutting steps again. Try as they might, they could not quite make the summit. They returned to the camp a few thousand feet below. Sunday came and went. On Monday, Peck asked her guides, "Up or down?" Down was the answer. They returned to Yungay, where they learned "it was feared that she had met with some accident." Indeed she was very much alive; she had been delayed because one of the porters in her party had fallen ill. She set about getting more food and clothing.

Ten days later they tried again. This time they followed a more direct route. The wind blew. The cold penetrated every layer of woolen clothing. Finally they reached the summit. "My first thought on reaching the goal was, 'I am here at last, after all these years; but shall we ever get down again?' I said nothing except, 'Give me the camera,' and as rapidly as possible took views towards the four quarters of the heavens, one including Gabriel [Zumtaugwald]. The click of the camera did not sound just right, and fearing that I was getting no pictures at all, I did not bother to have Gabriel try to take a photograph of me."

Peck took out her altimeter and measured. Hands frozen, they tried in vain to light the stove so they could use the hypsometer. They were running out of time; they would die of exposure if they stayed on the top much longer. She shoved the instrument back in her pack, and the three started the harrowing journey down the mountain. They walked, slid, and sometimes slipped their way down until they reached their tent. It was nearly 11:00 PM. Rudolf Taugwalder, who had lost both of his gloves, stared in horror at his hands. The digits were turning black.

Though Peck hadn't gotten the official recording she needed and wanted, she nonetheless reported the climb to the American Geographical Society. "If, as seems probable, the height is 24,000 feet I have the honor of breaking the world's record for men as well as women," she wrote in her exclusive for *Harper's Magazine*.

Henry G. Bryant, undersecretary for the American Alpine Club, sent his congratulations. He invited her to present an outline of her experiences to the club's annual meeting, slated for next January in Baltimore. Likewise Charles E. Fay extended his congratulations for her enthusiasm and persistent will. He hoped she would consider being included in *National Geographic*'s article "The World's Highest Altitudes and First Ascents."

News of Peck's claim spread fast, igniting one of climbing's most controversial episodes.

# 9

# A RECORD DISPUTED

THE SUN ROSE on a morning clear and cold. The Workmans melted snow for their morning tea while they waited for thirty of the nearly one hundred porters to return with more firewood. Wood was scarce, and Fanny wondered aloud if they should get going; she knew it could easily take the porters three days to find and bring enough dwarf willow bushes to keep the kettle boiling.

It was early summer 1908, and Fanny and Hunter were exploring the Hispar Glacier, a sixty-two-mile-long ribbon of ice. Having only glimpsed the glacier on earlier expeditions, the couple had looked forward to this trip for months. Following a route from Gilgit through Nagar, they planned to explore the Biafo-Hispar watershed and then retrace their route across Snow Lake—where Fanny had fallen into a crevasse back in 1898.

Connecting two ancient mountain kingdoms, Nagar in the west and Baltistan in the east, the glacier lay three miles above sea level. At twenty-five thousand feet and higher, the snow-covered mountains pressed the sky. Reaching the glacier required a significant amount of boulder hopping across the moraine. Vegetation was sparse here; it was as if the mountain had run out of shrubs and grass. The landscape grew ever more monotonous.

With them on this trip were some familiar faces: Dr. Karl Oestreich, who would serve as their topographer, and guides Giuseppe Müller and Matthias Zurbriggen. The porters tasked with carrying wood were expected to carry between forty and sixty pounds. At least that is what they'd told Workman they were capable of when they were hired. However, they usually only managed between sixteen and thirty-five pounds each. "They could have assembled that weight in a half hour, but chose to loaf a whole day instead," Workman later complained to a Boston newspaper, unable to tamp down her annoyance. "Had they been allowed to have a free hand, they would have burned the whole quantity brought by 30 of them in a single night," she wrote, complaining about the porters for "lingering, shirking work, deserting, demanding double rations, looting grain and mutinying."

As they waited, Workman opened her black leather journal and pulled out a fountain pen. She wanted to reread her glacier notes. In reviewing the entries of the previous two nights, she noticed she had forgotten to mention the "large, tall and very perfect earth pyramids" they had seen on their way to camp. What those pyramids were she had no idea. She also added a brief paragraph about the glacier's topography. She was particularly interested in how it "beckoned largely from the great snow basin" and noted its northern branch extended miles across, entering the glacier just below the Hispar Pass. To Workman, the glacier appeared to be composed of many great serac falls, several feeder branches, and a large clear, blue glacial lake.

Thoroughly absorbed in her notes, it took her a moment to notice her husband was standing over her shoulder saying something about a fast-moving sandstorm and closing the tent flaps. He tried to seal them as tightly as possible to prevent the blowing wind from bringing sand inside. For the next several hours, the incessant wind beating and sand scraping against the canvas kept them awake. Around two in the morning, a mighty gust almost ripped their tent from its stakes, which would have left them exposed to the fury of the elements. More than once Fanny prayed for the storm to end.

In the morning, after the sandstorm abated, they dressed and went outside to survey the campsite. They wanted to check everyone had escaped unharmed and that all the equipment was intact. Upon stepping outside she nearly stumbled over two dead chickens and a small basket filled with rock-hard plums sitting on the ground outside their tent. Apparently, the basket was a welcome gift from a local potentate, as his messengers explained, adding that they were fairly confident the chickens had been alive when they had left Nagar. But the birds simply had not survived the journey, what with no food and being carried upside down by the legs the whole way. Nonetheless, "after delivery of these delicacies, the messengers asked for seven days' rations."

As she unraveled the story of the chickens, the band of porters who had gone in search of firewood reappeared carrying firewood aplenty. A new lumberdar, or village officer, also accompanied them. Everyone was reassembled, and the Workmans announced it was time to cross the Hispar Pass. A cold wind discouraged clouds from gathering in the indigo sky.

---

On August 24, 1908, the Workmans became the first couple to traverse the ice highway on the way to the Hispar Pass.

Though the snow was in good condition, the constant cold and wind left Hunter aching. When the team finally reached the point where the road ascends from Biafo to Hispar, he and Fanny asked a porter to continue on and get more supplies. "They made a fearful row, howled and beat the *lambardar* [sic] who ordered them until we thought his end was near. They are simply a horde of savages," Hunter scribbled in his well-worn journal.

Like many privileged white explorers, the Workmans had a deeply rooted sense of superiority toward those in their employ, a superiority rooted in class and race. They extended more respect toward those locals who had higher positions of rank and wealth. This wasn't the first such incident of unrest among the porters—nor was it the first time the Workmans demonstrated racism toward their employees—but like before, tempers cooled and everyone returned to work. Nevertheless, the underlying condescension the Workmans had for the porters and the porters' distrust of a woman leader remained.

―――――――

Shortly after a breakfast of kola biscuits and weak tea, they went out on the ice. Suddenly Fanny felt a stabbing pain in her side. She ignored the sensation and kept on trekking, albeit with great difficulty. Glancing at her every so often, one of their guides grew increasingly concerned, but he held his tongue, not wanting to upset his boss. After about eight miles of her labored walking, he convinced Workman to rest on a rocky outcrop, even for just a moment. The pain subsided somewhat, and they finished the day's work, measuring and mapping.

Sometime before sunrise, Workman was roused from sleep by a "fearful pain in my right breast. . . . We feared it might be pneumonia. H. fired on hot water bag, but it did not help and I had to take more drugs but the severe pain continued all night and most of day following," she wrote, her penmanship cramped.

The pain forced her to remain under the covers the whole of the next day. Taking to bed did not come easily for the woman from Worcester. Lists of all the things she could be accomplishing ran through her head. She made a mental note of which supplies needed replenishing and which supplies were plentiful. They definitely needed more wood. The only wood they had was green, which was useless for fires, and there was of course no wood to forage here on the ice. She would ask Hunter to tell a group of porters to return to their previous camp and collect some there.

Then, as she fixated on the wood situation, she saw a shadow outside her tent. It was a new lumberdar. Three new porters stood by his side. She hoped the fresh faces meant the expedition would get back on track; perhaps this new lumberdar would put an end to the incessant bickering among the porters. She pulled herself up to a sitting position and motioned for him to come inside so she could introduce herself.

---

Workman still felt poorly the next day; her elbows and knees creaked, her chest ached, but push on she must. The morning survey would take the group five and a half hours from their camp. The snow was hard and their feet tired quickly. When they reached camp that evening, they found the porters had not brought the group's water supply along, and so Hunter ordered them back to the lower camp to retrieve what they could as the expedition was now short on provisions.

Once everyone had enough to fill their leather containers with several quarts, they could again go forth onto the glacier. She marveled at the terrain's variety. During the course of a day, they might find themselves on the ice, then navigating around seracs and moraine, and then back on the smooth ice. "This rough camp is wild and attractive wedged in between glaciers and glacial lakes and streams," she wrote.

The days turned into weeks as the Workman party explored the boundary of ice separating Tibet and Afghanistan. Before them were "dizzy precipices laden with snow and ice, which constantly fell in avalanches. . . . Through these perils the intrepid American woman—daughter of ex.-Gov. Bullock of Massachusetts—and her no less intrepid husband climbed, followed or preceded by their 200 coolies carrying supplies." They ascended and descended. They lunched sitting on rocks, and once they reached what she described a sandy camp. "Before reaching camp saw many bare footed human tracks, but no human beings," she said.

It took four weeks for the Workmans, their guides, and their dozens of porters to reach the head of the Hispar Glacier, where jagged peaks surrounded an enormous plain of snow.

---

By the end of August 1908, the same month Robert Peary's expedition sailed for the North Pole, the Workmans reached Askole, the last settlement in the Shigar Valley. A year had passed since their last visit. Just like the last time they were here, they couldn't find a decent field in which to pitch tents, and so, with permission from locals, they sheltered in the nearby Shigar Fort. "The Askole people seem anxious to provide us with everything, even sheep," Workman said.

On September 8, they left the village via a washed-out road to Loh. On the way, they climbed steep slopes and crossed rock-filled ravines while constantly dodging falling rocks. "No one is ever safe and one cannot hurry because of being on the deep in dry and or debris," Workman wrote. After more than a day of trekking, they reached their snow camp. Situated on the last northern branch of the glacier, with an altitude of 18,932 feet, it was the highest camp of their trip. It would also be their last.

In the meantime the Workmans lived on the ice for fifty-six days. They never went lower than twelve thousand feet and occasionally went as high as twenty-three thousand feet. Sometimes it was so cold they thought their eyelashes would splinter. It was an endurance test the likes of which they had never experienced. "Climbing up, up, up from ice peak to ice peak—such was the summer vacation last year of Mrs. Bullock Workman of Worcester Mass," reported the *Wide World Magazine*. Some of the photographs she and Hunter took during this part of the trip accompanied the article, "An American Woman's Climb to the Top of the World: A Brave Explorer's Record Breaking Journey Over Mountains of Ice to the Highest Peaks on Earth."

"Mrs. Workman has been further away from the centre of the earth, nearer the top of the world, and consequently, closer to heaven than any other woman who has ever lived, and her husband is the only man who has been higher than she—with the possible exception of two or three balloonists," recounted the article.

That the Duke of Abruzzi, who chased mountains with the same zeal he chased titles, was rumored to be interested in beating her record barely registered with Workman. After learning what the press in the United States was reporting, she had far more pressing concerns. Apparently Annie S. Peck had just announced that she was the new holder of the women's altitude record.

Until now, the rivalry between Workman and Peck had been contained within the tight-knit community of climbers. With this announcement, their sparring was now on display for the world at large. They were in open and direct competition for the women's altitude record. As the *Galveston Daily News* reported, Workman not only held the record for women but also had achieved a height "which has been attained by a very, very small number of mountain climbers, including guides." News editors knew their readers would clamor after this story. It had all the key ingredients—action, danger, and class differences—but above all, it was a controversy centering around two women who were passionate about their work. That two women could be so competitive was almost unheard of; competition was considered a distinctly male virtue. "For men, writing about their Alpine achievements was a way of cementing their position in society, giving credence to their authority, strength, power and outgoing nature. They were positioning themselves among their peers, hoping to impress, even further their careers. More importantly, attracting attention to the self was not something most women would entertain; it was unfeminine and ran against social mores," wrote historian Clare Roche more than a century later. To be sure, there had been women climbers, like Lucy Walker, who'd climbed the Matterhorn in 1871. However, because she had climbed with her father and brother, and had often sipped champagne and nibbled on sponge cake while climbing, she wasn't considered in the same vein. Indeed, this was a new kind of story for a new century.

---

Fanny and Hunter had been the subject of international attention for many years now, whether for their lectures and books, their exploration of parts unknown, or their partnership of equals. There was zero chance Workman was going to cede all she had accomplished so far to Annie Smith Peck. On the other hand, Peck, too, had been the subject of the world's gaze, for the way she dressed and for her work. She had lectured across the United States, penned numerous articles, and would eventually author two books, including *A Search for the Apex of America: High Mountain Climbing in Peru and Bolivia*. As a lecturer, she was in high demand in the United States, from New York to Michigan.

Audiences delighted in hearing Peck, who was described as having a "pleasing personality and unusually graceful manner, a charm of voice, which is clear, and distinct when telling a story of thrilling interest."

Separately, each woman was a story in her own right. But a story about the two women locked in competition for the female altitude record would have editors salivating over headlines and column inches. The *Salt Lake Tribune* wasn't exaggerating when it later wrote, "A scientific controversy that promises to over-shadow the Peary-Cook imbroglio and throw the mountain climbing contingent into a commotion, was precipitated today when Mrs. Bullock Workman, who claims to be the champion woman mountain-scaler of the world, boldly challenged the claims of Miss Annie Peck to preeminence, declared the latter would have to submit proofs of her achievements or stand discredited."

Until Peck had summited Mount Huascarán on her fifth try and claimed the highest record for women, Workman had held the title, except briefly in 1897, when, with backing from the *New York World*, Peck had climbed the 18,491-foot Orizaba in Mexico. But Workman had quickly surpassed her with her climb up the 21,001-foot Koser Gunge. Thereafter she'd held onto the title year after year—until now. When Peck stood atop Huascarán, she was likely as happy as she had ever been. The subsequent news likely made Workman as angry as she had ever been.

It angered her not only because Peck might actually have topped her record but also because—and this was more to the point—Peck's assertion lacked evidence since she didn't calculate altitude at the summit. When she neared the summit, Peck had tried to take observations with the hypsometer, "but on account of the wind, [we] were unable to light the candle. . . . Sadly I packed away the instruments, as I had counted on obtaining the height of the mountain. To break, perhaps, the world's record and not be able to prove it was a great disappointment, but to return alive seemed still more desirable." For someone who had invested so much in proving her achievements, Workman found Peck's lack of data to be a personal affront. When Peck failed to submit detailed proof of her climb, Workman felt it to be a betrayal of the climbing community. Ironically, as technology and mapping techniques improved, much of the Workmans' own glacier work would later be corrected.

The couple had discovered numerous glaciers and peaks over the years, and the British government in India held their work in high esteem; it was always ready to furnish the couple with the necessary guides, porters, and other attendants. Likewise, the French government recognized the geographical value of the Workmans' mountain climbing. Fanny had been honored by the Geographical Society of France and was now a member of the American Geographical Society as well. In short, at that time the Workmans were at the pinnacle of their career and truly believed their measurements would stand the test of time.

Although she had a stake in the matter, Fanny was far from the only person pressing for evidence from Peck. Peck had scarcely returned to Manhattan when George C. Hurlbut, the librarian of the American Geographical Society, asked her to speak about her climb. She obliged, and on February 23, 1909, she would give a lecture based on the article she'd written for *Harper's Magazine*. To her credit, she did add measurements, and subsequently her talk ran as an article, "The Conquest of Huascaran," in the *Journal of the American Geographical Society of New York*. Workman saw the article in *Harper's*, but what really jumped out was Peck's statement that "if future triangulations, or observations, made on the summit of the southern peak, which is probably a trifle higher, should prove, as I have hoped, the altitude of Huascaran to be

24,000, I shall have had the honor of breaking the world record for men as well as women."

Aside from the recognition from governments, the Workmans enjoyed favorable coverage from much of the press; perhaps Fanny received more attention than Hunter, as she was the face of the duo. She garnered a great deal of admiration, in part because of the couple's frequent ascents in the Himalayas and because they often faced death from overhanging ice walls, hidden crevasses, and avalanches; but also because she was a woman not content to let her husband speak for her.

While it's true that leading British alpinists such as Sir Martin Conway and A. F. Mummery had cracked open the mysterious Himalayas, it was equally true that the Workman duo led geographically significant and pioneering expeditions into the region. Most importantly, it was a widely held view that Fanny Bullock Workman was at the vanguard of these expeditions: "She was married to Dr. William Hunter Workman but it would in fact be more correct to say that he was married to her, for she was certainly the dominant partner. They never described themselves as Dr. and Mrs. Workman; it was always Fanny Bullock Workman and Dr. William H. Workman. Fanny liked it better that way."

The Huascarán story broke just as the Workmans' fifth book, *Peaks and Glaciers of Nun Kun: A Record of Pioneer-Exploration and Mountaineering in the Punjab Himalaya*, was released. It was their best-received work to date. The book contained Hunter's map with angles taken by prismatic compass (though many years later a Dr. Arthur Neve of the Mission Hospital in Srinagar corrected several aspects of the map). Fanny had spent much of 1907 and 1908 working on it, lying awake night after night, writing and rewriting drafts in her head.

Stories about the disputed record swirled, and the press reported on the quarrel with articles like the one from the September 10, 1909, *Philadelphia Press* headlined, WOMEN CLIMBERS IN CONTROVERSY: MRS. FANNY BULLOCK WORKMAN CHALLENGES ANNIE PECK'S CLAIM TO WORLD CHAMPIONSHIP. Peck didn't refrain from speaking with reporters. On the contrary, she readily spoke with the press. In covering the rivalry in 1909, the *Trenton Evening Times* told readers "Mountain climbing is not all she wants to do, while she is down there. She had a few more contributions, amounting to say to $200 she would venture on something that she really has a longing to do—the exploration of the source of the Amazon."

In other words, holding the record for the highest altitude meant a lot to Peck, but not everything. After all, she was already planning another trip; in 1911 she meant to find the apex of the American continent. She wanted to climb a summit higher than Aconcagua, which was located on the Argentinian and Chilean border. She sought volunteers, especially those with topographical science expertise, to join her adventure.

In the midst of their dispute, both Peck and Workman learned of an appeal made on behalf of the forty-one-year-old Swiss guide Rudolf Taugwalder, who "in the pursuit of his calling in the recent successful scaling of Mt. Huascaran, whereby, through the loss of a frost-bitten hand and foot, he is forever incapacitated from the exercise of his profession and the support of his numerous dependents is one that cannot but appeal to American lovers of the mountain and admirers of the sturdy and loyal race of men that the sport of mountaineering has called into being in Switzerland."

During the descent, Taugwalder had lost his gloves and been forced to grip his ice ax with his bare hands. He also had worn only one pair of stockings inside his alpine boots. By the end of the climb, his fingers and toes were black. It had taken three days to transport the injured man to the hospital in Yungay. Once there, he had been hospitalized for three months. While both hands and feet were affected by frostbite, the doctors amputated his right foot and most of his left hand; they were able to save the other extremities. Taugwalder would never climb another mountain.

Describing him as "a most faithful and competent guide," the appeal from the American Alpine Club described how Taugwalder had accompanied the Workmans on their first visit to the Himalayas. The appeal also called for a showing of American generosity for a man who served "to make Americans more than ever welcome in Switzerland." It must be noted the appeal mentioned both Fanny and Hunter Workman but not Peck, even though it was she who'd led the aforementioned climb up Mount Huascarán.

———————

Like Workman, Peck wanted to make her own contributions to science and topography. Also like Workman, Peck's achievements were overshadowed by the fact that so many identified her as a woman scholar, leaving her with a public identity resembling something of a caricature. She was a single woman and suffragist who earned her living as a climber, explorer, lecturer, and author. Yet, for the most part, the public saw her as merely a woman climber in pants.

For her part, Workman was most confident the matter would be settled in her favor. In many an interview, even she, who couldn't abide by the sexism she received, couldn't resist gibing her rival for wearing knickerbockers: "I have never found it necessary to dispense with the skirt."

Until the *Bulletin of the American Geographical Society*, the sister publication to the British *Geographical Journal*, published Peck's claim, which seemed to support Peck's assertion, Workman had seen fit to ignore the flurry of press coverage. She was, after all, deep in the Himalayas. But this was too much for the reserved Yankee. She was outraged that a reputable journal deigned to publish so flimsy a claim. Workman knew in this ever-escalating game of mountain climbing brinksmanship she couldn't let Peck's claim stand. She had worked too hard to be toppled by this parvenu.

Yet, here she was, still in the Himalayas, wrapping up their exploration of the snowy Hispar Glacier. It would be impossible for her to travel to South America, assemble a team, climb Mount Huascarán herself, and personally verify Peck's declaration. So she did the next best thing. About eight months later, in June 1909, she hired a pair of French geographers and surveyors, Franz Schrader and Henri Vallot of the Société Générale d'Études et de Travaux Topographiques of Paris, with instructions to go to Peru. Under the direction of Etienne de Larminant of the Service Géographique de l'Armée they would triangulate Huascarán and make an accurate relief of the Cordilleras Range from where it rose. Ever meticulous, Workman made sure the two men were outfitted with the most up-to-date instruments specially made for the purpose. "This was more than mere idle curiosity on Mrs. Workman's part, for she herself has done 23,300 feet in the Himalayas, which is the record achievement of womankind in getting toward the sky," stated an article in the *New York Times*.

Workman told reporters she had no doubt that Peck had assigned an absurdly exaggerated height to the mountain in question. Whether her private thoughts matched her outward display of confidence is impossible to know. She had grown accustomed to maintaining a certain stoicism and never publicly expressed self-doubt. In private she rarely confided uncertainty to her husband of twenty-eight years or even to the pages of her journals.

---

As the French survey team sailed to South America that June, the Workmans had met up with Rachel in India; she was now pursuing her own research work in geology. Like her mother, Rachel was multilingual, able to converse in French, Italian, Spanish, and German with ease.

On their return voyage to Europe in 1909, Rachel met Sir Alexander MacRobert, a self-made millionaire and widower whose first wife had died from cancer in 1905. At age fifty-five, he was thirty years Rachel's senior. The couple had known the Scotsman for several years, having first met him in 1907 when Fanny had given a lecture about their exploration in the Himalayas. Chatting with MacRobert afterward, the Workmans had persuaded him to join the Royal Scottish Geographical Society. Born in Aberdeen, Scotland, MacRobert had left school at the age of twelve. In 1884, at age thirty, he'd gone to India, where he was hired as a manager for a woolen mill in Cawnpore (now called Kanpur). Eventually he bought several other mills and amassed a small fortune. His wealth and interest in India appealed to the couple. These factors outweighed any hesitation they might have felt regarding the great gulf in years between their daughter and MacRobert when the two started courting.

---

Peck was furious when she heard Workman had sent a team to survey Huascarán. No, she felt more than simple fury. She resented the independently wealthy Workman. She couldn't stand that this starched one-time New Englander could finance a verification team without batting an eye. Why couldn't Workman and the mountaineering world take her word? At fifty-seven years old, Peck had attacked one of the most difficult mountains in the southern hemisphere. Her feat was so impressive that Eduardo Higginson, the consul general of Peru, congratulated her on her "marvelous endurance and courage" and presented her with a gold medal.

The Geographical Society of Lima awarded her a silver trophy shaped like a slipper. Coincidentally, the night she was given the slipper, she herself was wearing but a single slipper. The day before the banquet she had stepped on a nail, and her foot was swaddled in a bandage.

So proud of the award was Peck that she would make sure to hold it in the photograph of her in her widely acclaimed book *A Search for the Apex of America*. Yet, if she were being completely honest with herself, the slipper wasn't enough. She wanted the altitude record.

And so it was that Fanny Bullock Workman and Annie Smith Peck, who both shared an intense love of the outdoors, came to share an intense disdain for one another. Their climbing rivalry, one of the fiercest in the history of American mountaineering, was about to reach its peak.

# 10

# CLIMBERS IN CONTROVERSY

THE ENVELOPE ARRIVED bearing a return address from Zermatt, Switzerland. Annie S. Peck carefully slit it open. Although she guessed correctly that it was from her former guide Rudolf Taugwalder, she couldn't imagine what he had to say. As it turned out, he had a lot to say.

First, he wanted Peck to know he was sorry she thought he blamed her for his disfigurement. He assured her he had only the highest praise for her. However, he needed her to know he was suffering. Surely she understood that without his hand and foot his mountain guide days were forever over. Surely she knew he was in dire straits financially, that it was "indeed a very sad business for me I have had to go to Lausanne several times and must go again for my false hand and foot but it is all more expensive than one expects it to be," he wrote.

He pleaded. If she could send some amount of money, no matter how small, he would be forever thankful, because while he didn't want to seem ungrateful, the photos she had sent were useless. Didn't she realize tourists in Zermatt weren't interested in souvenir photos of a South American mountaintop? Didn't she understand they wanted picture postcards of horse-drawn sleighs or the Matterhorn capped in snow? Didn't she understand no one wanted photographs of her?

Rudolf Taugwalder (Guide de Zermatt)
Invalide ensuite de la 1ʳᵉ ascension du Mont Huascaran (Pérou) 1908

Swiss-born Rudolf Taugwalder accompanied Fanny
Bullock Workman and also her rival, Annie S. Peck.
After frostbite on Peck's Huascarán descent, he lost his
right foot and most of his left hand. This picture postcard was used to raise money afterward.

His letter, so earnest, so sincere, threw Peck off just a bit. It
arrived just as Fanny Workman, and to a lesser degree, Hunter, was
pushing back and as many in the climbing community had begun
chiming in with doubts about what was now a very public matter.

The way she viewed it, Workman was smearing her reputation,
painting her as the great exaggerator. She dismissed the suggestion
that she didn't actually climb the peaks but rather was "hauled to the
summits. . . . I regard it as beneath my notice to deny such a trivial
assertion, made by people who really know nothing about me, and
know less than a Swiss pack-pony about mountain climbing and

whose motives for making such statements appear to be inspired by but one feeling, that of jealousy."

It was hard for Peck to see anything but a gilded woman of privilege when she thought about Workman. She felt like the David to Workman's Goliath.

That anyone might actually think she lied about the height of Mount Huascarán for attention offended the fifty-nine-year-old former Latin teacher. She had invested so much of herself in her climbing career. Years she could never retrieve. Money she would never recoup, no matter how many lectures she delivered. Above all, she stood to lose her credibility.

The first inkling that she stood on shaky ground had come in January 1909, months before Workman sent the surveyors to Peru. Impressed with Peck's venture south of the equator, the American Alpine Club had invited her to speak at its annual meeting, scheduled for just after New Year's, in January 1909. Now, just a few months later, the club was considering rescinding its invitation, in part because they were hearing from readers.

For as the newspaper coverage ensued, readers, fans, and others also started questioning her claim. One of the first to question her was an attorney named Horatio G. Bent. A longtime fan, Bent had closely followed her climbing career, particularly her attempts to summit Mount Huascarán. Never before had he doubted her claims, but this time something seemed amiss. He noticed she sometimes gave the elevation as twenty-six thousand feet, sometimes twenty-five thousand, and most recently twenty-four thousand. He was confused. Since he was working on a paper about mountain climbing to be read before his club, he hoped she could provide some answers. "Now I wish to know from yourself the facts as to the elevation attained. Was your climb the highest ever reached by man or woman?" he wrote. He welcomed a reply from her, no matter how brief. He just wanted her to put the matter to rest.

Then came a letter published in *Harper's Weekly* that caused her further consternation. Virgil Bogue, vice president and chief engineer of the Western Pacific Railway Company, wrote about the excitement with which he read Peck's account of her Mount Huascarán adventure. He thought it a remarkable trip, a thorough test of her mettle. However, he wasn't writing to discuss her achievement. He was writing because he wanted to understand exactly how she'd ascertained Huascarán's elevation. Had she simply taken the guess of her two guides and herself and divided by three? He was baffled. He didn't understand why she hadn't taken along two or three aneroid barometers: "Unless some man suggested it and the lady resented the suggestion as she says she did others which emanated from members of the male sex. To start a mountain climb without an aneroid is a good deal like going fishing and leaving the line and hooks at home."

Some fans wrote to the Rhode Island native asking her to explain why she didn't seem to have the proper data to answer questions about the height. Others wondered about the inaccuracy in her observations. Yet she couldn't, or wouldn't, provide them with answers.

The pressure mounted. Finally, in April 1909, the American Geographical Society too demanded that Peck furnish answers. The society was running out of patience, wrote Cyrus C. Adams, the editor of the society's journal. It had been several months since he'd requested she send the scientific results of her climb. Without the report, they wouldn't pay her for her article.

Eventually the government of Peru entered the fray. The consul general Eduardo Higginson, who had presented Peck with a medal for her climb, questioned her much-publicized claim.

The affair of the altitude consumed Peck.

In the middle of the storm, she wrote to Admiral Robert E. Peary, who happened to be embroiled in his own controversy. In April 1909, Peary and his partner Matthew Henson sent word from Indian Harbour, Labrador, that they had reached the North Pole. Dr. Frederick A. Cook challenged their claim. Cook said he had reached the top of the world a full year before Peary and Henson, in April 1908. One journalist called the fight the story of the century, and it would play out in newspapers, the courtroom, and eventually Congress. Ultimately Peary would be recognized as the first to reach the Pole.

Nonetheless, Peck told Peary that the seemingly endless controversy over her altitude claim was harder to endure than the climb itself. Quite a statement, considering frostbite had claimed Taugwalder's hand and foot and, based on her own description, she had been forced to descend one of the highest peaks in the Andes in the pitch-black of night with high winds howling. Aware that Peary was steeped in his own problems, Peck dared not ask him to get involved in the matter. She merely wanted someone with whom she could commiserate.

While Peck had only herself to blame for the situation—she was the one who chose to announce she held the altitude record without verification—it was wearing on her nerves, so much so that she tried to recast her earlier remarks. Though she stopped well short of admitting she'd exaggerated, she wrote: "Concerning the altitude of Mt. Huascarán in regard to which there has been a rather one-sided controversy, a few words must be said. That I ever asserted the height of the mountain to be 24,000 feet is a deliberate misstatement, to which my articles published in *Harper's Magazine* for January, 1909, and in the *Bulletin* of the American Geographical Society for June of the same year bear witness."

It was too late; the story had legs. Peck might have had better success convincing her mother it was permissible for women to wear pants. In the early twentieth century, it was a novelty to have woman adventurers hashing out their rivalry in real time. People were curious to see what kind of sportsmanship came from this competition. They liked seeing the two women pitted against each other.

The *New-York Tribune* was one of many papers to cover the story in depth. It reported that at least a year, if not more, before Peck's final attempt to summit Huascarán, two of her compatriots had reported record-breaking achievements in the Himalayas: Hunter Workman, who computed his greatest altitude at 23,394 feet, and Fanny Bullock Workman, who reached 22,568 feet. Since then, it went on to report, Fanny Workman had "made an ascent which, in a letter to The Tribune, printed on Thursday, she says took her 23,300 feet above sea level."

There was something about the Workman-Peck affair that tantalized readers and editors alike. "Possibly there may be material for a feminine mountain climbing controversy arising out of the remarkable record reported by Fanny Bullock Workman in her new book *Peaks & Glaciers*, ascent Pinnacle peak, 23,000 feet thus breaking her own record of 22,568 feet. . . . One almost hesitates to express an opinion on so delicate a subject, since there have recently been reported some very remarkable and quite similar achievements by feminine explorers in the Andes," reported the *New York Times*.

The *New-York Tribune* continued pushing and probing for answers, insisting the matter could be resolved if both Peck and Workman submitted their original records, astronomical and otherwise, to a competent board of scientists. Meanwhile, the *New York Times* asserted, "it is entirely proper to admire the immense amount of pluck and energy shown by Mrs. Workman in her picturesque and successful experiences in the Himalayas."

Fanny was impatient. She couldn't wait for the surveyors to return with their results and let the scientific process take its course. No longer able to contain herself, she weighed in. She wrote a letter to the editor of the American Alpine Club's journal and opined that Peck hadn't mistakenly recorded the height of the Peruvian peak. Rather, she had intentionally misled the public, Workman said.

Otherwise, argued the Worcester native, why hadn't Peck simply come forward and proved, once and for all, the authenticity of her feat? Her failure to do so cast further doubt on her claims. Thus, Workman, without Hunter's input, worked the press. She intuited the need to stay ahead of the story. She wanted to be the one to frame the narrative—and the narrative according to her was quite simple. In her view, Peck had the power to end the matter anytime. All she had to do was step forward with her data.

In fact, Peck was trying to get a more accurate measurement of Huascarán's height. She forwarded all her records to the US Department of Agriculture's Weather Bureau. However, upon receipt of the data, D. F. Marvin told Peck he couldn't calculate the answer; he didn't have enough information. So Peck sent a photograph of the summit to a Fred E. Wright at the Carnegie Institution of Washington Geophysical Library. Again, she was told there was not enough information for a reasonable estimate.

Meanwhile Peck, too, courted the press. She cast herself as the bullied underdog. She played up the fact that Workman had the money, the husband, and the domestic help. Of course none of that was germane to the case. Certainly, Workman's wealth allowed her to finance the surveyors and engineers, but it had nothing to do with the height of the mountain. Likewise, Workman's marriage had nothing to do with Huascarán's altitude.

To Workman, it was poor form for her rival to conflate her personal finances and marital status with the quest for accurate measurements. Workman thought it an embarrassment that a scholar of Greek and classical literature such as Peck would stoop to ad hominem arguments to try to distract the public.

Even before the surveyors delivered their findings to Workman, in November 1909, Peck conceded she couldn't prove the height of the peak above sea level. She admitted she had based her claim on incomplete observations. She explained how a terrific gale had swept the mountain, making it impossible to take proper measurements. Furthermore, she didn't oppose Workman when she named herself champion with the Nun Kun climb of 23,300 feet: "Miss Peck has taken the sensible view of the situation especially as Mrs. Workman's claim hangs on a mere trifle of 200 feet."

One paper wrote, "Miss Annie S. Peck has shown magnanimity in her attitude toward Mrs. FBW, which is looked for in vain in the squabble between the North Pole explorers (Peary & Cook). Mrs. Workman asserts that her ascent of one of the highest peaks in the western Himalayas gives her the title of 'champion woman mountain climber.'"

Indeed, Peck's tone had shifted over the past year. Her willingness to admit to error on her part was winning her favor in the court of public opinion. She even started hearing from editors and readers who appeared to be in her camp. "My dear Miss Peck: I congratulate you on the dignified manner in which you have met the tiresome and undignified, publicity-seeking methods of Mrs. Fannie Bullock Workman," wrote a Caspar Whitney.

Her spirits were further buoyed when she opened a letter from one Mary Thaxter. A friend and admirer of Workman's, she asked Peck to keep the missive "entre-nous." "I feel a desire to write and express to you my admiration of your public letter to Mrs. F Bullock Workman in which your acknowledgement of her holding the record as a woman mountain climber is made. . . . I consider her a wonderful woman to have achieved what she has, even with her great advantages and facilities. Your letter struck others as well as myself as showing a spirit of fairness and calm dignity which under the circumstances must have been somewhat difficult to express with the courtesy which you did."

While these epistolary pep talks assuaged Peck's ego, they couldn't change the numbers. Finally the teacher turned climber addressed the public.

"I had never thought of my climbing as anything more than an amusement up to that time, but I had begun to lecture upon archaeology not long before, and I thought as I was going to climb the Matterhorn," she wrote. "I began to think that, as I seemed to be posing as a mountain climber, I had better really do something in that line worthwhile."

The statement struck Workman as simultaneously disingenuous and defensive. She was skeptical of Peck's sincerity when she said she never intended to make a business of climbing mountains. After all, Peck had agreed to be one of the faces of the Singer Sewing advertisement campaign. Peck was the one to announce the altitude of each mountain she climbed, and Peck was the one who wrote about the climbs in magazines and books.

From her perspective, if Peck truly didn't care about altitude or making a profession from climbing, then she wouldn't have begrudged Workman taking the scientific step of determining the mountain's height.

According to *National Geographic*, it was important to consider many factors when giving credit to those "who bring to us knowledge of the world's mysterious heights." One must consider the fact that each climb presents unique challenges, including its remoteness from civilization, the landscape necessary to cross to reach its base, the height of the snow line, and the climate. The article went on to note that the Workmans, in spite of extreme conditions, provided full data when they climbed in the Nun Kun back in 1906 (though their elevation measurements were later disputed).

---

October 1909 in Paris. Crimson, tangerine, and gold leaves dressed the trees along the Seine. Over at the Grand Palais, the first official Paris Air Show was in full swing. Workman, who was there to deliver a series of lectures, hadn't time to join the hundred thousand people who visited the 380 exhibitors. But she did have time to write Peck a letter.

The international press covered the Workman expeditions. This story appeared in a French magazine.

She smoothed the paper, composing the words in her head before pressing the nib to paper. She wanted to be just so in her response to Peck's September letter, which had included a photograph of the mountain at the center of this controversy. A nice touch, Workman thought. Yes, a fine-looking peak indeed.

Workman thought Peck had some nerve for taking her and Hunter to task for not providing boiling points in their writings. Her letter was vintage Workman—authoritative with a dash of condescension:

> As every one at all versed in the subject of altitude measurements knows, a boiling point or barometric reading taken by itself without reference to a similar simultaneous reading at a lower station, the height of which has been accurately fixed, is worthless as an exact measure of altitude, indicating a height that may vary by 1,500 feet or more according to the pressure of air at the time the reading is taken. To render individual readings of any value other data would have to be given, which would not interest the general reader and would only serve to pad a book with superfluous information. The statement of such readings may give a book the appearance of erudition to the uninitiated, but it gives no definite information and does not blind the eyes of those who understand the subject.

Not exactly light reading, but she made her point. Peck tried not to let the letter irritate her too much.

Meanwhile, Peck plucked another letter from her pile of correspondence. This one came from France. The writer told Peck he thought the "rather amusing controversy" might sell in French newspapers and magazines, including *L'illustration* or *Le Monde illustré*. Perhaps she would consider writing her story or letting

someone else write her story. It would give her a chance to inter-
rupt the story line; Workman was lecturing all over France.

Further bad news arrived in Peck's letter box. The Boston-based
publisher Little, Brown rejected her manuscript *A Search for the
Apex of America*. Originally Peck had planned to call her book
*Apex of America*, but having failed to nail down the altitude
record, she decided to change the title to *A Search for the Apex
of America*. She also recast it as a love letter of sorts to friendly
relations between the United States and Peru. Peck said she hoped
her expeditions there would foster friendship between the two
continents. The publishing house was of the opinion that Peck had
the ingredients to tell a thrilling story, but editors thought exces-
sive trivialities weighed it down. Moreover, at 150,000 words—
nearly twice the length of a standard manuscript—it was simply
too long.

Throughout the controversy, readers got an education in mountaineering. They learned about the kinds of equipment and conditions climbers faced. The Workman-Peck affair also shone a light
on the extremes these women were willing to chase in pursuit
of glory. Of course, as those who followed the controversy likely
knew, women were already testing boundaries through stunt and
sport. Indeed women "were active participants in almost thirty
different sports; individual sports, ranging from the fine motor
skills of archery to the gross bodily skills of lawn tennis and swimming." In 1901, Annie Taylor had become the first person to go
over Niagara Falls in a barrel, and in 1869, Ellen and Anna Pigeon
had hiked the Sesia Joch glacier between Zermatt, Switzerland,
and Alagna, Italy.

As Peck and Workman's drama played out, citizens around
the world were taking steps toward securing rights back home.
On February 18, 1909, the Socialist Party of America organized
the first National Woman's Day in honor of the 1908 garment

workers' strike in New York, where women protested hazardous working conditions.

At the same time, ideas about women's health were changing, albeit slowly. There were of course those physicians who insisted women should never walk when they could ride or stand when they could sit. Nevertheless, against the backdrop of the Workman-Peck dispute, the idea that activity contributed to a woman's well-being, both physically and spiritually, was gaining traction. For example, bicycling had become accepted as a sport. Tennis and swimming were not only acceptable, women were setting records. Alpine clubs were allowing women members. In 1909 Mary E. Crawford wrote an article promoting the health benefits for women who climbed. She wrote, "There was no reason why every woman shouldn't ask herself 'why should I not spend my holiday this year in the mountains?' . . . There is no recreation which, in all its aspects of surroundings and exercise, will bring about a quicker rejuvenation of worn out nerves, tired brains and flabby muscles than mountaineering." As for training, one need not do more than walk—a lot. "Mrs. Bullock Workman, who, as she says of herself, is not a light weight, made ascents of over 16,000 feet in the Himalayas without any [training], and her highest and hardest work was accomplished in the low levels and moist atmosphere of Ceylon and Java. She recommends for those who wish to reach the higher peaks, a previous residence of a few weeks at 11,000 feet," Crawford wrote.

In truth Peck and Workman had more in common than they might have cared to admit. Both felt an urgency to test their limits. Both knew that, unlike society, mountains made no judgments. They just were. It was only on a freshly cut step in the ice or while clambering over scree or striking a granite wall with an ax that these two different women truly felt free from the confines of society.

# 11

# A PLUCKY PERFORMANCE

I N August 1909 Franz Schrader and Henri Vallot arrived in Callao, the seaport of Lima, Peru. Their voyage had carried them across the Atlantic, around Cape Horn, and then up the coast of South America. They had been nearly forty days at sea.

Utterly exhausted, on arrival the pair found lodgings in a small inn. They required a good meal and a solid night's sleep. Before they could even think of closing their eyes, they unpacked their boxes, eager to see how the carefully packed instruments fared. They breathed a sigh of relief. Nothing was broken or bent. The glass on the barometer was intact, the needles on the compasses worked, and the hypsometer was in fine working order.

In the morning, they set forth on the long, bumpy road from Lima to Huaraz, a city that appeared to crawl up the foothills of the Cordillera Blanca. The saddlebags, packed with their instruments and maps, bounced against the horses' flanks. From Huaraz they continued on, following the same route Peck had taken just a couple years earlier. Only unlike Peck, Schrader and Vallot hardly noticed the landscape. They disregarded the condors flying above. They paid no mind to the people. They had one mission—Huascarán—and one master: Fanny Bullock Workman.

With a team of horses and a pair of mules in tow, they wound their way up and over the Musho trail. The steeples of Huascarán's twin peaks towered in the distance. In the foreground stood a brightly painted church. At one point the going got too difficult for the mules. The pair dismounted and, leaving the gray animals behind, continued on foot. They climbed over rock slabs and paths studded with stones until they found flat ground. No stranger to mountain climbing, the two men pitched their tents, unfurled their sleeping bags, and supped on tinned meat and biscuits. After a spot of tea, they slept. Neither man was very concerned about the jaguars that lived in the area. The moon hung pale and full over the horizon.

———————

Before the two men had left France, they'd cautioned Workman that their final figures might vary a bit. They thought their word of caution bore repeating, even though she already knew measuring mountains was notoriously difficult. In the age before satellites, surveyors used a theodolite to capture the angle of a peak's rise from two different locations. Dating back to the early 1500s, the tool had since been modified several times. By 1787, explorers and geographers considered it a most modern and accurate device. The precision instrument could measure both vertical and hor- izontal angles.

In the late eighteenth century, Jesse Ramsden introduced his new and improved theodolite to the world. He called it the Great Theodolite. It was used to survey Great Britain, and later variations of it were used to survey India. The aptly named Great Theodo- lite—it stood between five and six feet high—weighed about two hundred pounds and had to be transported by a carriage. Schrader and Vallot brought something slightly less unwieldy to Peru, but the principal use of the tool was the same: triangulation.

Triangulation was a centuries-old technique. Gemma Frisius, a Dutch physician, mathematician, cartographer, and philosopher, devised the method in 1533. It involved taking direction plots of surrounding landscape from two separate locations. Then the two graphing papers were superimposed, which provided a scale model of the landscape. Measuring one distance both in the real terrain and in the graphical representation let surveyors calculate the true scale. The Norwegian explorer Roald Amundsen used this method during his 1910 South Pole expedition.

While in Peru, Schrader and Vallot would determine Huascarán's height after they plugged the numbers into a trigonometric formula, which compensates for the curve of the Earth. The surveyors would use instruments specially made for the purpose. Of course, their results would only be as solid as the data they entered. The distance between the sight point and the summit must be accurate. If the distance is off even slightly, the altitude calculation will be off.

Today, GPS has mostly replaced triangulation as a way of calculating altitude since it's more accurate, though GPS requires someone stand on the summit, where they can get a strong satellite signal. That doesn't mean triangulation is obsolete. It's occasionally used for peaks that are either too dangerous to climb or that forbid climbers because of cultural or religious reasons, as is the case with several peaks in the Himalayas.

To smooth the path for Schrader and Vallot, Workman had enlisted the help of the Peruvian government, which was no small feat. After all, the nation openly admired Peck. In 1928, the Lima Geographical Society would name Huascarán's northern peak Cumbre Aña Peck.

After collecting the necessary data, Schrader and Vallot traveled back to Lima, spent a night there, and then boarded a ship bound for France. Knowing their reputations were on the line, the pair had been exacting in their work. They knew appearances were as important as facts and that any hint of bias would hurt their professional reputations in the long run. Upon returning to Europe, they spoke with no one about their results. Not the press. Not the alpine or geographical societies. Not Fanny Bullock Workman. Not yet.

The two engineers quietly prepared their report over the next several months. In November 1909, they sent it to London, where the Workmans were lecturing and visiting with their daughter and future son-in-law, Alexander MacRobert. Fanny forwarded the results to Henry G. Bryant, secretary of the American Alpine Club, who in turn sent a copy of the results to Peck. "My dear Miss Peck, I have received a cable from Mrs. Bullock-Workman relating to the height of Mt. Huascaran, a copy of which I herewith enclose for your information," Bryant wrote. "My mission despatched [sic] by Schrader and Vallot completed careful triangulation Huascarán North Peak 21,812, South 22,187. Possible variation only few feet."

The few feet in question were actually 1,311 feet less than Pinnacle Peak, the Himalayan mountain Workman had summited in 1908. To put it another way, that 1,311 feet was about nine-tenths as tall as the Eiffel Tower, or two and a half times as tall as the Great Pyramid of Giza. It wasn't a distance easily closed. Workman "officially retains the honor of the world's championship for women Alpinists," reported the *New York Times*.

In spite of the news, Peck insisted there were plenty of mountain climbing authorities who wouldn't agree with Schrader and Vallot's report. She cleaved to that belief when in February 1910 she sat down for an interview with the *New York Sun*.

"In reference to the accuracy of triangulation of figures I have only to cite the well known authority Arnold L. Mumm who in his recent book *Five Months in the Himalaya* declared 'the results of triangulation do not always agree. Even when they practically coincide they cannot be accepted as unimpeachable,'" she said.

Peck repeated Mumm's assertion that the science of refraction wasn't well understood. Therefore, the higher or more remote a summit, the greater chance for an error in the calculation. She also cited the work of Dr. John Norman Collie, a British-born scientist and mountaineer, who aside from being the first person to try to scale Nanga Parbat in the Himalayas also authored *Climbing on the Himalaya and Other Mountain Ranges*. But most important, from Peck's point of view, Mumm had said triangulation wasn't always accurate.

All this was true. Yet, repeating these assertions didn't make them any more powerful. They were not the bombshells she hoped for. Schrader and Vallot had already conceded triangulation's margin for error and discussed accuracy with Workman. So when they did hand in their work to Workman, they'd made sure to triple-check their calculations.

---

As the dispute churned, Peck considered Workman's contention as nothing more than a personal attack. She bristled at the way the press spun the story, so much so that she wrote to the editor of the *New York Evening Mail*. In her letter Peck said she respectfully protested the statement going the rounds of the newspapers that women explorers "are disputing, scrapping, engaged in a war of words and indulging in personalities equal to Commander Peary and Dr. Cook."

First of all, neither Cook nor Peary engaged in personal attacks even though many newspapers and private individuals roundly abused Peary, she said. "As to Mrs. Workman, so far as I know she has called me nothing worse than Miss A. Peck which, while not especially courteous, can hardly be designating as indulging in personalities," she wrote.

Peck wanted the paper and its readers to understand two more things. First, her letter to Workman had received many compliments. Second, she objected to the way the media presented the controversy as two women at each other's throats. To her, the press was sensationalizing the story and assigning roles for her and Workman to play—Peck, the upstart single woman, versus Workman, the imperious wife. Their competition was real, but it was also amplified by the press coverage of the day. Controversy sells and controversy between women really sells, especially since this particular dispute went against the picture of womanhood still reinforced in the press: that women must be devoted and obedient to the males in their lives, that they must keep house and look after children. Even before the controversy, countless newspaper columns had been devoted to these ideas, from the *New York Times*' Women Here and There—Their Frills and Fancies to the *Los Angeles Times*' The Times' Answers by Experts.

While Peck accepted that Workman was within her rights to send engineers to South America to triangulate Huascarán, she harshly criticized her for spending $13,000 to do so, an exorbitant sum to the frugal Rhode Islander. Peck's own climbing expedition had cost but $3,000. She complained that if she had had just $1,000 more for her expedition, she easily could have triangulated the peak. (She didn't mention that she had no background in triangulation.) Put another way, Peck said that with an additional $12,000 she could have triangulated and climbed even more mountains and accomplished other valuable exploration.

Peck was further aggrieved because she didn't think Workman pushed the issue in the interest of science. She believed ego motivated her rival more than anything.

Never one to show much sympathy, Workman insisted there was nothing personal in her quest to validate the peak's height; rather it was "in the interest of mountaineering science, which, among other things, demands that, as a matter of fair play to others, no claims should be made for altitude attained that has not been determined by a recognized method of measurement," she wrote. She felt that the only way women would be considered equal to men in mountaineering, or any other endeavor, would be if they were held to the same exacting standards. So if she came across as brusque, so be it. For her, winning and exactitude ranked before likability.

Indeed the editor of the British newspaper the *Independent* had only high praise for Workman and her achievements, though even in print he grappled with whether to qualify her achievements based on her sex: "I believe I am right in saying that the feats accomplished by Mrs. Workman are more remarkable in the way of mountaineering than those which have been accomplished ever before by any of her sex. Whether I ought to make that limitation or not I am rather doubtful, but, at all events, with that limitation it will not be denied."

---

In New York City, a reporter from the *Sun* tracked down Peck at the Hotel Alabama. Before going upstairs to interview the Rhode Islander, he chatted with the hotel's elevator operator. "She never uses his machine," according to the article. She preferred to keep in shape by climbing the stairs.

Peck had a few choice words regarding Workman, whom the paper described as another American woman who found no activity so intriguing as being the first to scale a previously unscaled peak. "If other women want to go around triangulating

William Hunter Workman and Fanny Bullock Workman.

her mountains and find profit in so doing that is their business," the *Sun* article stated. "As for herself, she believes that there are no women's records in mountain climbing that are worthwhile going after, and she hopes only that someday she may be able to compete with men for men's records over in the Himalayas."

Peck also accused the press of being hypocritical. She told the reporter it was unfair that her claim was being scrutinized while her rival's claims went unexamined. That was the real story, she said, the one the papers should be investigating. She later elaborated in a letter to the editor of the *Evening Mail*: "While Mrs. Workman has frequently announced her readiness to furnish evidences of altitude claimed by herself, she does not seem always ready to give them to inquirers. I wrote to her some time ago and said I would be interested in seeing some of the figures of altitudes she had taken in the Himalayas, and she replied that they had not been published, nor did she offer to give them to me personally." Peck was referring to her autumn 1909 correspondence with Workman. She omitted Workman's answer and explanation.

Peck explained, again, that she gave only a close approximation of Huascarán's height because she and her guides had arrived at the summit at 3:00 in the afternoon. One of her hands was frozen, and so she couldn't light the candle under the hypsometer. She'd asked her guide to try. Each time he'd struck a match, the wind sweeping over the peak had extinguished the flame. He'd tried twenty times. The hour grew late and the hazardous descent awaited; they had to abandon "efforts to make exact observations on this top of the mountain."

"Anyone who chooses to accept Mrs. Workman's figures is surely free to do so and if he likes he may call her the champion woman mountain climber as well. I have been much more concerned in my work to measure it with that of men rather than that of other women," she told the reporter.

Well, esteemed bodies did accept Workman's figures.

On March 26, 1911, nearly two years after the controversy exploded, the *New York Times* reported the Academy of Sciences officially ruled in favor of Fanny Workman. She maintained the world record for a woman in mountain climbing. Newspapers heralded the news of her victory. "MRS. WORKMAN WINS: Establishes Supremacy as Mountain Climber Over Peck" read a 1911 headline in the *New York Times*. The article went on to indicate Peck was perhaps not forthcoming when she first reported her claim: "Now Miss Peck insists that she scaled the Huascaran Peak of the Andes, but she gave no idea of the distance. Sometimes it is alleged to have been a climb of 24,000 feet. What is the public to think about it? Miss Peck has not submitted the record of any scientific measurement of her climb, and there is no evidence to indicate that any measurements except those of the human eye were made," reported the paper. Workman was in London lecturing when she heard the news. Surprisingly, she didn't mention the momentous victory in her journal. Likewise, it's unknown when and how Rachel Workman heard the news. She had just published her first academic paper, "Calcite as a Primary Constituent of Igneous Rocks," in *Geological Magazine.*

In pursuing the story of Workman's victory, the press pointed out that Peck could have hired her own surveyor and made a strictly scientific calculation of the elevation. If she lacked the funds to pay for it herself, she could have raised money for the work as she did for climbing expeditions. She was also at liberty to make an independent investigation of the Workmans' labors. "Although, if we are not mistaken, they employed barometers and other instruments to learn how high they went. As the case stands, her ascent of Huascaran must be regarded as an exceedingly plucky performance but the world will hardly be convinced that she has made a new record in the strenuous sport of which she is a devotee," reported the *New-York Tribune.*

Peck was irate. Five trips to Peru. Four attempts up the mountain before she finally stood on its summit. Her taste of glory dissolved. She had not achieved what she thought she had achieved.

"Though it would thus appear that Huascarán is not so lofty as I had hoped, my ten long years of effort had culminated in the conquest of a mountain at least 1,500 feet higher than Mt. McKinley, and 2,500 feet higher than any man residing in the United States had climbed. With this I must be content until opportunity is offered to investigate some other possibilities in regard to the Apex of America," said a resigned Peck upon hearing the news.

Peck's attempt to set a record was given special mention in Charles Fay's journal *Appalachia*: "She has crowned with a well merited success her persistent efforts to attain a lofty Andean summit." While some were concluding it might be time to stop calling attention to a climber's gender, Fay maintained that women faced greater challenges than men to even break into extreme sport and therefore deserved extra praise for their achievements.

Even after the results were announced, some in Peck's camp held the view that she "need not accept the figures which are now set down for the height of Huascarán. But Miss Peck does accept them. 'I don't say that I am convinced those figures are correct,'" she said, "'but I don't dispute them.'"

Nonetheless, behind the scenes, away from the spotlight, Workman's win sent Peck into a mild depression, for she would have to scrimp and scrape her entire life, sleeping in hostels, writing and lecturing her way to pay for her expeditions. She had hoped the achievement would boost her finances, but instead she felt Workman stole her moment of glory.

She reached out to Admiral Peary again. He was now a pen pal of sorts, and she wanted to send him her book *A Search for the Apex of America*, which was published by Dodd, Mead in 1911. From his home in South Harpswell, Maine, he thanked her for her thoughtfulness, generosity, and courtesy. He conveyed his "compliments and appreciation and best wishes for the fullest measure of success in her present efforts."

In time, Peck reconciled her feelings and realized she had indeed achieved a great deal. She had accomplished more than most people could ever dream of. She realized that even if she lost the altitude title, she was winning as a woman making history. "A woman who has done good work in the scholastic world doesn't like to be called a good woman scholar. Call her a good scholar, and let it go at that. Taking the figures given for Mount Huascaran by the triangulation, I have climbed 1,500 feet higher than any man in the US. Don't call me a woman mountain climber," she said.

While Peck knew she could never afford to send a team to triangulate Huascarán, or any peak for that matter, for several months afterward she felt annoyed by the Academy of Science's decision. Nevertheless, ever so slowly, the cloud of gloom lifted. The debate was over. She wanted to move forward. And "though the peak is not the hemisphere's loftiest it gave the Knickerbocker clad Miss Peck, then past 50, the distinction of having climbed 1,500 feet higher than any man in the USA." She decided to let the matter rest.

It was the danger itself that made climbing so exciting. She thrived on the constant and consistent tests the sport offered her. She knew she was happiest going where no human being had stepped before. She wanted to grip rocks that had previously never been clasped by human fingers.

Yet, as much as she wanted to move forward, the controversy never completely dissipated, for throughout the ensuing years Peck tried to claim altitudes and feats that weren't hers.

A few years after the Huascarán hullabaloo, in 1913, she became embroiled in another to-do with the American Alpine Club. She had requested her 1911 climb up Coropuna be inserted as a first ascent. However, Coropuna consists of six peaks, and she had not climbed the highest one, which by today's measurements is just around 21,000 feet. The club secretary, Howard Palmer (Bryant was now president), wrote asking for clarification. "Now this phraseology (through an oversight no doubt) is calculated to mislead the unwary by apparently claiming more than you actually accomplished," Palmer wrote.

He also reminded her in light of the club's action taken "in the case of Huascaran (the propriety of which later events fully justified) I feel confident that the Club would not countenance the inclusion of this claim in the hand-book."

Palmer sent her notice for revision. Rather than accept the written rebuke, she resigned her membership.

---

When Workman addressed audiences in Paris, Marseille, Nantes, and Algiers, no one saw her as weather-beaten—no dirt caked under her fingernails, no stained skirts, no wiry hair springing from beneath her helmet. They saw a fifty-two-year-old woman impeccably dressed in silk brocade, a fascinator pinned atop her graying hair. They heard a woman speak in measured tones about what was possible. They saw a woman who had carried out "the largest and only serious scientific expedition ever directed by a woman thus far, [and] received recognition of her explorations, the highest medal and diploma."

She, and her husband, Hunter, who seemed to increasingly prefer the shelter of his wife's shadow, were considered to have "done such important work in the exploration of the higher mountain regions that all the geographical societies in the world have recognized it."

"Mrs. FBW, who has just named a peak of the Himalayas after King George of England, has gone through hardships and dangers that would not disgrace a polar explorer," stated the *Japan Chronicle*.

---

In some ways the controversy hinted at something more, the idea that there were still worlds out there waiting to be explored. As the *New York Times* put it, "The ingenious devices of man, aided by the potent agency of steam and electricity, have brought the remotest corners of the earth within easy reach."

On July 1, 1911, the German gunboat *Panther* arrived off Agadir, allegedly to protect German interests and nationals in Morocco. The world was edging toward war.

# 12

# VOTES FOR WOMEN

WITH THE WOMEN'S altitude record firmly in her pocket, fifty-two-year-old Workman once again turned her gaze east. Over the course of the next two climbing seasons, in 1911 and then 1912, she and Hunter, who was now sixty-three, would explore all forty-seven miles of the Siachen Glacier, also known as the Rose Glacier. Theirs was an audacious agenda, for in addition to exploring the glacier, they would attempt to triangulate forty new peaks.

The superlatives come easy when describing the Rose Glacier. It is one of the most unwelcoming and foreboding places on earth. It is the longest glacier in the Karakoram Range and the second longest glacier in the world's subpolar regions. Located just south of the great divide separating the Eurasian Plate from the Indian subcontinent, some call the Karakoram the "Third Pole." During the 1911 season, the Workmans planned to reconnoiter the west and south approaches to Siachen, and then cross into Bilafond La. They would save the glacier valley for last. The "painstaking and diligent" surveyor Captain Cosmo Gordon Grant-Peterkin accompanied the Workmans with the goal of elevating their work to a new level. A graduate of the Royal Indian Engineering College, the thirty-three-year-old Scotsman had worked for the Ceylon

Survey Department. During his time as topographer and surveyor with the Workmans, he also collected stones and rocks, which he sent to the British Museum.

The couple left Dresden in late March 1911. Once again, Fanny draped dust cloths over their well-appointed furniture and, together with Hunter, carefully packed the instruments for the journey across Europe and into India. This would be their seventh season in the Himalayas; by this time each task felt mechanical and repetitive.

Just as she had so many years ago when walking out the door of their home on Elm Street in Worcester, Fanny swung her handbag over her arm and closed the door. Standing on the stoop, she was overcome with the oddest feeling. For the first time, she felt a twinge of ambivalence about the upcoming journey. It wasn't that she didn't relish making new discoveries. She did. It wasn't that she didn't want to set a new record. She did. However, she felt a sense of dread when she thought about hiring and firing porters, repairing equipment, and pitching tents.

"It was with a feeling of aversion that almost counterbalanced the lure of the magnificent mountain-world beyond," she wrote, adding that "with an enthusiasm sustained by the prospect of visiting once again the glorious regions beyond, we plunged into the tedious details of preparation for the proposed exploration, which after the experiences of six preceding ones had become unpleasantly familiar." A knot took up residence in her stomach. The feeling stayed with her on the train. It was still there when they stepped aboard the boat and when they cleared customs on the subcontinent and started on the two-hundred-mile trip to Srinagar. Germany was thousands of miles away and weeks behind them.

As soon as they cleared customs on April 14, they began the monotonous task of unboxing and checking the condition of their gear. Several rain-damaged boxes needed repacking, as did some cartons that appeared to have been pierced by four-inch wire nails.

On April 16, they started for the hinterlands. Passing through the valley on the way to Zoji La, the caravan wore deep ruts into the earth, which softened under the heat of the day. This made travel difficult and in some places treacherous. They stopped frequently to keep the ponies, weighed down with equipment, from sinking into the mud.

A few hours later, they crossed to a picturesque village situated on a slice of arable and well-cultivated land, "overhung on both sides by high, broken hills." They paused and "lunched beneath mulberry-trees bending under a heavy load of fruit, which furnished an excellent dessert to our al fresco repast." Because the Workmans couldn't find a suitable camping place, they continued on "over the rock-strewn and desert mountain-wastes to the village of Tagas."

The corners of Workman's eyes turned upward in a smile when she saw Wazir Abdul Karim's familiar weatherworn face. They hadn't seen the loquacious local leader since their 1906 expedition. They reviewed the plan for the next few weeks over steaming cups of tea. With a last sip, Karim said goodbye and mounted his sleek black mountain pony. He rode away, the pony kicking up a puff of dust. Karim scouted out campsites, procured supplies, hired porters, and helped keep the expedition on schedule.

The Workmans and a few dozen porters followed behind, albeit at a decidedly slower pace. Fanny made a mental note of the rock formations along the way. Most of the rocks were striated in shades of gray, brown, and white. She admired the way the layers folded and twisted in intricate curves. Slowly they made their way through the labyrinthine glacier-filled valley. "From wall to wall, no pathway can be found by their sides, in most cases, and one is obliged to ascend directly over their surface, clambering up and down the slopes of great hillocks and ridges heavily covered with rocks, interrupted by crevasses and chasms, or broken into ice-precipices, a fatiguing undertaking neither agreeable nor, by any means, devoid of danger. Moreover the upper, steeper, crevassed, and broken portions are wholly inaccessible," she wrote.

A woolen blanket loosely draped over her shoulders, Workman fought back a spell of nausea; she didn't know whether it was from altitude sickness. Hunter wrote in his journal and sketched a picture of the glacier as he imagined it to be. Between the back pages he pressed a little flower he'd plucked somewhere along the way.

Two days later the Workmans and their guide Siméon Quaizier scaled a thousand-foot hill above their camp. At the top they discovered a small, sandy terrace, which appeared to be protected from avalanches.

While Quaizier looked out onto the horizon, Hunter dug in his pack for his camera. Riven and gullied, the land stretched endlessly before them. As he viewed the world through his lens he chatted with Fanny. Then he couldn't hear her voice. He saw her mouth move, but no sound came out. The earth shook. A terrific roar filled the valley. Rocks and mud burst through the top of the gorge. Clouds billowed in its wake. Another cascade of moraine rocks followed, "a rolling tumbling mass of dark brown colour, mixed with mud," Hunter wrote. Though they stood a reasonable distance away, their bodies vibrated with the blast.

Nature's violent, ferocious display yanked the last vestiges of travel fatigue from the couple. They marched forward with sixty porters and a flock of sheep and goats in tow.

———————

Fanny was absorbed in her work, but not so much that she forgot her daughter Rachel's wedding. The night before, she and Hunter celebrated with a bottle of champagne. She also made a special journal entry the evening of July 8: "Rachel's Wedding Day." It was the only time she set aside a page for something personal, for something unrelated to mountain climbing. Nevertheless, because Fanny Workman garnered such interest among the public, news of the wedding reached across the Atlantic. The *New York Times* ran a story titled "Miss Workman Weds" about the nuptials taking place inside a Quaker meetinghouse.

Before leaving for this trip to the Eastern Karakoram, Fanny had mailed the invitations for the marriage of their daughter to Sir Alexander MacRobert of Douneside Tarland, Scotland,

Rachel Workman with her mother.

at York, England. The thick, creamy paper befitted a marriage of this status.

The Workmans approved the match; they thought their daughter's betrothed was a solid man, perhaps a bit aloof. Then a director of six companies, MacRobert would merge them in 1920 to form the British India Corporation. The move would be the highlight of his career. That he was wealthier than the Workmans and moved in a higher social strata appealed to Fanny's sense of class. By wedding MacRobert, their daughter the geologist would become a gentlewoman among the elites.

Though no letters from Fanny to Rachel survive, a June 8 letter from Hunter to his "Liebe Rachel" offers affectionate reflections on the occasion of her marriage:

> I can imagine various sentiments, which may float through your mind on this day and occasion. What you really may feel I do not know. . . . To me while I am glad if you are making a change that will add to your happiness, there is a sense of sadness connected with this day for I am losing my only daughter and child under her own name and can no longer address her as Miss Rachel Workman, but must henceforth commit her entirely to the care of another and address her by the unaccustomed name of Lady McRobert [sic]. However, my feelings in this matter are of no consequence. My race is nearly run, and the welfare and happiness of yourself and your husband are the main points at issue for which you both have my sincerest desire.

It wasn't that Fanny was entirely removed from the day. Before leaving for this trip, she and Rachel had planned the wedding together. They'd shopped for the dress, which cost $500, and, of course, the Workmans paid for the wedding. But work was work.

And she was about to become the first person—man or woman—
to map the world's least explored and least accessible subpolar
glacier. Rachel wasn't surprised by her mother's absence. All she
knew was a mother who walked in and out of her life, packing
and unpacking. She was neither bitter nor resentful. Rachel was
proud of her mother's achievements, and she was blazing her own
trail in academics and standing for women's rights. In 1913 she
would attend the annual general meeting of the Royal Geological
Society, where an "attempt was made to eject me. The Secretary
rushed up and said 'I was not a fellow,' so I explained this was
through no fault of mine but the Society's and waved him aside
and marched in. . . . He need not try any tricks with me because
I am a woman," she later remarked.

Rachel and Alexander MacRobert's new life would be full of
joys, sorrows, and separations. Home base would be the nine-
thousand-acre Cromar estate, near Douneside, that MacRobert had
purchased some years back. He would travel to and from India, a
place Rachel had little interest in. She would eventually birth and
bury all three of their sons, Alasdair, Roderic, and Iain. Two died
serving as Royal Air Force pilots during World War II; the other
died in an aviation accident before the war. But none of that had
yet come to pass when Fanny settled under her covers that July evening in 1911 and opened her journal to write one more time. For
now, the mother could think only happiness awaited the daughter.

"May all blessings be Rachel's in the new life opening," she
wrote, before pressing a four-leaf clover inside the journal and
slipping into slumber.

---

Massive walls of splintered rock rose toward the gray sky. It was
mid-July, and Workman and her husband were just a few days

into what would turn into a two-month stay on the ice. Living between fifteen thousand and twenty-one thousand feet, they encountered a "very great cold—almost as great as that experienced by Amundsen faced in the Antarctic. . . . Sometimes storms raged for 30 hours."

----

Three hours after Fanny, Hunter, Cesar Chenoz, and Quaizier had left camp, they stood atop a rocky perch. The Siachen Glacier stretched before them like a crystal sea. Fanny and Hunter snapped photograph after photograph. Many years from now, after Fanny died, Hunter would donate several of these photographs to the American Museum of Natural History in New York City. But for now the couple stood together, taking in the vista.

Thus each day passed. Striking out each morning to follow one branch of the glacier or another, they made measurements, sketched the terrain, and noted the location of various peaks. The work became almost routine. Until the evening when Hunter almost died.

Just before dinner, the cook asked the couple for their soup ration so he could prepare the meal. Engrossed in reviewing the day's work, Hunter reached for what he thought was a tin of pea soup from the tray of his *yakdan*, or serving trunk. Without looking up, he handed the paper-wrapped tin to the cook.

The soup was served. Sloshing about in the bowl it looked a little thinner, a lot darker, and a lot greasier than usual. Fanny, "eyeing it askance and tasting it with great caution, declined to have anything to do with it and sent it out forthwith," Hunter wrote, "while I, having dusted a liberal quantity of celery-salt into my portion, which effectually disguised any peculiar flavour it might possess, and remarking that the khansamah probably prepared it in a saucepan previously used for cooking meat or some greasy food, with that disregard for trifles which the 'simple life' is apt to beget in explorers, consumed almost the entire quantity in my plate."

After several spoonfuls, Hunter's mouth and throat dried up. He had a compulsive urge to swallow. He gulped cup after cup of water. Nothing worked, and the symptoms worsened. His appetite fled; even the "excellent custard pudding" couldn't tempt him. He suspected the soup was the culprit and half stumbled, half ran to the cook's tent. He asked if it had been prepared differently this evening. No, the cook said. Back in his tent, Hunter tried to sleep. His mouth and throat still felt parched. Swallowing was unbearable. Not wanting to wake his wife, he kept quiet. Finally, around three in the morning, his symptoms started to abate.

Shortly after daybreak, he again questioned the cook. Again the cook said he had prepared exactly what Hunter had given him, and to prove it, the cook showed him the tin. It was a tin of belladonna ointment, not pea soup. The cook hadn't realized the mistake because he was illiterate. Belladonna, which translates to "beautiful lady," has been used for centuries as a healing agent and as a poison. In Renaissance Italy, women used belladonna berry juice to enlarge their pupils, thinking it lent them an air of mystery. Others, like Hunter, used ointment made from the plant to soothe aching muscles. It is sometimes used today to treat bronchial spasms. The purple flowers and dark, inky berries of *Atropa belladonna*, or deadly nightshade, have chemicals that can block the body's nervous system, potentially affecting salivation, sweating, pupil size, urination, and digestive functions. If ingested it can also cause death. Today, atropine is sometimes used during anesthesia and surgery to help keep a normal heartbeat, and atropine sulfate can be used to block or reverse the adverse effects caused by some medicines and certain poisons.

"As circumstances turned out no serious harm resulted, but I have always felt, that they led me that night close along the brow of a precipice towering above an abyss of destruction, for as might easily have happened, had an additional plate of that soup been taken, another heretofore unheard of cause of danger to life in mountain-exploration would doubtless have been added to the list embracing sudden storms, avalanches, falling stones, floods, precipices, crevasses, gathering edelweiss, earthquake and lightning," he wrote.

---

The snow fell throughout most of the night. In the morning, Fanny looked at the thermometer. It registered twenty-eight degrees Fahrenheit, not completely uncomfortable for this elevation. She smoothed her hair as best she could and pulled on her favorite striped "valley sweater" over two shirts, tugging it over her hips. She buttoned her wool skirt over thick woolen tights. She laced her hobnailed boots and before leaving the tent fastened her helmet under her chin.

With threatening skies overhead, and several inches of new snow underfoot, they climbed over the moraine and rounded a large lake before they reached a mountain spur of the main Siachen Glacier. It was nearly noon when they reached the new campsite. They pitched tents. It was "a bleak nasty place for a base," she wrote of the camp, which had an altitude of 16,800 feet.

The days in Camp II Siachen were not much warmer than the nights. The sheep nibbled on the few blades of grass poking through the snow. For the first time, Workman seemed content with the porters and their work. As of yet she had made no complaints in the pages of her journal.

———————

Shortly after rising at 4:00 AM, the Workmans heated water for tea and dried socks and gloves over a Primus stove, proving that in the mountains the device was good for more than just cooking. They ate some tinned pâté and kola biscuits. About a half hour later, everyone was assembled for the day's trek. The late morning sun warmed their backs as they marched the eight miles toward what Fanny and the surveyors believed was the head of the glacier. Three grand peaks bounded the wide snow basin. There was no visible outlet. They kept going, moving ever so carefully over the rock ridge until they reached Camp III, at eighteen thousand feet.

"This jagged rock promontory of rotten granite overhangs a wonderful glacial basin and directly below the point of perch are two large blue glacial lakes nearly frozen over at noon hour. The snow running between huge white seracs produces a wonderful effect. This was the most interesting and wild passage of a glacier width we have made and appears near four miles wide," she wrote. Their first night here was no picnic. The wind shrieked and shook their tents from sunset to sunrise.

On the last day of August 1911, Fanny watched a hawk and a crow circle above. Numerous small gray birds with red-tinged wings flew away. Clouds covered the mountains, which moments before had been bathed in golden sun. The wind kicked up. The sky darkened, and the temperature plunged. A gust knocked off her hat. There was no way to tell how long the storm would last—weather in the mountains changed in an instant. They only knew they were going to be in its teeth.

Before Workman closed her journal for the night, she made a list of the books she wanted to read upon her return to Dresden. Topping the list were *Love's Privilege* by Stella M. During and Frank H. Desch and *A Bed of Roses* by W. L. George. Back in the United States, newspapers reported that she and her team were stranded on a "barren mountain on upper Siachen flank . . . in a violent snowstorm."

———————

At nineteen thousand feet, she and Hunter discovered a second tributary, which fed into the Siachen Glacier. They took some notations and kept on, climbing three hundred more feet, seven hundred more feet. At twenty-one thousand feet, the monsoon rains came fast and furious.

Water cascaded off their helmets and pooled inside their boots. At this time of year, the rain could just as quickly turn to snow. The party was forced to return to camp, where they discovered they wanted for wood, but not wildlife. "Thirty miles of the glacier were traversed without any sign of wood. A number of large Ibexes seen. Notwithstanding the storms and the difficulty of obtaining supplies, the expedition remained on the Siachen until September 15, and secured new and interesting glaciological and geographical information," Fanny wrote.

They placed eight large stone cairns on the Siachen. So ended two months on the ice.

"No, I won't come again," Workman thought, sitting in her snowed-in tent for two days at the end of the trip. "But no sooner had I turned my back to the Rose and reached again the top of the pass on that brilliant September 16th, than my mountain-ego reasserted itself, saying tant pis to the obstacles, 'Return you must.'"

Return they did, but not before spending time in Dresden, working on the first half of what would become *Two Summers in the Ice-Wilds of Eastern Karakoram* and lecturing. They also spent time with Rachel, who was pregnant with her first child, their first grandchild, due the following summer.

———————

Riding in the inflatable goatskin raft no longer felt strange, Workman noted as they moved swiftly down the Indus River. It was April 1912, and they had rehired several other porters who had accompanied them last season. Captain Grant-Peterkin and Surjan Singh of the Survey of India were also on hand to help survey the region. Fanny was designated "the responsible leader of this expedition," Hunter wrote.

At their campsite, local villagers watched the activity, mesmerized. Like a beehive, everyone had a job to do—pitching tents, lighting fires, gathering firewood—all in service of the queen bee: Fanny Bullock Workman. Spending a few nights here on a sand flat was Workman's first choice. To reach it they had to demolish two high stone walls, climb over the roof of a local woman's house, and then pass over a small field of grain belonging to the woman. "She sat looking at her overturned field till night and the next day when I left camp and begged of me. I amply satisfied her for her loss and she salaamed humbly," Workman wrote.

———————

Fanny and Hunter slept little; they spent most of the night clearing snow out of their tents. Their camp was just over seventeen thousand feet high.

They had left the Ali Bransa camp just before 7:00 AM, their usual time, on July 8, 1912. Heading over the Bilaphond Glacier, she and Chenoz led the party over seemingly solid snow. Hunter was back somewhere in the middle of the line. Two hours later they stood on a point below a ridge of seracs at an altitude of eighteen thousand feet. Workman turned to her husband and asked him to photograph her and Chenoz. While Hunter prepared the camera, Fanny walked a bit farther out onto the ice hummocks with Chenoz. She wanted the photograph to capture the terrain leading to the ridge. Chenoz carried the hemp rope, even though moments before he and Quaizier had agreed that roping for this portion of the excursion was quite unnecessary.

"I thought how rather soft the snow, but I saw no evidence of crevasses," she said.

After the photo, Chenoz flung the rope over his back and strode ahead. He was about eight feet ahead of Workman, taking a somewhat higher and faster tack to join the others farther up the trail. "I did not watch him to see if he was testing snow in front of us . . . but I did notice the yellowish colour of the small ridge we were on, but simply followed fast supposing he was as usual noticing carefully snow conditions," she later wrote. She asked him if they should rope up, but he told her not to worry, assuring her the surface was solid and crevasse free, in spite of the yellowish snow, which indicated otherwise. Then he quite simply vanished. "At not over two feet ahead of me he suddenly shot down out of sight and without uttering a cry into a great crevasse. I gave a cry and halted just this side of the brink of the great hole had disappeared into."

It took her a fraction of a second to realize what had happened. Workman stood stock still, as if her legs had taken root. All around her radiant, sunlit peaks jutted forth from the glacier. Before anyone noticed, she snapped to and her feet obeyed. She ordered the workers to bring ropes to the edge. They sprinted to her side. "The others rushed up very fast and I joined them descending directly from where I stood." Quaizier hollered down to Chenoz. The Italian guide's feeble voice rose from the depth of the huge crevasse, stating "that he was bien and could wait until Savoye was sent for, who had a second corde [rope], the first one being in crevasse with Chenoz." So Quaizier and a porter went over the pass to look for more porters.

There was nothing the group could do but stand "helpless waiting in the cloudless warm white snow. Whisky was got out and there we waited mad with anxiety for forty minutes, knowing how hopelessly frozen the man in the blue ice chasm must be." They leaned into each other against the biting wind, consumed with thoughts of Chenoz.

Savoye and Adolphe Rey, one of the smallest of the guides, returned and roped up. The others slowly lowered them until they reached Chenoz lying seventy-five feet below. He had ricocheted like a pinball when he fell. First, he'd hit an upper ice shelf, then crashed onto his back, and then tumbled to the bottom. Inside, the icy chamber icicles looked ready to break and fall on their heads. One of the porters opened a pack of smelling salts and waved them in front of Chenoz's nose, hoping to rouse the battered man.

Meanwhile up above, five porters stood on the edge of the crevasse holding the loose end of the rope, ready to lengthen or shorten it at Savoye's command. It was a full ten minutes before the signal came for the porters on the top to start pulling. They dug in their heels. Those in front went down on bended knee, putting all their weight on their supporting legs. They pulled on the rope, fist over fist. Backs, arms, and legs afire from the exertion, they kept their focus. The porters got up over the edge. Then the limp body of Chenoz, who was received by his "brother guides' sheltering arms and unroped." Savoye came last.

"Chenoz was hauled out with his hands black with cold and face covered with blood. When he was placed on snow and massaged by guides and servants for one hour and although conscious had no pulse and could barely drink small doses of hot coffee and whisky," Fanny wrote in her journal.

Hunter performed a cursory examination. He detected a faint glimmer of a pulse in one wrist but not the other. The retired physician directed six porters to carry Chenoz back to the Ali B camp on a litter crudely fashioned from sticks bound with ropes. Semiconscious, the guide clearly suffered from exposure. "The group looked exactly like Siegfried being brought in on his litter dead, as they sadly filed down the brilliant white glacier under the azure sky," Workman noted.

The entire group followed dirgelike behind the litter. She worried about Chenoz, her "dear good porter" who had spent four seasons with them. That she nearly missed her own death had yet to sink in.

Once Hunter settled Chenoz onto his cot, he examined him more closely, looking for broken bones and lacerations. The only visible signs of injury were severe bruising. Hunter administered morphine and listened to Chenoz's heart. The beat was regular but fluttering. At one point Chenoz took some more whisky and slept for close to three hours. At 9:00 PM he rolled over. Savoye asked his friend if he wished for a drink, but Chenoz declined. His eyelids fluttered over his marble-brown eyes one last time. "They thought he still slept when at 10:30 they touched his face and found it quite cold. So he passed in perfect peace," Hunter wrote.

Mere chance had saved Fanny's life. On any other day she would have been roped to Chenoz. Later she came to feel the accident was no one's fault and everyone's fault. Perhaps he should have been less cavalier about checking for crevasses. Perhaps she should have insisted everyone slow down just a bit. It was impossible to know whether he would have recovered, let alone survived, at a lower altitude, Hunter wrote in his red leather journal that night.

It was a ghastly night. "We were overcome by grief, yet action was imperative. We sat up into the small hours talking matters over with Savoye in a temperature of 16 degrees F. The only course possible was decided on during this awesome vigil," she noted.

The news reached the United States. However, the story focused on Fanny. Chenoz, who had spent four of six seasons with them, didn't even rate a solitary mention.

Morning broke. A light breeze ruffled Workman's hair as she watched Savoye leave camp with seven porters. They bore Chenoz's body on a litter down the glacier to the first sign of grass. There they delivered last rites to Chenoz. A large cairn marked his final resting place. They had no choice but to bury him in this spot since the climate wouldn't allow for remains to be carried all the way to the nearest village for a proper burial. Additionally, the porters warned Workman that villagers might desecrate the grave in search of clothes and other items.

Another forty porters went to the scene of the accident to retrieve what they could. Everyone else remained at "the camp of mourning."

"So ends this sad episode, the death and burial of my invaluable porter within 36 hours. He was a man of great strength and perfect health and died of shock and long exposure, which was not preventable in crevasse," Workman wrote. The guides and porters returned at dawn.

———————

They were now at the highest point of Siachen on the Indira Col. Grant-Peterkin, the surveyor who had accompanied the expedition, named the col for Lakshmi, the Hindu goddess of wealth, fortune, and prosperity. The expedition also named several other points in the region, including Teram Kangri, Apsarasas, Ghent, the Sia La, and Junction Peak.

Nearby the party stumbled on the crumbling remains of two cairns. Workman surmised they had been built "ages ago," as there were no locals in the area and that "no Europeans have ever been here before," she said of the small mystery. They were the first Americans or Europeans known to stand on this spot, 18,972 feet high. They were also the very first people to see this northward view toward the remote mountains of Xinjiang.

With nearly two more months ahead of them, Workman hit a mental wall. "This is hard work and we are nearly at end of our endurance of long snow marches and great heights and beastly cold snow camps," she said. Not to mention the tragedy of Chenoz.

And yet death hadn't finished visiting the expedition. A few days later, a porter slipped on the path, fell into a river, and drowned.

Workman arranged a pension for his family. Back in the United States, the *New York Times* and several other papers reported, erroneously, how "a great avalanche overwhelmed the Workman party killing one of them."

Then another porter, who was carrying one of the Workmans' specimen boxes and her favorite "valley sweater," fell into a glacial river. The porter escaped with his life, albeit with several nasty looking bruises. Two porters stripped and waded neck deep into the ice-cold water to retrieve the bags, lodged on the river bottom. Ever thankful, Workman was pleased to get the supplies back.

They trudged and they trekked and they made their way over the ice. Every few days, thirty porters went off in search of dwarf willow bushes to use for fuel. Meanwhile, Fanny and her husband conducted the largest and most serious scientific expedition ever before directed in this region. Her study of the sources, formation, and movement of the glaciers in this area endured for decades.

Workman was now a public figure and role model for female scientists and climbers—even if it was not what she had set out to be. "A Worcester woman over 50 years old has climbed one of the highest mountains in the world and began housekeeping on its top. Mrs. FBW is the famous conqueror of geographical obstacles who has accomplished this very thing and Dr. Dudley A. Sargent physical director of Harvard, and head of the school which bears his name, declares every American woman could do the same if she set her mind upon it," stated the *Boston Sunday Post*.

———————

Standing on the twenty-one-thousand-foot Silver Throne platcau, Fanny unfurled a banner. Hardly larger than a newspaper, and about as light, its three-word message was straight to the point: Votes for Women.

Uncovering the lens, Hunter slung his camera around his neck and snapped several photographs. The photo of Fanny Bullock Workman, hatted, with netting pulled back like a veil, clothed in her skirt and boots, with an ice ax planted in the snow next to her, exudes a sense of serenity that belies the fact that she was at that moment standing atop a peak in one of the most dangerous mountain ranges in the world. She held the sign in both hands to prevent the high-altitude winds from ripping it to shreds. Of all the photos of her, this one taken on the western source of the Siachen is the most iconic.

In *Two Summers in the Ice-Wilds of Eastern Karakoram*, published in 1916, Workman explained that she'd raised the sign

In 1912 Fanny Bullock Workman thrust her ice ax into the summit of the Silver Throne and held aloft this banner, Votes for Women.

[not] because I wish in any way to thrust myself forward, but solely that in the accomplishments of women, now and in the future, it should be known to them and stated in print that a woman was the initiator and special leader of this expedition. When, later, a woman occupies her acknowledged position as an individual worker in all fields, as well as those of exploration, no such emphasis of her work will be needed; but that day has not fully arrived, and at present it behooves women, for the benefit of their sex, to put what they do, at least, on record.

This book, the last the couple would ever write, was a departure. Using first-person narration, it struck a more emotional chord than any of their earlier works. Her account of Chenoz's death was the first time she showed readers her emotional side.

————————

One afternoon toward the end of the expedition, after an avalanche nearly buried them, the team built several small cairns under which they left notes about their adventure across the Siachen. Workman marked her initials and the date in black on a rock wall. The "Crows crying and cawing and following as usual," she said.

That evening Workman, never one to wax poetic, had a mystical experience. The entire expedition was camped on the upper plateau of the fabled city they called Tarim Shehr, or Oasis City, waiting to recross into Baltistan. She couldn't sleep, between the gusts of wind racking the tent and the praying of the porters, which rose above the howling wind. Exasperated, she threw on a fur coat and went outside. It was still snowing and blowing on the glacier. Above, the clouds had parted on a silvery full moon.

"As I stood there I beheld all about me the undulating hillocks covered with large, feathery, full-blown snow-roses. It was not a hallucination. . . . I buried my hands in their cold, silvery petals, and then, forgetting the zero temperature, stood chained by the poetry of the surroundings. . . . The weird glory of the scene and the discovery of the snow-roses so impressed me that I returned to my tent without stopping the chant."

————————

After reacclimating to life in Germany, the couple scheduled several lectures to talk about the expedition. She spoke about the climbs and the forays deep into the Himalayas and about the fragility of life and her hope to see more women join the ranks of mountaineering and science.

More than any other previous work, these past two expeditions cemented their influence on Himalayan exploration. They had broken the British stranglehold on Himalayan mountain climbing. The Bullock-Workman expeditions of 1911 and 1912 broke more new ground than their prior expeditions, and this time their original maps and charts were of higher quality. The triangulation of the Siachen glacier, done by their surveyor, remains the basis of current maps.

When they came home, they were surprised to learn of the sheer volume of obituary notices that had been written about them, about Hunter in particular. They were, however, pleased to read Sven Hedin's review of *Two Summers in the Ice-Wilds of Eastern Karakoram*. He described it as "one of the most important contributions ever given to our knowledge of these mountains." That the Workmans had fixed all prominent peaks along the Shaksgam watershed for position and height was, in Hedin's view, a "fine achievement." He wasn't the only one to praise their work. In his 1955 book *Abode of Snow: A History of Himalayan Exploration and Mountaineering from Earliest Times to the Ascent of Everest*, Kenneth Mason, a former superintendent of the Survey of India and a renowned professor of geography at Oxford, found the Workmans' work still useful. Perhaps the compliment they savored most came from Sir Martin Conway, who said the couple "added enormously to our knowledge of the greatest knot or group of mountains on the face of Earth."

It was to be their last expedition. As Hunter told Rachel in a letter written from the Siachen Glacier, "We have been very successful in our work this summer. As mama has probably written you, I have found it rather trying sleeping or rather not sleeping but roasting in snow camps at altitudes of 17 to 19,000 feet. I feel my age and cannot stand the [word unclear] as well as formerly. I have had much trouble with shortness of breath and have been much disturbed by this at night. . . . I see only too plainly that age has put a limit for me to this sort of work, and this will be my last expedition."

———————

In 1912, the controversy over the altitude record now well behind her, Annie S. Peck, now middle-aged, left her quest for record setting behind and started climbing more for pleasure. She embarked on a flying trip over South America and waged a letter-writing campaign, directly addressing President Woodrow Wilson, to protest American entry into World War I. And in 1914 she became the president of the Joan of Arc Suffrage League in New York.

In 1915, while on the lecture circuit, she strode up to the podium dressed in a gown of black net over green silk. Looking out at the richly attired audience she wondered, *What woman is authorized to speak for all suffragists?* There were too many men in politics, and of those men most were better suited for "hoeing corn or selling ribbon than for setting the affairs of state or nation," she remarked. It was time women were regarded as intelligent human beings, in charge of themselves, she said in one of her many lectures. She started to recognize there were differences between women's aspirations, but for now those differences needed to be set aside to advance the common goal of securing women's voting rights.

———————

As Fanny Bullock Workman worked on *Two Summers in the Ice-Wilds of Eastern Karakoram*, it was clear how far she had come from her earliest attempts at writing. In her first romantic fantasy, her heroine chose not to marry. In the second, the heroine fell in love, but with someone outside her racial and economic class, and chose not to marry. Now, decades later, Fanny favored writing about more grounded ideas, such as her travels and scientific work, and her progressive marriage. Through her writing she tried to show it was possible to travel the world and climb the highest mountains. She went further than any woman had gone before. She was a pioneer.

Studio portrait of Fanny Bullock Workman.

She never let domestic expectations hold her back from adventuring. Workman never "kept house" as much as she "kept help" in the house. The privileges of financial freedom allowed her to fulfill her passions for mountain climbing, but in matters of the heart she preferred to be off on the edges of the earth, alone in a Mummery tent with Hunter. Engaging with the mundane existence of home life never interested her. And yet she had struggled in her own way. In spite of the honors, and there were plenty; in spite of the fame, and there was much—she fought to be taken seriously, and in truth she never was fully accepted.

As for Peck, she had neither husband nor child. She seemed to live Workman's earliest fantasy: to escape the expectation that the only suitable role for a woman was as wife and mother. Peck had pursued, and attained, an education. She taught the classics and took up the cause of women's rights, while Workman lacked an advanced education but gained years of mountain climbing experience.

Annie S. Peck and Fanny Bullock Workman. Two healthy, strong, and skilled women. Two women who accomplished amazing feats of daring and prowess. Two women who challenged many assumptions and prejudices the public held about women's strengths and abilities.

# EPILOGUE

SOON AFTER THE 1914 assassination of Archduke Franz Ferdinand, a member of the Austrian nobility most Americans had never even heard of, the Great War engulfed the European continent, and Fanny Bullock Workman's exploring days ended. She and Hunter left Paris for London on September 14, 1914. "Liebe Rachel," Hunter wrote,

> We made a rush from Paris yesterday by auto bringing with us all the luggage we now have including cycles, and fortunately squeaked through without delay. We left Paris on the last day that the gates were open for autos to depart. Found the main road choked with military trains and lines of wagons of all sorts and sizes filled with fugitives escaping from Paris and the war zone. . . . There has been an awful scramble away from Paris since the aeroplanes with bombs began flying over the city. Mama has been frightened out of her senses. . . . We are fortunate to get away so easily and certainly could not have waited longer without being caught there. This bomb business is most devilish.

As Fanny and her husband of thirty-three years set aside thoughts of embarking on any more expeditions, her heart had begun to fail. It now took all of her effort to climb even the shortest flight of stairs, and with each passing week this sturdy, indomitable woman came to realize she might never recover. For the next eight years she suffered from ill health.

Fanny and Hunter, the once "indefatigable alpinists" retired to the South of France sometime after World War I, where they enjoyed visits with Rachel, her husband Alexander, and their three sons. Looking out on the Mediterranean, Fanny reflected on her achievements: during her life, ten European geographical societies bestowed her with medals. "The adventures of Mrs. Workman and her husband in mountainous regions have been read by scores of persons with the greatest interest, but the daring exploits of the famous American mountain climber in the Himalaya mountains in Asia are the most exciting of all," reported the *Boston Sunday Post*.

She had received a gold medal and high honors from the French Alpine Club partly because of her Himalayan work. She also received the Academic Palms from the French government, as well as recognition by the French Academy of Sports. She was honored alongside Georges Carpentier, the pugilist, and Marcel Brindejonc des Moulinais, who flew from Paris to St. Petersburg. Over the course of her life, numerous clubs elected her as member, including the American Alpine Club, the Club Alpino Italiano, the Club Alpin Français, the Royal Geographical Society, and the Royal Asiatic Society. She was also a corresponding member of the Brooklyn Institute of Arts and Sciences. She drew up a will that bequeathed $125,000 to four women's colleges—Radcliffe, Wellesley, Smith, and Bryn Mawr—testimony to her interest in the advancement of women's rights and the idea that women are equal to men.

Then, on January 22, 1925, at age sixty-six, the "Queen of the Lady Mountaineers" died from heart failure in a hotel in Cannes.

The staunch feminist who regarded herself as proof that women could equal and even outdo men was gone. At her death, she held the world record in altitude for woman mountaineers. One newspaper described her as "the most intrepid woman climber the world has so far known, who with her husband has conquered many of the most difficult Himalaya peaks, beating one world's record after another. Mrs. Workman's exploits gave her the name of premier woman mountain climber of the world. She explored and surveyed the Hispar and Biafo glaciers and lectured extensively before geographical scientific societies in America, Scotland, France, Germany, and Italy."

When the president of the Alpine Club of Great Britain sat down to write Workman's obituary for the 1925 issue of the *Alpine Journal*, he noted that she "was no quitter." Furthermore, he praised how "her enthusiastic nature induced her to sustain her opinions by vigorous arguments based on facts which it was difficult to controvert. It is not to be expected that a woman of such determination and energy, when assailed or assailing, would be other than a very doughty fighter, as indeed became her pure New England ancestry . . . but they who got to know her could not fail to recognize her warmness of heart, her enthusiasm, her humor, her buoyant delight in doing." It was very unusual for the *Alpine Journal* to carry obituaries of nonmembers, and in particular female climbers.

It is true that many of the couple's geographical reports raised a good deal of controversy, largely because they neglected to pay attention to the work of their predecessors. Still the couple was bold and persistent and was lauded for their work.

After Fanny's body was cremated in Marseille, Hunter sailed for America. Her remains were buried in the Rural Cemetery in Worcester, Massachusetts, on September 24, 1925, with only immediate family members there to bear witness. Fanny Bullock

Workman was home again. No longer would she show the way, ice ax in hand, topee perched atop her head.

A year after her death, Hunter sent a letter to the New York Public Library along with twenty-eight photographs of their alpine climbs. The library director appreciated the charming photographs and Hunter's continued interest in the library's alpine collection.

In 1937, at age ninety, William Hunter Workman, surgeon turned explorer, died in Newton, Massachusetts. He was buried alongside his wife. The inscription beneath the four-foot-high mountain-shaped stone reads: PIONEER HIMALAYAN EXPLORERS.

# ACKNOWLEDGMENTS

T HANK YOU, Jill D. Swenson of Swenson Book Development. I am grateful for your encouragement and astute suggestions to the manuscript that helped me shaped the narrative.

A special thanks to everyone at Chicago Review Press, especially my tireless editor Jerome Pohlen for his critical eye and enthusiasm regarding this project. Thanks to Ellen Hornor, whose narrative sensibility, rigor, and attention to detail made this manuscript better than it was.

I am grateful to the staff of the National Library of Scotland, including Dr. Emily Goetsch and Olive Geddes, curator of social history, archives and special collections, for helping me navigate the Workman papers during an intense week of research.

Thank you, Alison Donaldson at the MacRobert Trust, for answering questions and ferreting out correspondence from William Hunter Workman.

Thanks to Colleen Bradley-Sanders, Ted Hechtman, Pamela Kerns, and Marianne LaBatto at the Brooklyn College Library archives and special collections, for guiding me through the Annie S. Peck papers.

I am grateful to several specialty libraries and historical societies. At the Alpine Club Library UK, Nigel Buckley, honorary archivist Glyn Hughes, and Barbara Grigor-Taylor, thank you all for answering numerous questions on peak names, elevations, and itineraries. Both the American Alpine Club Library and the Worcester Historical Society helped round out my research.

Thank you to Dave Peck, a descendent of Annie S. Peck; Hayden Carpenter of Rock & Ice; Stuart Leggatt from Meridian Rare Books; and Jack Davis for answering questions and suggesting leads to follow.

Thank you to my parents, Norma and Marvin Prince, for your steady encouragement and constant support. Thank you to my children, Nathan and Zoë, for your good humor, conversation, and inspiration. And to my husband, Pierre, for being an early reader, for listening, for your advice, and, above all, for our life together.

# NOTES

## Abbreviations

ASP—Annie Smith Peck
FBW—Fanny Bullock Workman
WHW—William Hunter Workman

## Chapter 1: Mountaineering for Ladies

*"The real enjoyment"*: Charles Dudley Warner, *In the Wilderness* (Hartford, CT: Houghton, Mifflin, 1878), 126–27.

*"generous, sympathetic"*: Caroline E. Robinson, *The Hazard Family of Rhode Island 1635–1894: Being a Genealogy and History of the Descendants of Thomas Hazard, with Sketches of the Worthies of this Family and Anecdotes Illustrative of Their Traits and also of the Times in which They Lived* (Boston: Merrymount, 1896), 227.

*"physical health"*: Thomas Wentworth Higginson, *The Writings of Thomas Wentworth Higginson: Outdoor Studies; Poems* (Cambridge, MA: Riverside, 1899), 10.

*"Alpine Books Worth Reading"*: Commonplace Book of Fanny Bullock Workman, 1876, Workman Papers, Archives and Manuscript Collections, National Library of Scotland, Edinburgh. Hereafter referred to as Workman Papers.

*"The great society event"*: "Marriage Announcement," *New York Times*, June 16, 1881.

*"were in harmony"*: "Marriage Announcement," *New York Times*.

*"In the presence of"*: "A Notable Wedding. A Brilliant Gathering at All Saints Church," *New York Times*, June 16, 1881.

"profuse and costly": "A Notable Wedding," *New York Times*.

*"New Woman"*: Sarah Grand would later coin the term in her March 1894 *North American Review* article "The New Aspect of the Woman Question" (volume 158, no. 448, 270–76).

*"One bright afternoon"*: FBW, "A Romance of King Philip's War," *New England Magazine*, 1886, 330.

*"Marry you I never can"*: FBW, "King Philip's War," 332.

*"A most charming romance"*: "Title Review," *Sacramento (CA) Record-Union*, June 5, 1886.

*"For years these"*: "Club for Women Climbers: They Have Long Been Angry at Being Kept out of Alpine Club," *New York Times*, August 18, 1907.

*"gathered or plaited"*: Carol Mattingly, *Appropriate[ing] Dress: Women's Rhetorical Style in Nineteenth-Century America* (Carbondale: Southern Illinois University Press, 2002), 41.

## Chapter 2: No Time for Tea

*"boldest of knickerbockers"*: Jess Gant and Nicholas J. Hoffman, *Wheel Fever: How Wisconsin Became a Great Bicycling State* (Madison: Wisconsin Historical Society Press, 2013), xxiv.

*"Did women realize"*: FBW, "Bicycle Riding in Germany," *Outing: An Illustrated Monthly Magazine of Sport, Travel and Recreation*, October 1892–March 1893, 111.

*"without fireworks"*: Jeremy Bernstein, "Ascent I: Whymper and Mummery Reporter at Large," *New Yorker*, March 13, 1965, 44.

*"cheap trippers"*: A. F Mummery, *My Climbs in the Alps and Caucasus* (London: Basil Blackwell, 1936), 1.

*"pointers out of paths"*: Bernstein, "Ascent I," 138.

*"The morning was clear"*: FBW, journal entry, 31 August 1892, Germany and Italy 1892, Acc. 9893/3, Workman Papers.

*"The snow was thick"*: FBW, journal entry, 31 August 1892.

*"The wind, very curiously"*: FBW, journal entry, 31 August 1892.

*"altogether a narrow"*: FBW, journal entry, 18 September 1892, Germany and Italy 1892, Acc. 9893/3, Workman Papers.

"*good jolly supper*": FBW, journal entry, 18 September 1892.

"*nasty people*": FBW, journal entry, 18 September 1892.

"*Our family comes*": "The Healthiest Family Is the Happiest," *Syracuse (NY) Herald*, August 22, 1920.

"*contumacious disobedience*": Author email correspondence with David Peck, 30 August 2015.

"*felt that daughters*": Thomas B. Stockwell, *A History of Public Education in Rhode Island: From 1636–1876* (Providence: Providence Press, 1886), 15.

"*saw a giantess*": ASP, diary entry, 7 June 1865, 1862–1888, Series 1, Box 1, Annie Smith Peck Collection, Archives and Special Collections, Brooklyn College Library. Hereafter referred to as Peck Collection

"*but never hot biscuit*": "Healthiest Family," *Syracuse (NY) Herald*.

"*I hope you will*": Ann Power Smith Peck to ASP, 28 September 1873, Group 1, Series 2, Box 3, Folder 2, Peck Collection.

"*I do not esteem*": John Brownell Peck to ASP, 8 January 1873, Series 2, Box 2, Peck Collection.

"*Why you should recommend*": ASP to George Peck Sr., January 1874, Series 2, Box 2, Peck Collection.

"*raised eyebrows*": "Annie Peck Reached Dangerous Heights," *Appleton (WI) Post Crescent*, February 2, 1975.

"*it is expressibly silly*": A. G. Pitts to ASP, 16 February 1892, Group 1, Series 2, Box 11, Folder 1, Peck Collection.

"*complimented our sex*": ASP to John Brownell Peck, 3 November 1873, Group 1, Series 2A, Box 18, Peck Collection.

"*Where a chipmunk*": "Climbing High Mountains: Miss Annie S. Peck Tells How Her Love for It Finally Made Her a Record Breaker," *New York Times*, January 9, 1898.

"*Cried out great deal*": WHW, Notes of Siegfried's Last Illness, Acc. 9893/1, Workman Papers.

"*Perhaps within 12 hours*": WHW, Siegfried's Last Illness.

"*His eyes closed half*": WHW, Siegfried's Last Illness.

"*I write a line*": WHW to Lou Workman, Dresden, 28 June 1893, Acc. 9893/1, Workman Papers.

"*One year ago*": FBW, "Only a Year," included in file Acc.9893/1, Workman Papers.

## Chapter 3: The Wheels Go Round

*"a very long and tiresome"*: FBW, journal entry, 9 February 1894, Algeria 1894, Acc. 9893/5, Workman Papers.

*"the Arab dogs"*: FBW, journal entry, 13 February 1894, Algeria 1894, Acc. 9893/5, Workman Papers.

*"This was not encouraging"*: FBW, *Algerian Memories: A Bicycle Tour over the Atlas to the Sahara* (London: Fisher Unwin, 1895), 10.

*"leisure, stopping where"*: FBW and WHW, *Sketches Awheel in Modern Iberia* (New York: G. P. Putnam and Sons, 1897), v.

*"the opportunity offered"*: FBW, *Algerian Memories*, 13.

*"spiral stone stairways . . . who cruelly persecuted"*: FBW, *Algerian Memories*, 14.

*"some of the older Jews"*: FBW, *Algerian Memories*, 13.

*"particularly characteristic"*: FBW, journal entries, 15 and 16 February 1894, Algeria, Acc. 9893/5, Workman Papers.

*"the Jewish Sunday"*: FBW, journal entries, 15 and 16 February 1894.

*"for a sou"*: FBW, journal entries, 15 and 16 February 1894.

*"delicious and refreshing drink."*: FBW, *Algerian Memories*, 24.

*"Our frequent meetings"*: FBW, *Algerian Memories*, 5–6.

*"After rains the large feet"*: FBW, *Algerian Memories*, 5–6.

*"listening to the babbling"*: FBW quoted in Dorothy Middleton, *Victorian Lady Travellers* (Chicago: Academy Chicago, 1993), 77.

*"great sight was the monkeys"*: FBW, *Algerian Memories*, 24.

*"their* farine *and"*: FBW, journal entry, 27 February 1894, Algeria 1894, Acc. 9893/5, Workman Papers.

*"bright, pretty slaves"*: FBW quoted in Luree Miller, *On Top of the World: Five Women Explorers in Tibet* (New York: Paddington, 1976), 78.

*"cordial Amazons in trousers"*: FBW, *Algerian Memories*, 54.

*"At this he stepped"*: FBW, *Algerian Memories*, 38.

*"The muzzle of"*: FBW, *Algerian Memories*, 67.

*"The newly-born girl"*: FBW, *Algerian Memories*, 68.

*"It is to be hoped"*: Albert B. Southwick, "City's Pioneer Feminist Lived a Life of Adventure," *Worcester (MA) Sunday Telegram*, October 15, 2000.

*"advance of a nation"*: FBW, *Algerian Memories*, 67.

*"without [Fanny's] skill"*: "Sketches Awheel in Modern Iberia Is in One Sense a Family Book," *Milwaukee Weekly Wisconsin*, May 28, 1897.

*"We neither knew"*: FBW and WHW, *Sketches Awheel*, xiii.

*"thoroughly by heart"*: Richard Ford, *The Handbook for Travellers in Spain*, 8th ed. (London: John Murray, 1892), 39–45.

*"an obese, oily-looking"*: FBW and WHW, *Sketches Awheel*, xiii.

*"The lead bull"*: FBW, journal entry, 27 May 1895, Algeria and Spain 1895, Acc. 9893/9, Workman Papers.

*"He advanced toward us"*: FBW, journal entry, 16 April 1895, Spain, Acc. 9893/20, Workman Papers.

*"American bars"*: FBW, journal entry, 16 April 1895.

*"Barcelona is not"*: FBW and WHW, *Sketches Awheel*, 19.

*"then after repairing it"*: FBW, journal entry, 4 April 1895, Spain, Acc. 9893/20, Workman Papers.

*"We found it very endurable"*: FBW, *Algerian Memories*, 56.

*"he who planned"*: FBW and WHW, *Sketches Awheel*, 29–30.

*"ran towards us"*: FBW and WHW, *Sketches Awheel*, 53–54.

*"Lowering the mattock"*: FBW and WHW, *Sketches Awheel*, 53–54.

*"women rushed down"*: FBW, journal entry, 2 July 1895, Algeria and Spain 1895, Acc. 9893/9, Workman Papers.

*"were so glad"*: FBW, journal entry, 2 July 1895.

*"a huge bullheaded ruffianly"*: FBW and WHW, *Sketches Awheel*, 73.

*"his fiendish face"*: FBW and WHW, *Sketches Awheel*, 73.

*"This sort of adventure"*: FBW and WHW, *Sketches Awheel*, 74.

*"When the press pursued"*: FBW and WHW, *Sketches Awheel*, 188–89.

*"quite prepared to print"*: T. Fisher Unwin to WHW, 6 December 1896, Acc. 9893/2, Workman Papers.

*"We strongly object"*: WHW quoted in Michael Plint, "The Workmans: Travellers Extraordinary," *Himalayan Journal* 49 (1993): www.himalayanclub .org/hj/49/8/the-workmans-travellers-extraordinary.

*"From this it will"*: "Family Book," *Milwaukee Weekly Wisconsin*.

*"very simple, beds like"*: FBW, journal entry, 27 February 1898, Ceylon 1897–98, Acc. 9893/11, Workman Papers.

*"curious custom of greeting"*: FBW, journal entry, 27 February 1898.

*"kept here until 15"*: FBW, journal entry, 27 February 1898.

*"considerable literary taste"*: WHW and FBW, *Through Town and Jungle: Fourteen Thousand Miles Awheel Among the Temples and People of the Indian Plain* (London: T. Fisher Unwin, 1904), 85.

*"wretchedly kept carriage"*: WHW and FBW, *Town and Jungle*, 3.

*"principal* sirdar *would"*: FBW, "Our Climbs," *Wide World Magazine*, December 1900, 262.

*"make the proposed route"*: FBW, "Our Climbs," 262.

*"It was immediately noised"*: FBW, "Our Climbs," 262.

*"floating up from a"*: FBW, "Our Climbs," 262.

## Chapter 4: Steadfast in Skirts

*"we have never been able"*: FBW and WHW, *Ice-Bound Heights of the Mustagh: An Account of Two Seasons of Pioneer Exploration and High Climbing in the Baltistan Himalaya* (London: Archibald Constable, 1908), 396.

*"well-known character"*: FBW, "Our Climbs," 261.

*"When on march"*: FBW, "Our Climbs," 261.

*"Our yaks would"*: FBW, "Our Climbs," 261.

*"These afforded plenty"*: FBW, "Our Climbs," 261.

*"but the scenery"*: "Climbing High Mountains," *New York Times*.

*"people had said so much"*: "Climbing High Mountains," *New York Times*.

*"for the danger on"*: David Starr Jordan to ASP, 16 April 1895, Group 1, Series 2, Box 12, Folder 1, Peck Collection.

*"It makes me shudder"*: Jennie Cunningham Croly to ASP, 30 July 1895, Group 1, Subseries 2, Box 12, Folder 1, Peck Collection.

*"clothed in its scanty garb"*: ASP, "A Woman's Ascent of the Matterhorn," *McClure's Magazine*, July 1896, 96

*"Such a climb is enjoyable"*: ASP, "Ascent of the Matterhorn," 96.

*"Now don't let it happen again!"*: Minnie E. Young to ASP, 25 September 1895, Group 1, Subseries 2, Box 12, Folder 1, Peck Collection.

*"pushed financially."*: Ann Power Smith Peck to ASP, 8 November 1896, Group 1, Series 2, Box 12, Folder 18, Peck Collection.

*"whose fame as a mountain climber"*: Redpath Lyceum Bureau pamphlet, Peck Collection.

*"For a woman in"*: ASP quoted in Miller, *Adventurous Women: The Inspiring Lives of Nine Early Outdoorswomen* (Boulder, CO: Pruett, 2000), 40.

*"succeed in destroying"*: William M. Nevin, "The Bloomer Dress," *Ladies Wreath*, 1852, 253.

*"Our class at school"*: Fanny Henderson to ASP, 1 November 1895, Group 1, Series 2, Box 12, Folder 1, Peck Collection.

*"Dear Madam, I am a boy"*: Charles W. Slacks to ASP, 13 July 1896, Group 1, Series 2, Box 12, Folder 1, Peck Collection.

*"Obviously a college athlete"*: ASP, "Practical Mountain Climbing," *Outing*, 1901, 696.

*"to attain some height"*: ASP, "Practical Mountain Climbing," 696.

*"filching"*: ASP to Mortimer Brooks, 9 July 1896, Letters 1884–1900, #2A, Box 18, Peck Collection

*"were the first two ladies"*: ASP, "Practical Mountain Climbing," 696.

*"That she should take advantage"*: ASP to Mortimer Brooks, 9 July 1896, Letters 1884–1900, #2A, Box 18, Peck Collection.

*"striking costume"*: "What She Wears," *Pawtucket (RI) Evening Times*, June 24, 1898.

*"There is a lady"*: "A Mountain Climbing Record: Interview with Dr. and Mrs. Workman," *New York Times*, August 20, 1900.

*"It has been a grievance"*: Letter quoted in Ann C. Colley, *Victorians in the Mountains: Sinking the Sublime* (Burlington, VT: Ashgate, 2010), 115.

## Chapter 5: The Glass Jar

*"a thoroughly modern land"*: FBW, journal entry, 22 March 1899, Acc. 9893/13, Workman Papers.

*"fairly clean steamer"*: FBW, journal entry, 22 March 1899.

*"had to call a boy"*: FBW, journal entry, 4 April 1899, Acc. 9893/13, Workman Papers.

*"with irresistible power"*: Mary Blair Beebe, "A Quest in the Himalayas," *Harper's Monthly Magazine*, March 1911, 489.

*"kept running away"*: FBW, journal entry, 5 July 1899, Himalayas 1899–1900, Acc. 9893/14, Workman Papers.

*"four days in the wilderness."*: FBW, journal entry, 5 July 1899.

*"a grand immense"*: FBW, journal entry, 8 July 1899, Himalayas 1899–1900, Acc. 9893/14, Workman Papers.

*"Now, the mosquito"*: FBW, "Our Climbs," 263.

*"The question of dress"*: "Climbed Skyward Over Four Miles," *Boston Globe*, October 16, 1904.

*"the wild and beautiful"* and *"simply exquisite"*: FBW, journal entry, 13 June 1899, India 1898–99, Acc. 9893/12, Workman Papers.

*"The sun burns hot"*: FBW, journal entry, 13 June 1899.

*"fine effect on the mountains"*: FBW, journal entry, 13 June 1899.

*"The Askole people . . . a sweet-smelling"*: FBW, "Our Climbs," 263.

*"bridge sways and swings"*: FBW, journal entry, 13 July 1899, Himalayas 1899–1900, Acc. 9893/14, Workman Papers.

*"a lively-looking sheep"*: FBW, "Our Climbs," 270.

*"hefted the whole bundles"*: FBW, journal entry, 17 July 1899, Himalayas 1899–1900, Acc. 9893/14, Workman Papers.

*"When we sat down"*: FBW, journal entry, 17 July 1899.

*"should not hesitate to speak . . . He ended his food"*: FBW, journal entry, 17 July 1899.

*"An absurd accusation"*: FBW, journal entry, 17 July 1899.

*"But like most"*: ASP quoted in David Mazel, ed., *Mountaineering Women: Stories by Early Climbers* (College Station: Texas A&M University Press, 1994), 109.

*"We then refused to pay"*: FBW, journal entry, 21 July 1899, Himalayas 1899–1900, Acc. 9893/14, Workman Papers.

*"fired a shot"*: FBW, journal entry, 21 July 1899.

*"Weird, ice-covered towers"*: FBW, journal entry, 21 July 1899.

*"Z who keeps filling"*: FBW, journal entry, 21 July 1899.

*"Beyond all comparison"*: Sir William Martin Conway, *Climbing and Exploration in the Karakoram-Himalayas* (London: T. F. Unwin, 1894), 1:377.

*"Pull on the rope"*: FBW, "Our Climbs," 267.

*"after the bumbling"*: FBW, "Our Climbs," 267.

*"We had the satisfaction"*: FBW and WHW, *In the Ice World of Himálaya* (London: T. F. Unwin, 1900), 178.

*"I had reached"*: "Mountain Climbing Record," *New York Times*, August 20, 1900.

*"As the sun flung"*: FBW, "Our Climbs," 267.

*"bounded by chains"*: FBW, "Our Climbs," 267.

*"And so ended"*: FBW, "Our Climbs," 267.

*"there is nothing in it"*: "Noted Travelers—Dr. and Mrs. Workman Are Now in India," *Boston Sunday Globe*, November 9, 1902.

*"dark, serpentine object"*: FBW, "Our Climbs," 268.

*"ragged, shaly wall"*: FBW and WHW, *In the Ice World*, 140.

*"gained the most extraordinarily"*: "Mountain Climbing Record," *New York Times*, August 20, 1900.

*"For the benefit of women"*: FBW and WHW, *In the Ice World*, 182.

*"An ordinary Swiss guide"*: FBW, "Our Climbs," 269.

*"monarch among the snow giants"*: Arthur Winslow Tarbell, "Mrs. Fanny Bullock Workman: Explorer and Alpinist," *New England Magazine: An Illustrated Monthly*, n.s., September 1905–February 1906, 489.

*"No other woman"*: "Woman Climbs Himalayan Peaks," *Boston Globe*, September 11, 1912.

*"the slides showed"*: *Aberdeen Journal*, December 11, 1900, quoted in Jo Woolf, "Fanny Bullock Workman—A Woman of Substance," Jo Woolf's personal blog, October 15, 2016, https://rsgsexplorers .com/2016/10/15/fanny-bullock-workman-a-woman-of-substance.

## Chapter 6: Into the Death Zone

*"capable and energetic"*: Sir Francis Edward Younghusband, *India and Tibet: A History of the Relations which Have Subsisted Between the Two Countries from the Time of Warren Hastings to 1910; with a Particular Account of the Mission to Lhasa of 1904* (London: John Murray, 1910), 237.

*"if that one can endure"*: FBW and WHW, *Ice-Bound Heights*, 8.

*"carried in a* dandi": FBW and WHW, *Ice-Bound Heights*, 9.

*"dilapidated, dust-covered"*: FBW and WHW, *Ice-Bound Heights*, 15.

*"I remained in slight shade"*: FBW, journal entry, 28 June 1902, Indian notebook 1902–3, Acc. 9893/15, Workman Papers.

*"We took a photo"*: FBW, journal entry, 28 June 1902.

*"a hard day"*: FBW, journal entry, 28 June 1902.

*"soft and lovely morning"*: FBW, journal entry, 6 July 1902, Indian notebook 1902–3, Acc. 9893/15, Workman Papers.

*"Whirling round and round"*: FBW, journal entry, 9 July 1902, Himalayas 1902–3, Acc. 9893/26, Workman Papers.

*"glistening like a gigantic whale"*: FBW, journal entry, 13 July 1902, Himalayas 1902–3, Acc.9893/27, Workman Papers.

*"carry off a sheep"*: FBW and WHW, *Ice-Bound Heights*, 73–74.

*"On an exposed mountain-side"*: FBW and WHW, *Ice-Bound Heights*, 52–53.

*"in this white wilderness"*: FBW and WHW, *Ice-Bound Heights*, 79.

*"singing a dismal chant"*: FBW and WHW, *Ice-Bound Heights*, 89.

*"Those not used to camping"*: FBW and WHW, *Ice-Bound Heights*, 117–18.

*"Our faces are burned purple"*: FBW, journal entry, 15 August 1903, Himalayas 1903, Acc. 9893/27, Workman Papers.

*"large as small houses"*: FBW and WHW, *Ice-Bound Heights*, 165.

*"he is a perfect brute"*: FBW, journal entry, 15 August 1903, Himalayas 1903, Acc. 9893/27, Workman Papers.

*"valley sweater"*: FBW, journal entry, 14 August 1903, Indian notebook 1902–3, Acc. 9893/15, Workman Papers.

*"It was exceedingly dangerous"*: FBW, journal entry, 14 August 1903.

"Es ist sehr": FBW and WHW, *Ice-Bound Heights*, 146.

*"the tongue began to crack"*: FBW, journal entry, 29 August 1903, Indian notebook, 1902–3, Acc. 9893/15, Workman Papers.

*"This was insulting . . . take away the jaded"*: "Noted Travelers," *Boston Sunday Globe*.

*"educative and purifying power"*: Mummery, *My Climbs*, 235.

*"These people are"*: WHW, journal entry, 12 August 1903, Himalayas 1903, Acc. 9893/27, Workman Papers.

*"They were in no danger"*: WHW, journal entry, 12 August 1903.

*"First Exploration of"*: "Proceedings of the Club," *Appalachia* 11 (1908): 85, https://archive.org/stream/appalachia01clubgoog/appalachia01clubgoog _djvu.txt.

*"their comfortable home"*: "Noted Travelers," *Boston Sunday Globe*.

*"absolute silence reigned"*: FBW, "First Ascent of the Hoh Lumba," *Independent* 55 (January–December 1903): 311.

*"it is not surprising"*: FBW and WHW, *Ice-Bound Heights*, 326.

*"chilly to the woman explorer"*: Mazel, *Mountaineering Women*, 93.

*"whose courage, endurance"*: FBW and WHW, *Sketches Awheel*, dedication.

*"A combination of good living"*: J. A. Fowler, "Mountain Climbing a Pleasure and a Science: What Miss Annie S. Peck Has Accomplished; Her Mental

and Physical Equipment," *Phrenological Journal of Science and Health* 119, no. 5 (May 1906): 140.

"*as to what is fitting*": ASP to "Dear Sir," 7 January 1906, Letters 1901 to 1935, Series 2, Folder 7, Peck Collection.

"*If I can demonstrate*": ASP to "Dear Sir," 26 April 1906.

## Chapter 7: Camp America

"*particularly of the upper*": FBW and WHW, *Peaks and Glaciers of Nun Kun: A Record of Pioneer-Exploration and Mountaineering in the Punjab Himalaya* (London: Constable, 1909), 16.

"*We had more than enough*": FBW and WHW, *Peaks and Glaciers*, 2.

"*The crops having failed*": FBW and WHW, *Peaks and Glaciers*, 2.

"*It cannot boast*": WHW, "The Nun Kun and Its Glaciers," *Journal of the Manchester Geographical Society* 24 (1908): 85.

"*nasty and rainy*": FBW, journal entry, 17 June 1906, Himalayas 1906, 1908, Acc. 9893/17, Workman Papers.

"*If the traveler wished*": FBW and WHW, *Peaks and Glaciers*, 20.

"*They seemed to take*": FBW and WHW, *Peaks and Glaciers*, 22.

"*under a shade tree*": FBW, journal entry, 25 June 1907, Himalayas 1907–8, 1911, Acc. 9893/29, Workman Papers.

"*the whole scene*": FBW, journal entry, 28 July 1907, 1907–8, Acc. 9893/16, Workman Papers.

"*impossible a feat*": FBW and WHW, *Peaks and Glaciers*, 27.

"*Armed with our bergstocks*": FBW and WHW, *Peaks and Glaciers*, 35–36.

"*had to play the part*": FBW and WHW, *Peaks and Glaciers*, 37.

"*A bakhshish of money*": FBW and WHW, *Peaks and Glaciers*, 37.

"*not grudge him*": FBW and WHW, *Peaks and Glaciers*, 37.

"*Burrows pierced the ground*": FBW and WHW, *Peaks and Glaciers*, 39.

"*down upon us*": FBW and WHW, *Peaks and Glaciers*, 47.

"*For more than a mile*": FBW and WHW, *Peaks and Glaciers*, 48.

"*Ice-axes were tested*": FBW and WHW, *Peaks and Glaciers*, 49.

"*First we went over . . . over long ascending*": FBW, journal entry, 26 July 1906, India 1906, Acc. 9893/16, Workman Papers.

"*This did not tend*": FBW and WHW, *Peaks and Glaciers*, 49.

*"Or if we passed"*: FBW and WHW, *Peaks and Glaciers*, 65.

*"There is plenty of opportunity"*: FBW and WHW, *Peaks and Glaciers*, 65.

*"physical suffering"*: Hayden Carpenter, email correspondence with author, 17 August 2017.

*"And if any snow-leopards"*: FBW and WHW, *Peaks and Glaciers*, 67–68.

*"We did not fancy"*: FBW and WHW, *Peaks and Glaciers*, 74.

*"So we camped here alone"*: FBW, journal entry, 28 July 1905, Acc. 9893/16, Workman Papers.

*"a man 'personally thinks'"*: FBW and WHW, *Peaks and Glaciers*, 79.

*"but an atom . . . leaving the ice-wilderness"*: FBW and WHW, *Peaks and Glaciers*, 80.

## Chapter 8: Pinnacle Peak

*"snow-work"*: FBW and WHW, *Peaks and Glaciers*, 49. They used this term in several of their books.

*"The absolute silence"*: FBW and WHW, *Peaks and Glaciers*, 81–82.

*"On putting our heads out"*: FBW and WHW, *Peaks and Glaciers*, 81–82.

*"and, last but not easiest"*: FBW and WHW, *Peaks and Glaciers*, 82.

*"It would be a boon"*: FBW and WHW, *Ice-Bound Heights*, 298.

*"which one recognizes"*: FBW and WHW, *Peaks and Glaciers*, 99.

*"the highest point up to date"*: FBW and WHW, *Peaks and Glaciers*, 76.

*"suffered much the last"*: WHW, journal entry, Himalayas 1905–1906, Acc. 9893/28, Workman Papers.

*"The view . . . is one"*: FBW, journal entry, 2 August 1906, Himalayas 1905–1906, Acc. 9893/29, Workman Papers.

*"Taken in moderate quantity"*: FBW, journal entry, 29 July 1906, Himalayas 1906, Acc. 9893/16, Workman Papers.

*"Some days ago"*: FBW, journal entry, 1 August 1906, Himalayas 1905–6, Acc. 9893/28, Workman Papers.

*"showed no spirit"*: "Noted Travelers," *Boston Sunday Globe*.

*"A misstep here might hurl"*: FBW and WHW, *Peaks and Glaciers*, 65.

*"a wide galaxy"*: FBW and WHW, *Peaks and Glaciers*, 86.

*"we had ascended plunged"*: FBW and WHW, *Peaks and Glaciers*, 86.

*"I made another record"*: FBW quoted Tarbell, "Mrs. Fanny Bullock Workman," 487.

*"Of great importance"*: Sven Hedin, "Mr. and Mrs. Workman in Southern Tibet," in *Southern Tibet* (Stockholm: Lithographic Institute of the General Staff of the Swedish Army, 1922), 441.

*"[Her] enthusiasm"*: WHW quoted in Miller, *On Top of the World*, 122.

*"One of the chief difficulties"*: ASP, "The First Ascent of Mount Huascaran," *Harper's Monthly Magazine*, January 1909, 112.

*"I had not really needed"*: ASP, "Ascent of Mount Huascaran," 112.

*"they aren't as good as men"*: ASP, "Ascent of Mount Huascaran," 112.

*"Many persons suppose that"*: ASP, "Practical Mountain Climbing," 695.

*"yawning chasms"*: ASP, "Ascent of Mount Huascaran," 178.

*"the steps were so far apart"*: ASP, *A Search for the Apex of America: High Mountain Climbing in Peru and Bolivia Including the Conquest of Huascaran, With Some Observations on the Country and the People Below* (New York: Dodd, Mead, 1911), 325.

*"toiled upward"*: ASP, "Ascent of Mount Huascaran," 179.

*"Up or down?"*: ASP, *Apex of America*, 329.

*"it was feared that she"*: "Miss Peck Is Safe: Returns from Climb of 25,000 Feet Up Mount Huascaran," *New York Times*, August 20, 1908.

*"My first thought"*: ASP, "Ascent of Mount Huascaran," 112.

*"If, as seems probable"*: ASP, "Ascent of Mount Huascaran," 187.

*"The World's Highest"*: Charles Fay to ASP, 25 October 1908, Subgroup 1, Series 3, Box 14, Folder 5, Peck Collection.

## Chapter 9: A Record Disputed

*"They could have assembled . . . lingering, shirking work"*: "Keeping House," *Boston Sunday Post*, July 5, 1914.

*"large, tall and very perfect . . . beckoned largely"*: FBW, journal entry, 13 August 1908, Acc. 9893/17, Workman Papers.

*"after delivery of these delicacies"*: "Keeping House," *Boston Sunday Post*.

*"They made a fearful row"*: WHW, journal entry, 16 August 1908, Acc. 9893/17, Workman Papers.

*"fearful pain in"*: FBW, journal entry, 17 August 1908, Acc. 9893/17, Workman Papers.

*"This rough camp is wild"*: FBW, journal entry, 17 August 1908.

*"dizzy precipices laden with snow"*: "Keeping House," *Boston Sunday Post.*

*"Before reaching camp"*: FBW, journal entry, 22 August 1908, Himalayas 1906, 1908, Acc. 9893/17, Workman Papers.

*"The Askole people seem anxious"*: FBW, journal entry, 26 August 1908, Acc. 9893/17, Workman Papers.

*"No one is ever safe"*: FBW, journal entry, 8 September 1908, Acc. 9893/17, Workman Papers.

*"Climbing up, up, up"*: "An American Woman's Climb to the Top of the World: A Brave Explorer's Record Breaking Journey Over Mountains of Ice to the Highest Peaks on Earth," *Wide World Magazine,* July 11, 1909, 6.

*"Mrs. Workman has been further"*: "American Woman's Climb," 6.

*"which has been attained"*: John S. Harwood, "The Most Thrilling Sport of All," *Galveston (TX) Daily News,* September 13, 1908.

*"For men, writing about"*: Clare Roche, "Women Climbers 1850–1900: A Challenge to Male Hegemony," *Sport in History* 33, no. 3 (February 9, 2013): 17.

*"pleasing personality and"*: Fowler, "Pleasure and a Science," 142.

*"A scientific controversy that promises"*: "Mountain Climbing Laurels," *Salt Lake (UT) Tribune,* November 7, 1909.

*"but on account"*: ASP, "Conquest of Mount Huascaran," *Journal of the American Geographical Society of New York* 40 (January 1, 1909): 363.

*"if future triangulations"*: ASP, "Ascent of Mount Huascaran," 187.

*"She was married to"*: "The Sportsman's Library," *Illustrated Sporting and Dramatic News,* April 18, 1908, 246.

*"mountain climbing is not all"*: "Peck for Championship," *Trenton (NJ) Evening Times,* September 13, 1909.

*"in the pursuit of his calling"*: "An Appeal Made on Behalf of Rudolf Taugwalder, the Swiss Guide," *Appalachia Bulletin* 1, no. 6 (April 1908): 52–53.

*"a most faithful . . . to make Americans"*: "In Aid of Rudolf Taugwalder," *Bulletin of the Appalachian Club* 1, no. 1 (November 1907): 52.

*"I have never found"*: "Peck for Championship," *Trenton (NJ) Evening Times.*

*"This was more than"*: "Miss Peck Goes Out to Climb the Heights; Huascarán not Being the Top of America, She's Going to Find the Top and Stand on It," *New York Times,* June 3, 1911.

*"marvelous endurance and courage"*: Eduardo Higginson to ASP, 20 February 1909, Subgroup 1, Series 2, Box 14, Folder 6, Peck Collection.

## Chapter 10: Climbers in Controversy

*"indeed a very sad"*: Rudolf Taugwalder to ASP, 26 May 1909, Subgroup 1, Series 2, Box 14, Folder 6, Peck Collection.

*"that I did not really climb"*: ASP quoted in Southwick, "City's Pioneer Feminist."

*"Now I wish to know"*: Horatio G. Bent to ASP, 23 December 1908, Subgroup 1, Series 2, Box 14, Peck Collection.

*"Unless some man suggested"*: Virgil Bogue to ASP, 14 January 1909, Subgroup 1, Series 2, Box 14, Peck Collection.

*"Concerning the altitude"*: ASP quoted in Mazel, *Mountaineering Women*, 116.

*"made an ascent"*: "Andean and Other Summits," *New-York Tribune*, January 21, 1910, Collections of the American Alpine Club Library, http://library.americanalpineclub.org/items/show/126.

*"Possibly there may be"*: "Topics of the Week: Feminine Mountain Climbing," *New York Times*, January 15, 1910.

*"it is entirely proper"*: "Feminine Mountain Climbing," *New York Times*.

*"Miss Peck has taken"*: "Miss Peck Declines Controversy," *Suburbanite Economist* (Chicago, IL), January 7, 1910.

*"Miss Annie S. Peck"*: "Declines Controversy," *Suburbanite Economist*.

*"My dear Miss Peck"*: Caspar Whitney to ASP, 13 September 1909, Subgroup 1, Series 2, Box 14, Folder 7, Peck Collection.

*"I feel a desire to write"*: Mrs. Mary G. Thaxter to ASP, 27 September 1909, Subgroup 1, Series 2, Box 14, Folder 7, Peck Collection.

*"I had never thought"*: "Climbing High Mountains," *New York Times*.

*"who bring to us"*: "The World's Highest Altitudes," *National Geographic*, June 1909, 504.

*"As every one at all"*: FBW to ASP, 23 October 1909, Subgroup 1, Series 2, Box 14, Folder 7, Peck Collection.

*"rather amusing controversy"*: FH Burlingham to ASP, 15 March 1910, Subgroup 1, Series 3, Box 15, Folder 1, Peck Collection.

*"were active participants"*: Catriona M. Parratt, "Athletic 'Womanhood': Exploring Sources for Female Sport in Victorian and Edwardian England," *Journal of Sport History* 16, no. 2 (Summer 1989): 311.

*"There was no reason"*: Mary Crawford, "Mountain Climbing for Women," *Canadian Alpine Journal* 2 (1909): 74.

*"Mrs. Bullock Workman"*: Crawford, "Mountain Climbing," 75.

## Chapter 11: A Plucky Performance

*"My dear Miss Peck"*: Henry Bryant to ASP, 19 November 1909, Subgroup 1, Series 2, Box 14, Peck Collection.

*"officially retains the honor"*: "Mrs. Workman Wins. Establishes Supremacy as Mountain Climber over Miss Peck," *New York Times*, March 26, 1911.

*"In reference to the accuracy"*: "Miss Peck at the Top, Anyhow," *New York Sun*, February 23, 1910.

*"are disputing, scrapping"*: ASP to *Evening Mail*, Subgroup 1, Series 3, Box 15, Folder 13, Peck Collection.

*"As to Mrs. Workman"*: Letters to the Editor, *New York Evening Mail*, Subgroup 1, Series 3, Box 25, Folder 13, Peck Collection.

*"in the interest of mountaineering"*: WHW and FBW, *The Call of the Snowy Hispar: A Narrative of Exploration and Mountaineering* (London: Constable, 1910), 239–40.

*"I believe I am right"*: "Recent First Ascents in the Himalayas," *Independent* (London), June 2, 1910.

*"She never uses this machine"*: "Miss Peck at the Top," *New York Sun*.

*"If other women want"*: "Miss Peck at the Top," *New York Sun*.

*"While Mrs. Workman"*: Letters to the Editor, *New York Evening Mail*, Folder 13, Subgroup 1, Series 3, Box 25, Peck Collection.

*"efforts to make exact"*: "Miss Peck at the Top," *New York Sun*.

*"Anyone who chooses"*: "Miss Peck at the Top," *New York Sun*.

*"Now Miss Peck insists"*: "Mrs. Workman Wins," *New York Times*.

*"Calcite as a Primary"*: Rachel Workman MacRobert, "Calcite as a Primary Constituent of Igneous Rocks," *Geological Magazine* 8, no. 5 (May 1911): 193.

*"Although, if we are not mistaken"*: "Andean and Other Summits," *New-York Tribune*.

"*Though it would thus appear*": ASP quoted in Mazel, *Mountaineering Women*, 116.

"*She has crowned with*": "Alpina," *Appalachia: The Journal of the Appalachian Mountain Club* 12, (1909–1912): 59.

"*need not accept the figures*": "Miss Peck Goes out to Climb the Heights," *New York Times*, June 3, 1911.

"*compliments and appreciation*": Admiral Robert Peary to ASP, 2 October 1911, Subgroup 1, Series 3, Box 15, Folder 2, Peck Collection.

"*A woman who has done*": "Miss Peck Goes out to Climb the Heights," *New York Times*, June 3, 1911.

"*though the peak is not*": "Ladies Seek Mountains to Climb," *Mason City (IA) Gazette*, October 25, 1956.

"*Now this phraseology*": Howard Palmer to ASP, 21 April 1911, Subgroup 1, Series 3, Box 5, Folder 5, Peck Collection.

"*in the case of Huascaran*": Howard Palmer to ASP, 21 April 1911.

"*the largest and only*": "French Honor Woman," *New York Times*, February 20, 1910.

"*done such important work*": "Climbed Skyward," *Boston Globe*.

"*Mrs. FBW, who has just*": *Japan Chronical* quoted in "Personal and General," *Chestertimes* (Chester, PA), August 8, 1913.

"*the ingenious devices of man*": "Workmans Climbed 21,000 Feet Peaks," *New York Times*, May 10, 1913.

## Chapter 12: Votes for Women

"*painstaking and diligent*": FBW and WHW, *Two Summers in the Ice-Wilds of Eastern Karakoram: The Exploration of Nineteen Hundred Square Miles of Mountain and Glacier* (London: T. Fisher Unwin, 1917), 124.

"*It was with a feeling*": FBW and WHW, *Two Summers*, 23.

"*overhung on both sides . . . over the rock-strewn*": FBW and WHW, *Two Summers*, 47.

"*From wall to wall*": FBW and WHW, *Two Summers*, 50.

"*a rolling tumbling mass*": WHW, journal entry, n.d., Himalayas 1911, Acc. 9893/30, Workman Papers.

"*Rachel's Wedding Day*": FBW, journal entry, 8 July 1911, Himalayas 1911, Acc. 9893/18, Workman Papers.

*"Liebe Rachel . . . I can imagine various"*: WHW to Rachel Workman Mac-
   Robert, 8 July 1911, MacRobert Trust, Aberdeenshire, Scotland. Hereafter referred to as MacRobert Trust.

*"attempt was made to eject"*: Alison McCall, "Lady Rachel Workman Mac-
   Robert: Mother, Millionaire, and . . . Geologist?!" *Trowel Blazers* (blog),
   edited by Jessica Mint and Suzie Burch, accessed January 15, 2018,
   https://trowelblazers.com/rachel-workman-macrobert.

*"May all blessings be"*: FBW, journal entry, 8 July 1911.

*"very great cold"*: FBW, journal entry, 8 July 1911.

*"eyeing it askance"*: FBW and WHW, *Two Summers*, 97.

*"excellent custard pudding"*: FBW and WHW, *Two Summers*, 97.

*"As circumstances turned"*: FBW and WHW, *Two Summers*, 96–99.

*"a bleak nasty place"*: FBW, journal entry, 19 August 1911, Himalayas 1911,
   Acc. 9893/18, Workman Papers.

*"This jagged rock promontory"*: FBW, journal entry, 19 August 1911.

*"barren mountain on"*: "Woman on Glacier—Base of Her Camp Made at Height
   of Over 16,000 Feet," *Grand Rapids (MI) Tribune*, November 29, 1911.

*"Thirty miles of the glacier"*: "Woman on Glacier," *Grand Rapids (MI) Tribune*.

*"No, I won't come again"*: FBW and WHW, *Two Summers*, 123.

*"the responsible leader"*: FBW and WHW, *Two Summers*, 123.

*"She sat looking at her"*: FBW, journal entry, 23 June 1912, Himalayas 1912,
   Acc. 9893/19, Workman Papers.

*"I thought how rather soft . . . helpless waiting in"*: FBW, journal entry, 8 July
   1912, Himalayas 1912, Acc. 9893/19, Workman Papers. All intervening
   quotes from this incident were taken from the July 8 journal entry.

*"brother guides' sheltering"*: FBW and WHW, *Two Summers*, 138.

*"Chenoz was hauled out"*: FBW, journal entry, 8 July 1912.

*"The group looked exactly"*: FBW, journal entry, 8 July 1912.

*"dear good porter"*: FBW, journal entry, 8 July 1912.

*"They thought he still slept"*: WHW, journal entry, 8 July 1912.

*"We were overcome by grief"*: FBW, journal entry, 9 July 1912, Himalayas
   1912, Acc. 9893/19, Workman Papers.

*"the camp of mourning"*: FBW and WHW, *Two Summers*, 139.

*"So ends this sad episode"*: FBW, journal entry, 9 July 1912.

*"ages ago . . . no Europeans"*: FBW, journal entry, 9 July 1912.

*"This is hard work"*: FBW, journal entry, 31 July 1912, Himalayas 1912, Acc. 9893/19, Workman Papers.

*"a great avalanche"*: "American Killed—Reported Overcome by an Avalanche in the Himalayan Range," *Mansfield (OH) News*, August 17, 1912.

*"A Worcester woman"*: "Keeping House," *Boston Sunday Post*.

*"[not] because I wish"*: FBW and WHW, *Two Summers*, dedication.

*"Crows crying and cawing"*: FBW, journal entry, 25 August 1912, Himalayas 1912, Acc. 9893/19, Workman Papers.

*"As I stood there"*: FBW and WHW, *Two Summers*, 164–65.

*"one of the most important . . . fine achievement"*: Hedin, "The Expedition of Dr. and Mrs. Workman 1911–1912," in *Southern Tibet*, 486.

*"added enormously to our"*: Martin Conway quoted in Hedin, "Expedition of Dr. and Mrs. Workman," in *Southern Tibet*, 486.

*"We have been very successful"*: WHW to Rachel Workman MacRobert, 6 August 1912, MacRobert Trust.

*"hoeing corn or selling ribbon"*: "Annie S. Peck's Views: 'Too Many Men in Politics Better Qualified for Hoeing Corn or Selling Ribbons,' Says Well Known Author," *New York Times*, February 28, 1915.

## Epilogue

*"Liebe Rachel . . . We made"*: WHW to Rachel Workman MacRobert, 4 September 1914, MacRobert Trust.

*"indefatigable alpinists"*: J. H. Richards, ed., "Notes," *Nation*, February 14, 1918, 189.

*"The adventures of"*: "Keeping House," *Boston Sunday Post*.

*"Queen of the Lady Mountaineers"*: "Can a Woman Climb Mt. Everest?" *Queenslander* (Brisbane, Australia), October 12, 1933.

*"The most intrepid"*: "The 'Queen of Women Mountaineers' Is Mrs. Fanny Bullock Workman," *Otterbein (IN) Press*, June 30, 1921.

*"was no quitter . . . her enthusiastic nature"*: John Percy Fararr, "In Memoriam: Mrs. Fanny Bullock Workman," *Alpine Journal* 37 (1925): 182.

# BIBLIOGRAPHY

## Books

Adams, Katherine H., Michael L. Keene, and Melanie McKay.
  *Controlling Representations: Depictions of Women in a Mainstream
  Newspaper, 1900–1950*. Cresskill, NJ: Hampton, 2009.

Attaway, Doris E., and Marjorie Rabe Barritt. *Women's Voices: Early
  Years at the University of Michigan*. Ann Arbor: Scholarly Publishing
  Office, University of Michigan Library, 2000.

Back, George, Rear Adm. Richard Collinson, and Francis Galton, eds.
  *Hints to Travellers*. London: Royal Geographical Society, 1865.

Ball, John, ed. *Peaks, Passes, and Glaciers: A Series of Excursions by
  Members of the Alpine Club*. London: Longman, Grenn, Longman,
  Roberts, 1860.

Berenbaum, Edwin. *Sacred Mountains of the World*. Berkeley: University
  of California Press, 1997.

Blunt, Alison. *Travel, Gender, and Imperialism: Mary Kingsley and West
  Africa*. New York: Guilford, 1994.

Bradley, Patricia. *Women and the Press: The Struggle for Equality*.
  Evanston, IL: Northwestern University Press, 2005.

Brown, Rebecca A. *Women on High: Pioneers of Mountaineering*.
  Guilford, CT: Appalachian Mountain Club Books, 2002.

Cameron, Ian. *To the Farthest Ends of the Earth: 150 Years of World
  Exploration by the Royal Geographical Society*. New York: Dutton, 1980.

Campbell, Karlyn Kohrs. *Man Cannot Speak for Her: A Critical Study of
  Early Feminist Rhetoric*. Vol. 1. Westport, CT: Greenwood, 1989.

Clark, Ronald. *The Victorian Mountaineers*. London: B. T. Batsford, 1953.

Colley, Ann C. *Victorians in the Mountains: Sinking the Sublime*. Burlington, VT: Ashgate, 2010.

Collie, Dr. Norman J. *Climbing on the Himalayas and Other Mountain Ranges*. Edinburgh, UK: David Douglas, 1902. www.cse.iitk.ac.in /users/amit/books/collie-1902-climbing-on-himalaya.html.

Conefrey, Mick. *How to Climb Mt. Blanc in a Skirt: A Handbook for the Lady Adventurer*. New York: St. Martin's, 2011.

Conway, William Martin. *Aconcagua and Tierra del Fuego: A Book of Climbing, Travel and Exploration*. London: Kessinger, 2010.

———. *Climbing and Exploration in the Karakoram-Himalayas*. London: Fisher Unwin, 1894.

Cott, Nancy. *The Grounding of Modern Feminism*. New Haven, CT: Yale University Press, 1987.

Creese, Mary R. S. *Ladies in the Laboratory: American and British Women in Science, 1800–1900*. Lanham, MD: Scarecrow, 2004.

Cross, Gary. *Social History of Leisure since 1600*. State College, PA: Venture, 1990.

Darwin, Charles. *Journal of Researches into the Geology and Natural History of the Various Countries Visited by H.M.S. Beagle, Under the Command of Captain Fitz Roy, R.N., 1832 to 1836*. London: H. Colburn, 1839.

Davidson, Lillias Campbell. *Hints to Lady Travellers at Home and Abroad*. London: Elliott and Thompson, 2011.

Degler, Carl N. "Revolution without Ideology: The Changing Place of Women in America." In *The Woman in America*, edited by Robert J. Lifton, 193–210. Boston: Beacon, 1965.

Dent, Clinton. *Above the Snowline: Mountaineering Sketches Between 1870 and 1880*. London: Longmans, Green, 1885.

Douglas, Ann. *The Feminization of American Culture*. New York: Knopf, 1977.

Ellis, Reuben. *Vertical Margins: Mountaineering and the Landscapes of Neoimperialsim*. Madison: University of Wisconsin Press, 2002.

Fitzgerald, Edward. *The Highest Andes: A Record of the First Ascent of Aconcagua and Tupungato in Argentina, & The Exploration of the Surrounding Valleys.* London: Methuen, 1899.

Flexner, Eleanor. *Century of Struggle: The Woman's Rights Movement in the United States.* Rev. ed. Cambridge, MA: Belknap-Harvard University Press, 1975.

Ford, Richard. *The Handbook for Travellers in Spain.* 8th ed. London: John Murray, 1892.

Freshfield, Douglas, and W. L. J. Wharton, eds. *Hints to Travellers.* London: Royal Geographical Society, 1893.

Gant, Jesse, and Nicholas J. Hoffman. *Wheel Fever: How Wisconsin Became a Great Bicycling State.* Madison: Wisconsin Historical Society Press, 2013.

Gardner, Arthur. *The Art and Sport of Alpine Photography.* London: Alpine Club, 1927.

Gilman, Charlotte Perkins. *The Man-Made World: or, Our Androcentric Culture.* 3rd ed. New York: Charlton, 1914.

Gómez Reus, Teresea, and T. Giffon, eds. *Women in Transit Through Literary Liminal Spaces.* London: Palgrave Macmillan UK, 2013.

Harriman, Florence Jaffray Hurst. *From Pinafores to Politics.* New York: H. Holt, 1923.

Harris, Barbara J. *Beyond Her Sphere: Women and the Profession in American History.* Westport, CT: Greenwood, 1978.

Henry, Emil. *Triumph and Tragedy: The Life of Edward Whymper.* Leicester, UK: Troubador, 2011.

Herzog, Maurice. *Annapurna: The First Conquest of an 8,000-Meter Peak.* Guilford, CT: Lyons, 1997.

Isserman, Maurice. *Continental Divide: A History of American Mountaineering.* New York: W. W. Norton, 2016.

———, and Stewart Weaver. *Fallen Giants: A History of Himalayan Mountaineering from the Age of Empire to the Age of Extremes.* New Haven, CT: Yale University Press, 2008.

James, Edward T., Janet Wilson James, and Paul S. Boyer. *Notable American Women, 1607–1950: A Biographical Dictionary.* Vol. 3. Cambridge, MA: Harvard University Press, 1971.

Kapadia, Harish. *Into the Untravelled Himalaya: Travels, Treks and Climbs.* New Delhi: Indus, 2005.

Krakauer, Jon. *Eiger Dreams: Ventures Among Men and Mountains.* Guilford, CT: Lyons, 1990.

———. *Into Thin Air: A Personal Account of the Mt. Everest Disaster.* New York: Anchor Books, 1997.

Lamphier, Peg A., and Rosanne Welch, eds. *Women in American History: A Social, Political, and Cultural Encyclopedia and Document Collection.* Santa Barbara, CA: ABC-CLIO, 2017.

LaPierre, Alexandra, and Christel Mouchard. *Women Travelers: A Century of Trailblazing Adventures, 1850–1950.* New York: Flammarion/Rizzoli, 2007.

Leach, Hugh, and Susan Maria Farrington. *Strolling About on the Roof of the World: The First Hundred Years of the Royal Society for Asian Affairs.* New York: Routledge Curzon, 2003.

Mason, Kenneth. *Abode of Snow: A History of Himalayan Exploration and Mountaineering.* New York: Dutton, 1955.

Mattingly, Carol. *Appropriate[ing] Dress: Women's Rhetorical Style in Nineteenth-Century America.* Carbondale: Southern Illinois University Press, 2002.

Mazel, David, ed. *Mountaineering Women: Stories by Early Climbers.* College Station: Texas A&M University Press, 1994.

McClone, Margo. *Women Explorers of the Mountains: Nina Mazuchelli, Fanny Bullock Workman, Mary Vaux Walcott, Gertrude Benham, Junko Tabei.* North Mankato, MN: Capstone, 1999.

Middleton, Dorothy. *Victorian Lady Travellers.* Chicago: Academy Chicago, 1993.

Miller, Luree. *On Top of the World: Five Women Explorers in Tibet.* New York: Paddington, 1976.

Miller, Marion. *Cawnpore to Cromar: The MacRoberts of Douneside.* Moray, UK: Librario, 2014.

Muir, John. "A Perilous Night on Shasta's Summit." In *Mountaineering Essays*, edited by Richard F. Fleck, 57–81. Salt Lake City: Peregrine Smith, 1984.

Mumm, Arnold L. *Five Months in the Himalaya: A Record of Mountain Travel in Garhwal and Kashmir*. New York: Longmans, Green, 1909.

Mummery, A. F. *My Climbs in the Alps and Caucasus*. London: Basil Blackwell, 1936.

Olds, Elizabeth Fagg. *Women of the Four Winds: The Adventures of Four of America's First Women Explorers*. Boston: Mariner, 1985.

Osborne, Michael A. *The Emergence of Tropical Medicine in France*. Chicago: University of Chicago Press, 2014.

Pauly, Thomas. *Game Faces: Five Early American Champions and the Sports They Changed*. Lincoln: University of Nebraska Press, 2012.

Peck, Annie Smith. *Flying Over South America: Twenty Thousand Miles by Air*. Boston: Houghton Mifflin, 1932.

———. *Industrial and Commercial South America*. New York: Dutton, 1922.

———. *A Search for the Apex of America: High Mountain Climbing in Peru and Bolivia Including the Conquest of Huascarán, With Some Observations on the Country and People Below*. London: Forgotten Books, 2012. Originally published 1911 by Dodd, Mead (New York).

Penn, Patricia E. "Annie S. Peck." In *American Women Writers*, edited by Lina Mainiero, 95–134. 4 vols. New York: Unger, 1981.

Pennell, Elizabeth Robins. "Cycling." In *Ladies in the Field: Sketches of Sport*, edited by the Lady Greville, 245–65. New York: D. Appleton, 1894.

———. *To Gispyland*. New York: Century, 1893.

———. *Over the Alps on a Bicycle*. London: T. Fisher Unwin, 1898.

Pennell, Joseph, and Elizabeth Robins Pennell. *A Canterbury Pilgrimage*. London: Seeley, 1885.

———. *An Italian Pilgrimage*. London: Seeley, 1887.

———. *Our Sentimental Journey Through France and Italy*. New York: Longmans, Green, 1888.

Polk, Milbry, and Mary Tiegreen. *Women of Discovery: A Celebration of Intrepid Women Who Explored the World*. New York: Clarkson Potter, 2001.

*Representative Men and Old Families of Rhode Island: Genealogical Records and Historical Sketches of Prominent and Representative*

*Citizens and of Many of the Old Families, Providence, Rhode Island.* Chicago: J. H. Beers, 1908.

Reus, Teresea Gómez, and T. Gifford Springer, eds. *Women in Transit Through Literary Liminal Spaces.* New York: Palgrave MacMillan, 2013.

Richardson, Hugh E. *Tibet and Its History.* 2nd ed. Boulder, CO: Shambhala, 1984.

Robinson, Caroline E. *The Hazard Family of Rhode Island 1635–1894.* Boston: Merrymount, 1896.

Shaw, Robert Kendall. *All Saints Church, Worcester, Massachusetts: A Centennial History, 1835–1935.* Boston: Commonwealth, 1935.

Smith, Catherine, and Cynthia Greig. *Women in Pants: Manly Maidens, Cowgirls, and Other Renegades.* New York: Harry N. Abrams, 2003.

Stearns, Precious McKenzie, ed. *Women Rewriting Boundaries: Victorian Women Travel Writers.* Newcastle upon Tyne, UK: Cambridge Scholars Publishing, 2016.

Stockwell, Thomas B. *A History of Public Education in Rhode Island: From 1636–1876.* Providence: Providence Press, 1886.

Stout, Glenn, and Christopher McDougall. *The Best American Sports Writing.* Boston: Houghton Mifflin Harcourt, October 2014.

Styles, Showell. *On Top of the World: An Illustrated History of Mountaineering and Mountaineers.* New York: Macmillan, 1967.

Tinling, Marion. *Women into the Unknown: A Sourcebook on Women Explorers and Travelers.* Westport, CT: Greenwood, 1989.

Tinker, Edward Laroque. *The Pennells.* Self-published by Frances and E. L. Tinker: 1951.

Tweed, William C. *History of Outdoor Recreation Development in National Forests 1891–1942.* Washington: US Forest Service, 1989.

Vause, Laurence Mikel. *On Mountains and Mountaineers.* Las Crescenta, CA: Mountain N'Air Books, 1993.

Waterman, Laura, and Guy Waterman. *A Fine Kind of Madness: Mountain Adventures Tall and True.* Seattle: Mountaineers Books, 2000.

Whymper, Edward. *Scrambles Amongst the Alps in the Years 1860–69.* First published 1871 by John Murray (London). Reprinted 2002 by National Geographic Society.

*The Worcester Directory, Containing a General Directory of the Citizens, a Business Directory, and the City and County Register.* Worcester, MA: Drew, Allis, 1885.

Workman, Fanny Bullock. *Algerian Memories: A Bicycle Tour over the Atlas to the Sahara.* London: T. Fisher Unwin, 1895.

Workman, Fanny Bullock, and William Hunter Workman. *Ice-Bound Heights of the Mustagh: An Account of Two Seasons of Pioneer Exploration and High Climbing in the Baltistan Himalaya.* London: Archibald Constable, 1908.

———. *In the Ice World of Himálaya.* London: T. F. Unwin, 1900.

    . *Peaks and Glaciers of Nun Kun: A Record of Pioneer-Exploration and Mountaineering in the Punjab Himalaya.* London: T. Fisher Unwin, 1909.

———. *Two Summers in the Ice-Wilds of Eastern Karakoram: The Exploration of Nineteen Hundred Square Miles of Mountain and Glacier.* London: T. Fisher Unwin, 1917.

Workman, William Hunter, and Fanny Bullock Workman. *The Call of the Snowy Hispar: A Narrative of Exploration and Mountaineering.* London: Constable, 1910.

———. *Sketches Awheel in Modern Iberia.* New York: G. P. Putnam and Sons, 1897.

———. *Through Town and Jungle: Fourteen Thousand Miles Awheel Among the Temples and People of the Indian Plain.* London: T. Fisher Unwin, 1904.

Younghusband, Sir Francis Edward. *India and Tibet: A History of the Relations which Have Subsisted Between the Two Countries from the Time of Warren Hastings to 1910; with a Particular Account of the Mission to Lhasa of 1904.* London: John Murray, 1910.

## Periodicals

Abraham, George D. "Pioneers of the Year on the Matterhorn." *Wide World Magazine,* October 1900–March 1901.

Adams, Cyrus C. "Lieut. Peary's Arctic Work." *Geographical Journal,* n.s., 2 (1893): 303–16.

*Appalachia.* "Proceedings of the Club." Vol. 11 (1908): 85. https://
    archive.org/stream/appalachia01clubgoog/appalachia01clubgoog
    _djvu.txt.

*Appalachia Bulletin.* "An Appeal Made on Behalf of Rudolf Taugwalder,
    the Swiss Guide." Vol. 1, no. 6 (April 1908): 52–53.

*Appleton (WI) Post Crescent.* "Annie Peck Reached Dangerous Heights."
    February 2, 1975.

*Atchison (KS) Daily Globe.* "Matron and Maid." December 1, 1903.

Bahrke, S. M., and B. Shukitt-Hale. "Effects of Altitude on Mood,
    Behaviour and Cognitive Functioning." *Sports Medicine* 16 (1993):
    97–125.

Baker, Paula. "The Domestication of Politics: Women and the American
    Political Society, 1780–1920." *American Historical Review* 89, no. 3
    (1984): 620–47.

Beebe, Mary Blair. "A Quest in the Himalayas." *Harper's Monthly
    Magazine,* March 1911.

Bell, Morag, and Cheryl McEwan. "The Admission of Women Fellows
    to the Royal Geographical Society, 1892–1914: The Controversy and
    the Outcome." *Geographical Journal* 162, no. 3, (November 1996):
    295–312.

Bernstein, Jeremy. "Ascent I: Whymper and Mummery Reporter at
    Large." *New Yorker,* March 13, 1965.

Betterton, M. D. "Theory of Structure Formation in Snowfields Motivated
    by Penitentes, Suncups, and Dirt Cones." *Physical Review E* 63, no. 5
    (April 26, 2001). https://doi.org/10.1103/PhysRevE.63.056129.

Bhandari, Rajneesh, and Jonah Engel Bromwich. "A Renowned
    Mountain Climber Dies Near Everest." *New York Times,* May 1,
    2017.

Blakeney, T. S. "The *Alpine Journal* and Its Editors, 1863–95." *Alpine
    Journal* 79 (1974): 166–73.

*Boston Daily Globe.* "They Scaled Mt. Sorata—Miss Annie Peck, Dr. W.
    G. Tight and Two Swiss Guides Accomplish Feat." September 3,
    1903.

*Boston Globe.* "Climbed Skyward Over Four Miles." October 16, 1904.

*Boston Sunday Globe.* "Noted Travelers—Dr. and Mrs. Workman Are Now in India." November 9, 1902.

Breivik, G. "Personality, Sensation Seeking and Risk Taking Among Everest Climbers." *International Journal of Sport Psychology* 27 (1996): 308–20.

*Bulletin of the American Geographical Society.* "The Conquest of Huascarán." 41, no. 6. (1909): 355–65.

Burek, Cynthia V. "The First Female Fellows and the Status of Women in the Geological Society of London." Geological Society of London Special Publication. *The Making of the Geological Society of London* 317 (August 21, 2009): 373–407.

Cavaletti, R., and G. Tredici. "Effects of Exposure to Low Oxygen Pressure on the Central Nervous System." *Sports Medicine* 13, no. 1 (1992): 1–7.

*Chicago Heights Star.* "Review On Top of the World: Five Women." February 10, 1985.

*Collier's.* "How I Prepared to Climb Mt. Huascaràn." March 13, 1909.

Conway, William Martin. "Exploration in the Mustagh Mountains." *Geographical Journal,* n.s., 2 (1893): 291–303.

Conway, W. M., C. T. Dent, and J. H. Wicks. "Report of the Special Committee on Equipment for Mountaineers." *Alpine Journal: A Record of Mountain Adventure and Scientific Observation* 15, nos. 107–114 (February 1890–November 1891): 3–32.

Crawford, Mary. "Mountain Climbing for Women." *Canadian Alpine Journal* 2 (1909): 73–76.

Danielli, G. "A Journey to the glaciers of the Eastern Karakoram." *Geographical Journal* 79 (1932): 257–68.

*East Liverpool (OH) Review.* "Famous Woman Explorer." February 5, 1909.

*El Paso (TX) Daily Herald.* "Woman's World." November 26, 1900.

Ellison, Julie. "Climbing Media Is Not Sexist, You Are." *Climbing Magazine,* July 21, 2015. www.climbing.com/news/climbing -media-is-not-sexist-you-are.

*Escanaba (MI) Daily Press.* "Noted Woman Explorer Climbs Lofty Himalayas." June 21, 1911.

Fay, Charles E. "The Appalachian Mountain Club." *Annals of the American Academy of Political and Social Science* 35 (March 1910): 393–400.

Fowler, J. A. "Mountain Climbing a Pleasure and a Science: What Miss Annie S. Peck Has Accomplished; Her Mental and Physical Equipment." *Phrenological Journal of Science and Health* 119, no. 5 (May 1906): 139–45.

*Gettysburg (PA) Times.* "Miss Annie S. Peck Mt. Climber to Search for Andes Highest Peak." May 25, 1911.

Grand, Sarah. "The New Aspect of the Woman Question." *North American Review* 158, no. 448 (March 1894): 270–76.

*Grand Rapids (MI) Tribune.* "Woman on Glacier—Base of Her Camp Made at Height of Over 16,000 Feet." November 29, 1911.

Gray, Eliza. "How British Suffragettes Radicalized American Women." *Time*, October 23, 2015. http://time.com/4084759/how-british -suffragettes-radicalized-american-women.

Henderson, Bruce. "Who Discovered the North Pole?" *Smithsonian*, April 2009. www.smithsonianmag.com/history/who-discovered-the -north-pole-116633746.

Hulbe, Christina L., Weili Wang, and Simon Ommanney. "Women in Glaciology: A Historical Perspective." *Journal of Glaciology* 56, no. 200 (2010): 944–64.

*Illustrated Sporting and Dramatic News.* "The Sportsman's Library." April 18, 1908.

*Independent* (London). "Recent First Ascents in the Himalayas." June 2, 1910.

Jones, Susanna. "For the Female Mountaineering Pioneers, It Was an Uphill Struggle." *Guardian* (US edition), March 26, 2012.

Kick, Wilhelm. "Chogo Lungma Glacier, Karakoram." *Geographical Journal* 122, no. 1 (March 1956): 93–96.

Krane, V. "We Can Be Athletic and Feminine, but Do We Want To? Challenging Hegemonic Femininity in Women's Sport." *Quest* 53 (2001): 115–33.

Krane, V., P. Y. L. Choi, S. M. Baird, C. M. Aimar, and K. J. Kauer. "Living the Paradox: Female Athletes Negotiate Femininity and Muscularity." *Sex Roles* (2004): 315–29.

Krane, V., J. Waldron, J. Michalenok, and J. Stiles-Shipley. "Body Image, and Eating and Exercise Behaviors: A Feminist Cultural Studies Perspective." *Women in Sport and Physical Activity Journal* 10, no. 1 (2001): 17–54.

*La Crosse (WI) Tribune.* "Honor VS. Sportswoman." January 19, 1914.

Leonard, Brendin. "Climber and Explorer Fanny Bullock Workman." *Adventure Journal,* November 14, 2012.

Lliboutry, L. "The Origin of Penitentes." *Journal of Glaciology* 2 (1954): 331–38.

Longstaff, T. G. "Six Months' Wandering in the Himalaya." *Alpine Journal* 23 (1906): 202–28.

*Los Angeles Times.* "The Times' Answers by Experts." January 5, 1903.

MacDonald, Cheyenne. "What Travel Looked Like 100 years go." *Daily Mail* (UK), November 30, 2015. www.dailymail.co.uk/sciencetech /article-3339902/What-travel-looked-like-100-years-ago-Map-shows -DAYS-took-travel-abroad-1900s.html.

MacRobert, Rachel Workman. "Calcite as a Primary Constituent of Igneous Rocks." *Geological Magazine* 8, no. 5 (May 1911): 193–201.

Madame Vallot. "Annuaire du club alpin français." *Alpine Journal* 14 (1888–1889): 150–51.

*Madison (WI) Capital Times.* "Inferiority Complex Is Seen in Copying of Men's Manners." May 13, 1928.

*Mansfield (OH) News.* "American Killed—Reported Overcome by an Avalanche in the Himalayan Range." August 17, 1912.

Mason, Kenneth. "A Note on the Topography of the Nun Kun Massive in Ladakh." *Geographical Journal* 56 (1920): 124–28.

———. "The Shaksgam Valley and Aghil Range." *Geographical Journal* 67 (1927): 351–52.

*Mason City (IA) Gazette.* "Ladies Seek Mountains to Climb." October 25, 1956.

*McClure's Magazine.* "A Woman's Ascent of the Matterhorn." July 1896.

*Milwaukee Weekly Wisconsin.* "Sketches Awheel in Modern Iberia Is in One Sense a Family Book." May 28, 1897.

*National Geographic.* "Record Ascents in the Himalayas." April 1903.

*New Castle (PA) News.* "Fanny Workman Is Dead in France." January 28, 1925.

*New York Evening World Late Edition.* "Brilliant Army of Women in White in Fifth Avenue Parade of Votes." October 23, 1915.

*New York Sun.* "Miss Peck at the Top, Anyhow," February 23, 1910.

———. "25,000 Get in Line for Parade of Suffragists in Face of Biting Wind." October 24, 1915.

*New York Times.* "Among the Magazines." September 18, 1909.

———. "Annie S. Peck's Views: 'Too Many Men in Politics Better Qualified for Hoeing Corn or Selling Ribbons,' Says Well-Known Author." February 28, 1915.

———. "A Brilliant Gathering at All Saints Church." June 16, 1881.

———. "Climbing High Mountains: Miss Annie S. Peck Tells How Her Love for It Finally Made Her a Record Breaker." January 9, 1898.

———. "Club for Women Climbers: They Have Long Been Angry at Being Kept Out of the Alpine Club." August 18, 1907.

———. "Cold to Women Orators: Sacramento Disappoints the Hughes Tourists." October 17, 1916.

———. "Dr. W. H. Workman, Explorer, 90, Dies." October 10, 1937.

———. "Feminine Mountain Climbing." January 15, 1910.

———. "50,000 Are Expected in Suffrage Parade." October 23, 1915.

———. "French Honors for Mrs. F.B. Workman." November 27, 1904.

———. "Hunter Workman Killed?" August 17, 1912.

———. "In Rock Climbing, Women Find Their Own Path to the Top." May 22, 2010.

———. "Marriage Announcement." June 16, 1881.

———. "Miss Peck Goes Out to Climb the Heights; Huascaran not Being the Top of America, She's Going to Find the Top and Stand on It." June 3, 1911.

———. "Miss Peck Returns from Andean Climb: She Planted a Suffrage Flag on Coropuna Peak, 21,000 Feet Above the Sea." February 5, 1912.

———. "Motherhood the Duty of Women—Roosevelt." March 14, 1905.

———. "A Mountain Climbing Record: Interview with Dr. and Mrs. Workman, Americans, Who Together Conquered the Himalayas." August 20, 1900.

———. "Mrs. Workman Wins: Establishes Supremacy as Mountain Climber over Miss Peck." March 26, 1911.

———. "A Notable Wedding." June 16, 1824.

———. "Oppose Artemas Ward: The Woman Suffragists Hold a Meeting and Decide to Fight Him." October 23, 1910.

———. "Roosevelt Is For Woman Suffrage; but Favors Letting Her Sex Decide the Matter by a Referendum Vote." February 3, 1912.

———. "Suffragettes Meet the Antis in Debate: Arguments For and Against Votes for Women Voiced at Woman's University Club." April 24, 1909. https://timesmachine.nytimes.com/timesmachine /1909/04/24/101035248.pdf.

———. "Women Here and There—Their Frills and Fancies." June 17, 1900.

———. "Workmans Climbed 21,000 Feet Peaks." May 10, 1913.

*Newark (NJ) Advocate.* "New York Women in Big Parade: Suffragettes to the Number of 1500 March Down 5th Avenue." April 6, 1911.

*New-York Tribune.* "45,000 March for Suffrage, Braving Wind and Darkness in Greatest Woman's Parade." October 24, 1915.

Nevin, Wm. M. "The Bloomer Dress." *Ladies Wreath,* 1852.

*Otterbein (IN) Press.* "The 'Queen of Women Mountaineers' Is Mrs. Fanny Bullock Workman." June 30, 1921.

*Outing.* "Men and Women of the Outdoor Word." May 1904.

Pauly, Thomas H. "Vita: Fanny Bullock Workman: Brief Life of a Feisty Mountaineer: 1859–1925." *Harvard Magazine,* March–April 2012.

*Pawtucket (RI) Evening Times.* "What She Wears." June 24, 1898.

Peck, Annie Smith. "The First Ascent of Mount Huascaran." *Harper's Monthly Magazine,* January 1909.

———. "Greece and Modern Athens." *Journal of the American Geographical Society of New York* 25, no. 1 (1893): 483–511.

———. "Miss Peck Replies to Mrs. Workman." *Scientific American* 102 (1910): 183.

———. "Practical Mountain Climbing." *Outing,* 1901.

———. "Scenic Wonders of South America" *Mentor,* January 1, 1920.

———. "A Woman in the Andes: My Attempt to Ascend Mount Huascaran." *Harper's Monthly Magazine,* December 1906.

———. "A Woman's Ascent of the Matterhorn." *McClure's Magazine,* July 1896.

Peck, Annie S., and Fanny Bullock Workman. "Mrs. Workman Answers Miss Peck." *Scientific American*, February 12, 1910.

Pennell, Elizabeth Robins. "Cycling." *St. Nicholas*, July 1890.

Perkins, Matt. "Rock Climbing Ethics: A Historical Perspective." *Northwest Mountaineering Journal*, issue 2 (2005): www.alpenglow .org/nwmj/05/051_Ethics.html.

Phillips, Noël. "No Man's Land: The Rise of Women in Climbing." *Climbing*, October 25, 2017.

Plint, Michael. "The Workmans: Travellers Extraordinary." *Himalayan Journal* 49 (1993): 231–37.

Relph, Edward. "An Inquiry into the Relations Between Phenomenology and Geography." *Canadian Geographer* 14 (1970): 193–201.

"Review of *A Search for the Apex of America*, by Annie Smith Peck." *Book Review Digest*, 1911.

Richards, J. H., ed. "Notes." *Nation*, February 14, 1918.

Richards, N. Phelps. "Mountaineering in the Australian Alps." *Wide World Magazine*, 454–58.

Robinson, Charles Turek. "Peck's Bad Girl." *Yankee*, February 1997.

Roche, Clare. "Women Climbers 1850–1900: A Challenge to Male Hegemony." *Sport in History* 33, no. 3 (February 9, 2013): 236–59.

Ross, Forrest. "A Lady Mountaineer in the New Zealand." *Wide World Magazine*, November 1900.

*Sacramento (CA) Record-Union*. "Title Review." June 5, 1886.

Senthilingam, Meera. "The Biological Secrets That Make Sherpas Superhuman Mountaineers." CNN, October 6, 2016. www.cnn .com/2015/11/11/health/sherpas-superhuman-mountaineers/index.html.

Sohn, Emily. "How Does a Nepalese Sherpa Carry So Much Weight?" NPR, March 12, 2017. www.npr.org/sections/goatsandsoda/2017 /03/12/517923490/how-does-a-nepalese-sherpa-carry-so-much-weight.

Southwick, Albert B. "City's Pioneer Feminist Lived a Life of Adventure." *Sunday Worcester (MA) Telegram*, October 15, 2000.

*Spectator* (London). "Bulls and Bull Fights." July 28, 1894.

*Suburbanite Economist* (Chicago, IL). "Miss Peck Declines Controversy." January 7, 1910.

*Syracuse (NY) Herald.* "The Healthiest Family Is the Happiest." August 22, 1920.

Tarbell, Arthur Winslow. "Mrs. Fanny Bullock Workman: Explorer and Alpinist." *New England Magazine: An Illustrated Monthly,* n.s., September 1905–February 1906.

*Trenton (NJ) Evening Times.* "Peck for Championship." September 13, 1909.

———. "Said She Is Head Mountain Climber: Mrs. Workman Disputes Claim of Miss Annie Peck for Championship." September 13, 1909.

Tucker, Richard P. "The Facts of the Western Himalayas: The Legacy of British Colonial Administration." *Journal of Forest History* 26, no. 3 (July 1982): 112–23.

Weeks, Linton. "American Women Who Were Anti-Suffragettes." NPR, October 22, 2015. www.npr.org/sections/npr-history-dept/2015/10/22/450221328/american-women-who-were-anti-suffragettes.

Williams, Cicely. "The Feminine Share in Mountain Adventure. Pt. 1." *Alpine Journal.* Accessed August 22, 2017. www.alpincjournal.org.uk/Contents/Contents_1976_files/AJ%201976%2090-100%20Williams%20Women.pdf.

*Worcester (MA) Gazette.* "Mrs. Workman Buried at Rural." September 24, 1925.

*Worcester (MA) Telegram.* "Dr. Workman Dies in Newton—Physician and Explorer Native of Worcester." October 14, 1937.

———. "Lady MacRobert Dies in Scotland." September 2, 1959.

———. "Late Noblewoman's Building on Main Street Up for Sale." October 26, 1955.

*Worcester (MA) Sunday Telegram.* "Worcester Women Found Athletic Pursuits to Their Liking." June 22, 2003.

*Worcester Magazine.* "The Slave Catcher's Riot." February 28, 2008. https://worcestermag.com/2008/02/28/the-slave-catcher39s-riot/4329.

Workman, Fanny Bullock. "Amid the Snows of Baltistan." *Scottish Geographical Magazine,* 1901.

———. "Ascent of the Biafo Glacier and Hispar Pass: Two Pioneer Ascents in the Karakoram." *Scottish Geographical Magazine,* 1899.

———. "Bicycle Riding in Germany." *Outing: An Illustrated Monthly Magazine of Sport, Travel and Recreation*, October 1892–March 1893.

———. "Conquering the Great Rose: An Account of the First Ascent of the World's Longest Non-Polar Glacier." *Harper's Monthly Magazine*, June–November 1914.

———. "Exploring the Glaciers of the Himalayas." *Harper's Monthly Magazine*, October 1909.

———. "Highest Camps and Climbs." *Appalachia* 11 (June 1907): 257–59.

———. "Our Climbs." *Wide World Magazine*, December 1900.

———. "A Romance of King Philip's War." *New England Magazine*, April 1886.

———. "Some Little Known Chalukyan Temples." *Journal of the Royal Asiatic Society of Great Britain & Ireland* (1904): 419.

———. "Some Notes on My 1912 Expedition to the Siachen, on Rose Glacier, Eastern Karakoram." *Scottish Geographical Magazine*, 1913.

Workman, William Hunter. "An Exploration of the Nun Kun Group and Its Glaciers: Discussion." *Geographical Journal* 31 (January 1908): 41.

Visser, PC. "Explorations in the Karakoram." *Geographical Journal* 68 (1926): 457–69.

Younghusband, Sir Francis Edward. "The Expedition to Western Tibet." *Geographical Journal* 25 (1905): 295–96.

———. "The Problem of Shaksgam Valley." *Geographical Journal* 68 (1926): 229.

## Blogs and Websites

Downing, Emily. "Op-Ed: The Thing About Climbing Media and First Female Ascents." *REI Co-Op Journal* (blog). Accessed August 4, 2017. www.rei.com/blog/climb/op-ed-the-thing-about-climbing-media-and-first-female-ascents.

Hanlon, Sheila. "Imperial Bicyclists: Women Travel Writers on Wheels in the Late Nineteenth and Early Twentieth Century World." August 8, 2014. www.sheilahanlon.com/?p=1343.

Heit, Judi. "Fanny Bullock Workman—Explorer and Mountaineer." *Women Without Boundaries* (blog). March 7, 2012. http://womenwhodare.blogspot.com/2012/03/fanny-bullock-workman.html.

Holland, Evangeline. "Fascinating Women: Fanny Bullock Workman."
    *Edwardian Promenade* (blog). May 22, 2011. www.edwardianpromenade
    .com/women/fascinating-women-fanny-bullock-workman.

Lavender, Catherine. "Notes on New Womanhood." Prepared for
    students in HST 386: Women in the City, Department of History,
    College of Staten Island/CUNY. 1998. https://csivc.csi.cuny.edu
    /history/files/lavender/386/newwoman.pdf.

McCall, Alison. "Lady Rachel Workman MacRobert: Mother, Millionaire,
    and . . . Geologist?!" *Trowel Blazers* (blog). Edited by Jessica Mint
    and Suzie Burch. Accessed January 15, 2018. www.trowelblazers.com
    /rachel-workman-macrobert.

Paloian, Andrea. "The Female/Athlete Paradox: Managing Traditional
    Views of Masculinity and Femininity." Applied Psychology OPUS
    (Online Publication of Undergraduate Studies). Fall 2012. http://
    steinhardt.nyu.edu/appsych/opus/issues/2012/fall/female.

Saunders, Anthony Victor. "The Golden Pillar: Spantik." American
    Alpine Club Publications. http://publications.americanalpineclub.org
    /articles/12198802100/print.

## Document Collections, Archives, and Historical Societies

Alpine Club, United Kingdom.

American Alpine Library, http://library.americanalpineclub.org.

Annie Smith Peck Collection, Archives and Special Collections, Brooklyn
    College Library.

MacRobert Trust, Aberdeenshire, Scotland.

Worcester Historical Museum.

Workman Papers, Archives and Manuscript Collections, National
    Library of Scotland, Edinburgh.

## Author Interviews and Correspondence

Hayden Carpenter                    Glyn Hughes

Jack Davis                          Stuart Leggat

Barbara Grigor-Taylor               David Peck

# INDEX